A Bouquet of Garden Writing

A Bouquet of
GARDEN WRITING

Selected from Five Grand Masters

Edited and introduced by

Ursula Buchan

David R. Godine · Publisher · Boston

First U.S. edition published in 1987 by
David R. Godine, Publisher, Inc.
Horticultural Hall, 300 Massachusetts Avenue
Boston, Massachusetts 02115

Originally published in the U.K. in 1986 by
Croom Helm Publishers Limited,
Beckenham, U.K. and Sydney, Australia

LC 86-82000
ISBN 0-87923-658-2

First printing
Printed and bound in the U.K.

❧ Contents ❧

		List of Colour Plates	6
		List of Black and White Figures	6
		Acknowledgements	8
		Introduction	9
Chapter	1	William Robinson 1838–1935	13
Chapter	2	Gertrude Jekyll 1843–1932	23
Chapter	3	E.A. Bowles 1865–1954	35
Chapter	4	Reginald Farrer 1880–1920	45
Chapter	5	Vita Sackville-West 1892–1962	57
Chapter	6	Plant-hunting	69
Chapter	7	Garden Design	79
Chapter	8	Growing Plants	99
Chapter	9	Herbaceous Plants	107
Chapter	10	Rock-gardens and Alpines	115
Chapter	11	Trees and Shrubs, including Roses	133
Chapter	12	Bulbs	143
Chapter	13	The Protected Garden—Greenhouses and Flower Arranging	151
Chapter	14	Water Gardens: Scent: the Seasons	159
Chapter	15	The Gardener's Enemies	169
Chapter	16	The Philosophy of Gardening	177
		Bibliography	185
		Indices	187

List of Colour Plates

1. Gravetye Manor—the West Garden in flower
2. Gravetye Manor—the Alpine Meadow
3. A cottage garden
4. A modern bedding-out scheme
5. *Gentiana verna*
6. Hellebores and anemones in light woodland
7. The Pergola—Hestercombe, Somerset
8. The 'Plat'—Hestercombe, Somerset
9. *Crocus chrysanthus* 'E.A. Bowles'
10. *Iris unguicularis*
11. *Narcissus* 'Weardale Perfection', painted by E.A. Bowles
12. *Galanthus nivalis var. scharlokii*, painted by E.A. Bowles
13. *Gentiana farreri*, painted by Reginald Farrer
14. *Eritrichium nanum*, photographed in the Pordoi Pass in the Dolomites where Farrer found it
15. A group of Oncocyclus irises
16. The old Alpine House at Wisley in early spring
17. The White Garden—Sissinghurst
18. The Rose Garden—Sissinghurst
19. The South Cottage Garden—Sissinghurst
20. *Cardiocrinum giganteum*

List of Black & White Figures

1.1 Etching of William Robinson by Francis Dodd — 13
1.2 The Reverend Samuel Reynolds Hole, after 1888 Dean of Rochester — 14
1.3 Portrait of William Robinson, aged 84 — 15
1.4 View across West Garden, Gravetye Manor — 18
1.5 William Robinson lying amongst Tufted Pansies, Gravetye — 19
1.6 View across West Garden, Gravetye, 'After my beds were completed' — 20
1.7 'Colony of Starworts among Rhododendrons' by H.G. Moon — 20
2.1 Gertrude Jekyll by Sir William Nicholson (1920) — 23
2.2 South Front of Munstead Wood with Scotch Briars. On the grass may be seen one of her much-loved cats — 25
2.3 The Circular Water-Court, Hestercombe, Somerset — 26
2.4 The Garden Court, Munstead Wood — 29
2.5 Part of a Border at Munstead Wood, with Lilies, Yuccas, *Euphorbia*, and *Eryngium* — 30
2.6 Munstead Bunch Primroses in the Nut Walk — 31
2.7 Approach to the House, through the Wood — 32
2.8 General Plan of the Garden at Munstead Wood — 33
3.1 E.A. Bowles with his dog, Kip — 35

3.2 Canon Henry N. Ellacombe, Rector of Bitton, Gloucestershire — 36
3.3 E.A. Bowles at 88 — 38
3.4 The Morning-Room at Myddelton House in May — 40
3.5 The Tulip Beds by the New River in the Garden of Myddelton House — 40
3.6 The Iris Beds by the New River — 41
3.7 The Market-Cross in the Rose Garden at Myddelton — 42
3.8 The Rock-Garden at Myddelton — 43
3.9 A Crocus Frame in the Kitchen Garden at Myddelton House — 43
4.1 Reginald John Farrer — 45
4.2 Ingleborough House, Clapham, West Yorkshire — 46
4.3 William Purdom dressed as a Coolie — 47
4.4 Facsimile of a Page of Farrer's Field Notes for the Expedition to Western China in 1914 — 48
4.5 The Craven Nursery, Ingleborough — 53
4.6 The Terrace at Ingleborough House — 54
5.1 Studio Portrait of Vita Sackville-West, 1934 — 57
5.2 Vita Sackville-West, photographed by Cecil Beaton — 60
5.3 The Tower and Tower Lawn in 1942 — 61
5.4 The Rose Garden, 1942 — 62
5.5 Vita Sackville-West and Harold Nicolson, by Cecil Beaton — 64
5.6 The Tower at Sissinghurst — 64
5.7 The Gate onto the Tower Lawn, Sissinghurst, 1942 — 65
5.8 Plan of the Garden at Sissinghurst (present-day) — 66
7.1 'Bed of alpine succulents, crested with dwarf Agave'. (From First Edition of *Alpine Flowers for English Gardens*, by William Robinson) — 80
7.2 Plan of the Main Flower Border at Munstead Wood — 92–3
8.1 Miss Jekyll's Boots by Sir William Nicholson — 103
10.1 'Frontispiece of a book on alpine plants'. (From Alpine Flowers for English Gardens, by William Robinson) — 116
10.2 'After Loudon'. (From *Alpine Flowers for English Gardens*, by William Robinson) — 118
10.3 'A truly laudable attack on monotony' from 'a botanic garden not one hundred miles from London.' — 118
10.4 Sir Frank Crisp of Friar Park, Henley-on-Thames — 119
10.5 Miss Ellen Willmott of Warley Place, Essex — 120
10.6 The Limestone Cliff Beside Ingleborough Lake — 126
10.7 *Anemone robinsoniana* — 128
11.1 White Climbing Rose Scrambling over Old Catalpa Tree — 138
12.1 A Drawing done by Bowles of *Narcissus bulbocodium citrinus* for *A Handbook of Narcissus* — 146
13.1 Christmas Roses in a Munstead Vase — 156
14.1 Water-Garden with Paved 'Rills', Hestercombe, Somerset — 162

❧ *Acknowledgements* ❧

I should like gratefully to acknowledge the assistance of the following people in the preparation of this book: Mr Michael Felgate Catt who first had the idea and encouraged me to undertake the project; Mr Peter Herbert who kindly showed me the garden at Gravetye Manor and gave me access to William Robinson's photographs; Dr J.A. and Mrs Farrer who conducted me round the garden at Ingleborough; Mr Geoffrey Stebbings, the head gardener at Myddelton House. They all patiently answered many questions. I should like to thank Dr Brent Elliott and his staff at the Royal Horticultural Society's Lindley Library; the staff of the Cambridge University Library; Miss Valerie Finnis; Miss Sarah Hawkey; Mrs Ian Stewart; Miss Pamela Schwerdt; Miss Linda Wade and Mrs Rosalie Wingate. To my brother, Toby Buchan, who read the typescript and gave me unstintingly of his time and invaluable expert advice, I owe an enormous debt of gratitude, and also to my husband, Charles Wide, for his encouragement, forbearance, and word-processor.

I should like to thank Curtis Brown Ltd for permission to quote from the works of Vita Sackville-West, and Thomas Nelson and Sons Ltd for permission to reproduce extracts from the books of E.A. Bowles.

I should also like to thank all those whose names appear below, who took photographs, lent me pictures, or who granted me permission to reproduce pictures for which they held the copyright.

Colour Plates

Plate 1, Barry Hicks, courtesy of Peter Herbert. Plate 2, Peter Herbert. Plates 3, 4, 5, 6, 9, 10, 14, 15, 16, 17, 20, Valerie Finnis. Plates 11, 12, 13, Cressida Pemberton-Pigott, courtesy of The Royal Horticultural Society, Lindley Library. Plate 18, Jeremy Whitaker, courtesy of The National Trust Photographic Library. Plate 19, John Bethell, courtesy of The National Trust Photographic Library.

Black and White Figures

Figs. 1.1, 1.3, 1.4, 1.5, 1.6, 1.7, courtesy of Peter Herbert. Figs 1.2, 5.1, courtesy of the National Portrait Gallery, London. Fig 2.1, courtesy of the copyright holder and the National Portrait Gallery, London. Figs. 2.5, 2.7, 5.3, 5.4, 5.7, courtesy of *Country Life*. Figs. 2.2, 2.3, 2.4, 2.6, 2.8, 4.3, 4.4, 7.1, 7.2, 10.1, 10.2, 10.3, 10.7, 11.1, 13.1, 14.1, by permission of the Syndics of Cambridge University Library. Figs 3.1, 3.3, 3.5, 3.6, 3.8, 3.9, 12.1, Cressida Pemberton-Pigott, courtesy of The Royal Horticultural Society, Lindley Library. Figs. 3.2, 10.4, 10.5, courtesy of the Trustees of the Royal Botanic Gardens, Kew. Fig. 3.4, courtesy of Thomas Nelson and Sons Ltd. Figs 4.1, 4.5, 4.6, courtesy of Dr J.A. and Mrs Farrer. Fig. 4.4, courtesy of The Alpine Garden Society. Figs. 5.2, 5.5, Cecil Beaton, courtesy of Sotheby's, London. Fig. 5.8, courtesy of Michael Joseph Ltd. Fig. 10.6, Dr G.C. Farnell. Fig. 8.1, courtesy of the copyright holder and the Tate Gallery, London.

Plates 7, 8; Figs. 3.7, 4.2, 5.6, are from photographs taken by the editor.

Ursula Buchan

❧ • *Introduction* • ❧

Writers have always been attracted to the cause of gardening, and the making of gardens, to explain, to encourage and to extol. Since the days of Pliny the Elder, such writing has provided not just the commentary but even, at times, the spur to changing fashions and customs, and neither wars, nor rumours of wars, have ever staunched the flow of ink. At no time, however, has that writing been more prolific, or more influential on a mass public, than in the century after 1870. It was, of course, a time of the most rapid and profound technological, economic, and social change in industrial Britain, and the rumblings of great conflicts and the creakings of painful adjustment could be heard quite clearly in the seemingly detached and cosy world of the garden. The upheaval resulted very quickly in changes in circumstances which put 'gardening' within the reach of ordinary people; people whose interests and aspirations differed markedly from those of the owners of the large estates, the arbiters of fashion in the preceding century. The most inspired chroniclers of these changes in horticultural taste and preoccupations were William Robinson, Miss Gertrude Jekyll, E.A. Bowles, Reginald Farrer, and the Hon. Victoria (Vita) Sackville-West. They were by no means alone, nor were they unaffected by contemporary opinion, but in their different ways, their work encompasses all that was best and most influential in garden writing from the mid-Victorian era until 1960. Without them, the history of gardening and garden design in the last hundred years would have been very different.

On one level, their writings are fascinating as period pieces, opening the door on a world that has disappeared as completely as gas-lamps and kitchen maids. These writers did not think as we do. For Miss Sackville-West, a very small garden was half an acre; Miss Jekyll considered that her house at Munstead Wood was a cottage;

Robinson was able to plant hundreds of thousands of trees around his estate; neither Farrer nor Bowles needed to work for their livings, and could spend their time walking in the mountains and freely collecting plants that were rare then and are now strictly protected. Labour was cheap, as were plants, and garden writing generally assumed that the reader had not only the time available for planning on a large scale but also the means and the will to bring such plans to fruition. In the early years of this century Miss Ellen Willmott, a friend of Robinson, employed 104 garden staff at Warley Place and, although gardening on that scale was unusual, it was not thought astonishing or excessive. There was, as nannies used to say, no such word as 'can't'.

Yet although that world has disappeared, there are many people still alive who knew these writers, or who worked for them, so that they are not so far removed from us as we may think. Robinson's story may strike us as a moral tale, drawn from an uplifting Victorian tract, of the rewards that follow from energy and enterprise, but his time is linked to our own, and there are strands of thought in his work that connect him to us.

In any case, the works of these five writers should not be appreciated primarily as period pieces. Although much of what they created has now gone (gardens rarely survive quite intact and unchanged the death or leaving of their creators), their writing lives on, as fresh and as comprehensible as when it was first published. The manners and attitudes of their day may have changed beyond recognition, but we may still tap the flow of their knowledge and inspiration. Not only does what they wrote give immense pleasure on its own account, but there is much of lasting practical and aesthetic value in these pages, born of first-hand experience, and recounted with relish. Slugs did for Farrer's campanulas as surely as they will destroy ours;

we may derive the same sort of enjoyment that Bowles did in the raising of new hybrids; plant associations and colour combinations concern us as they did Miss Jekyll—indeed, it is largely because of Miss Jekyll that we know that they matter.

Over the years, gardeners have absorbed their advice so completely that it is sometimes hard to comprehend the enormous influence that they exerted in their own lifetimes. It was not because they were the first to express new ideas, but rather because of their ability to convey those ideas attractively and persuasively. Robinson and Miss Jekyll shaped the present-day flower garden; Farrer and Bowles did the same for the rock-garden; fired by the example of the first two, Miss Sackville-West made visible at Sissinghurst all that was best in their writing and her own, and thereby realised that ideal of a pastoral but ordered simplicity towards which they had striven. Farrer and Bowles represented the complementary but parallel tradition of the botanist/gardener, as interested in individual plants and their habits as in the use of plants to paint a garden-picture. They did not, however, ignore the garden itself completely, as too many specialist growers have done since. All five embraced the idea of a plant's inherent value rather than its place merely as an atom in a molecular structure, or an extra in a crowd scene, without individual identity. Such ideas may now seem commonplace or obvious, but without them it is unlikely that today's gardening would display a tithe of its present artistry, variety and skill.

Miss Sackville-West's death in 1962 can be said to mark the end of the era. It is true that these five have successors, both as gardeners and as writers, but in the cramped world of the now-prevalent small garden, ingenuity in dealing with a limited space has become all important—we have moved into the age of the compromise. The demands of 'leisure' (a word never found in its new meaning in the writings of these people) now supersede the requirements of beauty and the congruous relationship of space, height, light, shade and colour. The search for attainable leisure has ensured the pre-eminence of gardens to be played in, sat in, or be seen in—anything, in fact, but gardened in. Such gardens are for those who are not keen gardeners; for those who are, the desire for beauty has resolved itself into specialisation, in the growing of alpines, say, or greenhouse plants, orchids, roses. The general has necessarily been sacrificed in favour of the particular.

With the shrinking in space has come a shrinking-away from the grand scheme. There is a small, but prominent, band of gardening writers who keep the adventurous and risk-taking spirit alive, in their search for better plants and better effects. Readers of this collection will find echoes of many of the modern gardening journalist's preoccupations, but it is apparent that the nerve and self-assurance that so distinguishes these five writers barely survives. It is significant that there is as much, if not more, harking back to the past in garden design than there is looking to the future.

With care and thought, yesterday's influence will spur today's innovation, but I have not chosen these five writers just because of their influence; they are represented here because they also wrote exceptionally well. Their work is full of wit, irony, lyricism, vivid imagery and profound feeling which has successfully found expression in words, and even humility. The writing is in most cases refreshingly undidactic, and is also wonderfully discursive, for these people saw gardening as part of life, rather than as some discrete occupation to be described solely within its own narrow terms of reference. They were merciless critics of the second-rate but we should not be cast down by their rigorous counsels of seemingly unattainable perfection, for their energy was exceptional even by the measure of their own energetic time.

By comparison, much modern garden-writing is accurate and painstakingly informative yet almost impossible to read with any pleasure or excitement. It is dull, timid and undiscerning. Senseless adjectives are piled high on top of each other so that 'beautiful's, 'lovely's, 'superb's, pepper the pages but even so we may learn little from it. It is in marked contrast with the vigorous, partisan, self-confident, opinionated writing of these five writers, not afraid to call a plant hideous if it is so, or to enter the lists in defence of one style of gardening at the expense of another. They could be partial, even prejudiced, and there are echoes in this book of skirmishes fought out on long-forgotten battlefields, the atmosphere of which I have tried to recapture.

The horticultural world then, as now, was small and tightly knit. These five all knew at least some of the others and, in many instances, they seem, in their writing, to be speaking more to each other than to their readers. The same friends and contemporaries appear in their books and in the biographies of them, as though they were part of a gardening *Dance to the Music of Time*. It is interesting, too, to remember that gardening has always been accepted as a 'fit recreation for a gentleman' even if, at some periods, practical work was thought the proper occupation of the hired man alone. Even Miss Sackville-West, with her aristocratic connections, received no condemnation for her pursuit of such a hobby; rather the reverse. Since gardening embraces all classes, it is not surprising that Robinson, the Irish professional gardener of dim origins, should have found himself treated as an equal by his gentlemanly neighbours when he had become rich enough to buy Gravetye Manor.

Selection, if not the secret of art, is certainly necessary and desirable. In compiling this anthology my first consideration has been good writing, capable of being read for its own sake as well as for what it teaches. To that end I have occasionally sacrificed the useful in favour of the readable. Second, the pieces should be original, even if the circumstances which prompted them have changed; or they should be historically interesting, closely observed, or practically valuable.

It is inevitable that I should have missed out some readers' favourite passages, for which they may condemn me, but, while I hope that I have covered every major aspect of these writers' lives and writing, this selection is essentially personal. I can only assure anyone thus disappointed of the agonies I have endured to keep the material within the compass of a single volume, which has meant leaving out much that I should dearly have liked to include. At the same time it must be said (indeed, I freely and gladly admit it) that this anthology falls some way short of being a truly representative collection. I have, as it were, censored some indifferent writing, believing that it is unnecessary for the reader to plough through much that is unworthy, thoughtless, or just plain bad. Each of these five writers could be repetitive and they were occasionally guilty of switching onto literary autopilot. There are, too, some instances of duplication when the same advice, and even the same phrases, can be found in several books. Robinson was particu-

larly given to this, so that it is a little misleading to state that he wrote nineteen books, for some passages were copied from one book to another; much of *Hardy Flowers*, for example, is lifted from *Alpine Flowers for English Gardens*. In this case I have concentrated on what I am certain was written by Robinson himself since in *The English Flower Garden* there are contributions by many other writers.

The chapters are arranged thematically, although it is true that a few of the extracts would fit happily under more than one heading. The reader who is allergic to rock gardens, but nurses a passion for greenhouse plants, will know what to skip. Not every aspect of horticulture is exhaustively covered: some may wonder, for example, about the dearth of material on kitchen-gardens, or herbs, or fruit-growing. This is simply because I could not find enough on these subjects by all five to justify including any extracts.

As a general rule, I have left the writers to speak for themselves. Where modern practice widely diverges, however, or where what they wrote has now been thoroughly superseded by modern innovations or theory, I have said so. I have applied the same rule to the use of Latin names (the frequent changing of which is the bane of the conscientious gardener's life) and therefore only occasionally, when a whole genus has been renamed, have I commented. I have not attempted to correct trivial mistakes, or to point out what varieties are no longer available, although I have been unable to resist remarking on inconsistencies or eccentricities.

In the end, I have been guided by my own interests and enthusiasms, and thus the selection may say more about me than about the five writers I have chosen. I wished to give myself pleasure in the collection of those passages that amused, inspired, and even exasperated me and to pass on what I could of that pleasure to others who had yet to discover these writers, many of whose books are, in any case, difficult or expensive to obtain. In the course of preparing this anthology I have learnt a great deal, so lightly and with so little pain. Both as a reader and a gardener I have been inspired by their vision, and I have come to share their enjoyment of what Bowles called 'the bright and happy days'.

Ursula Buchan

CHAPTER
❧ 1 ❧

William Robinson

1838~1935

Figure 1.1 Etching of William Robinson by Francis Dodd

William Robinson was born on 15 July 1838, in Ireland; precisely where is a mystery. There is some debate as to his parentage; originally it was thought he was of peasant stock but it seems more likely he was the son of Lord St George's land agent, who ran off to America with Lady St George, when William was about ten years old. This rather undesirable family fact is presumably the reason why he never said much at all about his early years.

After working as a garden boy at Curraghmore, employed by the Marquis of Waterford, he went to work for the Reverend Sir Henry Hunt Johnson-Walsh, a landowner, clergyman and keen gardener, at Ballykilcavan in County Laois. By the age of 21 Robinson had risen to be foreman in charge of the glasshouses and would perhaps have stayed in Ireland all his life if it had not been for an unfortunate incident that occurred in the winter of 1861. The story goes that he quarrelled either with his employer or the head gardener, let the fires go out in the glasshouses, knowing that on such a cold night all the tender plants would die, and set off for Dublin. It may have been that after the row he walked out immediately only to remember on the road that he had not stoked the fires. We will probably never know the exact truth of this but it is hard to imagine a man so passionately devoted to the care of plants doing such a thing on purpose, even in a fit of the hot temper which he undoubtedly possessed and it is unlikely, too, that he would have received anything but a cold reception from David Moore, the Director of the Botanic Gardens at Glasnevin in Dublin, to whom he straightaway presented himself, if the latter considered that he had misbehaved. It may be a story that has lost nothing in the telling.

Moore did see him, however, and recommended him to Robert Marnock, the Curator at the Royal Botanic Society's garden in the Regent's Park in London. Marnock was a talented and influential garden designer and under his hand the Regent's Park flourished. He became a lifelong friend of Robinson's. The young man was not put in charge of the greenhouses, it must be said, but instead rose quickly to be Foreman of the Educational and Herbaceous Department which had a unique small garden of British native flowers. He became most interested in the British flora, hunting the woods and lanes of rural England and even the cliffs of the South Coast for unusual plants. This interest can be traced in his writing all through his life. In the following year, 1862, he became engaged for the only time in his life, but he was jilted for another, richer man and he never married, or indeed, it is thought, ever formed a strong attachment again. With Marnock as a sponsor, he was elected a Fellow of the Linnaean Society in April 1866, which was a signal honour for a young professional gardener: his drive, enthusiasm and botanical expertise had been swiftly recognised. The following month he resigned from his job.

Three years before, he had begun to contribute pieces to *The Gardener's Chronicle*, and in 1867 he went to Paris as the horticultural correspondent of *The Times*, to cover some aspects of the French International Exhibition. He was most impressed by French gardens and also Parisian parks, such as the Parc Monceau. He thoroughly approved of French methods of fruit culture. His first book *Gleanings from French Gardens* came out in April 1868. There are remarks in it which, though mildly expressed, are the forerunners of his later obsessions. He told his readers in England 'how far we have diverged from Nature's ways of displaying the beauty of vegetation'.[1] He was evidently profoundly influenced by the writings of John Ruskin. He was sufficiently outspoken in this book for it to make a considerable impact, and it went into a second edition the following year.

In 1868 he made his first visit to the Alps, which quite enthralled him and made a lasting impression and, in 1870, *Alpine Flowers for Gardens* was published. This was not the very first book on the subject but proved most influential

Figure 1.2 The Reverend Samuel Reynolds Hole, after 1888 Dean of Rochester

as did *The Wild Garden*, also published in that year. Both were quite gentle in their criticism of current gardening practices and, indeed, even approbatory of certain features which later were to incur Robinson's wholehearted disapproval. The second edition of *The Wild Garden*, however, was substantially revised. Also out in 1870 and 1871 were *Hardy Flowers* and *The Subtropical Garden*. His energy was prodigious.

In 1870 he went to North America, both to see the flora and to meet the people. He and his brother James sought out their father and asked him for money which they received. This may well have spurred Robinson to start on a venture which he had discussed with the well-known rosarian, the Reverend Samuel Reynolds Hole, in the Regent's Park in 1865, that of setting up a weekly paper entirely devoted to gardening matters.

This magazine, *The Garden*, though it never made money, had, with its opinionated stance, a tremendous impact on interested gardeners, especially of the wealthier sort. Its contributors included Miss Jekyll after her meeting with Robinson at the paper's office, 37 Southampton Street in 1875, and clerical gardeners like Hole and Canon Ellacombe, whose rectory garden at

Bitton in Gloucestershire was a haven for rare and interesting plants. Even John Ruskin occasionally contributed articles. Robinson continued to edit it till 1899, when he handed the editorship to Miss Jekyll briefly, and then to E. T. Cook. This magazine, sold by Robinson in 1919, merged with *Homes and Gardens* in 1927.

In 1879 he founded another paper, *Gardening Illustrated*, which he sold 40 years later, in 1919. It joined with *The Gardener's Chronicle* in 1956. This periodical, practical and often technical, was aimed at suburban and villa gardeners, of which there were now a great many, and it was such a financial success—it sold 30,000 copies a week in 1881—that Robinson was able to invest heavily and profitably in London property and became quite well-to-do. Financial independence freed him to publish other magazines, notably *Cottage Gardening* (1892–8) and the expensively produced, but nevertheless short-lived, *Flora and Sylva* (1903–5).

1883 saw the publication of Robinson's most famous work, *The English Flower Garden*, which went into 15 editions and nine reprints in his lifetime, and was revised as late as 1956 by Roy Hay. It is upon this book that Robinson's reputation with future generations principally depends. His purpose was radically to change the direction of gardening in this country, although it is fair to say that a great deal that he said in this book was not absolutely new. He actually wrote no more than a fifth of the first edition, acknowledging the contributions of 71 others, so in effect it was an anthology of the writings of the most influential horticulturists of the day, under Robinson's editorial direction. As a directory of plants hardy in the British Isles it was without rival.

So rich did he become that he was able, in 1883, to buy the Elizabethan manor-house of Gravetye and 360 acres at West Hoathly in Sussex. Here he settled down for the rest of his life, and here he created his first and only garden. He renovated the house, adding a new hall that was completed in 1890, and planned the garden according to the precepts that he had set down in so many articles and books. He also did some designing of other people's gardens, including work for Miss Jekyll's mother at Munstead. The garden of which he was most proud was Shrubland Park in Suffolk which had been one of the most excessive examples of bedding-out with narrow beds of different-coloured brick and house-walls naked of climbers.

Figure 1.3 Portrait of William Robinson, aged 84

He was a man of varied enthusiasms. He took up the cause of cremation or urn-burial, writing *God's Acre Beautiful: or the Cemeteries of the Future*, which was published in 1880. He had been a moving spirit in the foundation of the Cremation Society in 1874 and his book undoubtedly had an effect on government policy. Cremation was made legal in 1884.

He was also concerned about air pollution and insisted that only wood should be burned at Gravetye. He engaged a French fumiste to improve the chimneys for, when he arrived at the house, every fireplace smoked. The fruits of his experiences are to be found in *My Wood Fires and their Story*, 1917, extended and retitled *Wood Fires for the Country House and Cottage* in 1924.

He was a passionate and discerning collector of late nineteenth-century artworks, especially by Corot, and he patronised English artists like H. Moon and Alfred Parsons, both as illustrators for his papers and also as painters of the landscape at Gravetye. He loved the countryside deeply and was very interested in what we now call conservation; this spurred him to plant many thousands of trees around the garden and on the estate. It also led him into a venture as a local farmer, for which he was not really suited and which he eventually gave up. As the years went by he went to London less often, leaving the running of his papers more and more to others.

In 1909, when he was 71, he had a bad fall and hurt his back. He failed to get better and syphilis was diagnosed. It is probable that he had suffered from this for many years, but it had not shown itself till his spine was injured. He was paralysed and spent the rest of his life in a wheelchair. This was a bitter blow for him but he mitigated the worst effects by buying a car and, after the First World War, a custom-built Citröen half-track vehicle so that he could get around the large estate. (Miss Sackville-West recalled a terrifying ride she endured in this on a visit to Gravetye in the late twenties.) A man of his determination was not to be defeated by illness. In 1911 he caused to be published, by the Oxford University Press, a beautiful volume, on hand-made paper, called *Gravetye Manor, or Twenty Years' Work Round an old Manor House*, which comprised extracts from the diaries that he had methodically kept. In 1914, the companion volume, *Home Landscapes*, appeared, which was primarily concerned with trees in the estate's landscape. In 1910 he recruited Ernest Markham as head gardener to oversee his staff in the way he no longer could. This was a happy choice, for Markham shared Robinson's devotion to trees and shrubs, especially clematis, about which they both wrote books. The head gardener's name is commemorated by such fine clematis as *C. markhamii*, 'Ernest Markham' and 'Markham's Pink'.

Despite his disability Robinson remained active to the end of his life, even travelling abroad accompanied by his nurse and he managed to make the 30 mile journey, in December 1932, to Miss Jekyll's funeral. In 1933, the year of the fifteenth and last edition of *The English Flower Garden* he was offered, and refused, a knighthood. He died on 12 May 1935, at Gravetye, at the age of 97 and his remains were cremated.

In 1888, Viscountess Wolseley (as she later became), who founded the Glynde School for Lady Gardeners, went to Gravetye and described her host as six foot tall with a black beard and a keen face. Many people commented on the softness of his voice and the Irish twinkle in his eye. Although he never married he was by no means misogynistic, and he was kind to children. His last words are reputed to have been, 'Children are always very delightful'.[2] He was

well-read, with an enquiring mind and an encyclopaedic memory. He was largely self-taught, making himself fluent in French in a short time. The lack of formal education shows occasionally in the over-elaborateness of his prose-style, and his weakness for quoting high-flown poetry. It may also explain his allergy to Latin names, however venerable and widely-used they were.

He was liked and respected by most of his staff, neighbours and gardening associates; by those, that is, who looked beyond his reputation for formidability. He did not, however, encourage close friendships, and some found him distant and detached. Those who admired him, did so for his unflagging enthusiasm, courageous determination and his perfectionism, for he had no patience with the second-rate. With all those gifts, he made at Gravetye a garden of rare beauty and serenity.

He is remembered, it must be said, as a man who became increasingly quirky as the years went by. It is tempting to attribute this entirely to his illness but, even as a young man, his pugnacity could antagonise his colleagues or opponents, and his contradictory nature exasperate it is possible to trace his progressive angularity in the later editions of his books, and his battle with Sir Reginald Blomfield over 'formalism' was nothing short of ridiculous overreaction. I should add that Blomfield was capable of just as much ill-judged combativeness, but he did not start the fight, and Robinson also attacked John Sedding, whose *Garden-Craft, Old and New* was published posthumously, so the man had no chance to refute the charges.

He fought with the villagers over a right of way, a dispute which in the end involved a law suit, which he won. He wrote belligerent letters to Sir Joseph Hooker, the director of Kew, over the bedding-out schemes there, which Hooker took in surprisingly good part.

The conclusion cannot be avoided that at times he enhanced his own reputation unduly and when, for example, he changed his mind about carpet-bedding, he did his best to suppress his earlier and by then rejected opinions. It was not unknown for him to lift material from other magazines without acknowledgement and he treated some contributors to *The English Flower Garden* with an attitude which bordered on the cavalier. To cite just one example, in the sixth edition he dropped completely the attribution to William Wildsmith, who had written nearly all the chapter on summer bedding. In the later editions it is often hard to say who wrote what.

His standing has remained so enormous partly because, in the course of a long life, which saw the predecease of his opponents and detractors, he did not do much to deny his reputation as the great gardening innovator. That is not to say, of course, that he did not deserve a great deal of the credit which accrued to him for, as far as the full-scale attack on the bedding-out system is concerned, the advocacy of hardy plants and the suggestion that the garden could be a place of beauty all the year round, if Robinson was not exactly a lone voice, his certainly made the most noise. But it is as a propagandist of genius that he should be remembered principally, and not as an originator.

He never claimed, as some have claimed for him, to have invented the herbaceous border as a more satisfactory alternative to summer bedding because it was filled with permanent and hardy plants. Certainly *The English Flower Garden* was a revelation to many because of the numbers of them that he described. But there were herbaceous borders at Arley Hall in Cheshire, which incidentally still survive, as early as 1846 and the horticultural journalist, Shirley Hibberd, referred in the 1850s to them as existing in the seventeenth century. Nor did he ever deny the existence of the 'mixed border' but it was not strictly accurate of him to maintain that till his championing of them, hardy plants had been virtually eliminated from nursery catalogues, by the prevailing fashion for half-hardy bedding.

It is probable that Robinson was the first to use the expression 'wild garden' to describe an area of ground beyond the garden proper where exotic hardy species could grow and should look after themselves, but it is also true that the nurseryman Peter Barr had been selling bulbs and annual seeds for naturalising in woodland from 1861.

He may have been the first to see the beauty and potential of the cottage garden, but it seems likely that Miss Jekyll was as strong a contemporary influence. Nor was he alone in rejecting the extravagant use of topiary when it was taken to illogical conclusions.

One may say that as Robinson was such a very skilled propagator of ideas, it matters little that those ideas were not his own. However, he has irritated some modern garden historians because they believe he puffed up his own reputation for originality at the expense of others and, in the process, misled future generations. It would be a pity if a fault like this should tarnish, even slightly, the reputation of a man who was such a great gardener. My own view is that he should be protected as much from his friends as his enemies, for the legend of his great originality began long before his death. In 1918, Sir Herbert Maxwell told him,

> I look back to the early seventies when your precepts were first taking effect, and I marvel at the change that has come over British gardens. You must surely feel gratified that it is owing to your books and the original *Garden* that, for every amateur who took an intelligent interest in horticulture fifty years ago there are now hundreds ...[3]

The headline in the *London Evening News* on his 95th birthday read: 'He changed the Face of England. Grand Old Man of the New Gardening'.[4]

What his critics cannot overlook is his sure touch for effective publicity and his fervour in pursuing his objectives. In the course of his long life he wrote 19 books and edited and wrote forewords for several more. He was a prodigious writer of articles, both signed and unsigned, in his periodicals. It cannot be denied, of course, that as a result his work could become repetitive. His hobbyhorses continued to be flogged long after they had died the death. His writing style, often most lively and inspired, could sometimes revert to turgid reiteration.

To keep the matter in perspective, however, it is important to think of Robinson as a missionary who felt there was a vast core of ignorance and error to break down and his skill as a polemicist, helped by an exceptional energy, earns him a place not only as one of the great garden writers of the last hundred years but also as one of the founders of the modern style of gardening. What use was it, after all, for innovative gardeners to pursue new horticultural practices if there were not the Robinsons, Jekylls and Farrers to trumpet their achievements to a receptive and ever-growing gardening public.

Gravetye

The legacy of three of our authors lies not just in their writings on gardening but also in the gardens themselves, which somehow have survived many vicissitudes and now flourish. It is true that much has disappeared at Munstead

Wood and at Ingleborough, which are both fragmented in ownership. However, seeing how personal a creation a garden is and of such evanescent quality, it is remarkable that, in a century that has seen such profound social and economic changes, the news is so encouraging. Sissinghurst still grows and thrives in a way that Miss Sackville-West would surely have commended, because of the foresight of her son in handing it over to the care of the National Trust; Myddelton House garden is in the process of restoration, with Bowles' books as ample guide; and Gravetye is enjoying a renaissance.

The man responsible for this last, Peter Herbert, who came to Gravetye in 1957 to open a country house hotel, has recreated what seemed irretrievably lost. When he arrived the weeds were so bad in the Formal Garden, that he had no idea there were paved paths there and although renovation of the house had to come first and work in the garden waited on a period of increased prosperity, he has gradually, using Robinson's published diary, *Gravetye Manor*, brought the garden back to that which Robinson would have known. He has been faithful to the spirit, although not a slavish adherent to the letter, for the small and frankly fussy beds in the

West Garden have been replaced by larger ones and the planting now owes more to Miss Jekyll's ideas on colour than to Robinson's rather more restricted conception. Nevertheless it is very likely that Robinson would have approved wholeheartedly.

'Fate gave me a piece of land in which all had to be done', he wrote of the garden when he first acquired the Gravetye estate. For many years it had been in the hands of local farmers and, although it was cultivated, it was done so in the execrable Victorian taste that he so inveighed against, with bedding-out round the house, a rockery close by and what trees and shrubs there were, were muddled and miscellaneous. The house was placed halfway up a hillside which, though not steep, was, as he saw at once, in need of terracing to give opportunities for level gardening. The estate did have the advantage of two large lakes in the valley to the south of the house. The making of the garden took several years and required a great deal of moving of earth, felling of trees where they blocked views and sight-lines and, at the same time, massive operations in the woods nearby to plant trees and create an idyllic English setting of wood- and pasture-land. He took full account of the situation of the

Figure 1.4 View across West Garden, Gravetye Manor

house and grounds. The air was cooler there than in more low-lying Sussex, but it was not a frost-pocket and the range of plants that would thrive was extensive.

First he levelled the large but ugly site to the north and east of the house, which he called The Playground (now the Long Lawn). This had contained rockery, fernery and rose-garden; it is now a serene and uncluttered length of grass. In the retaining walls and on the sloping ground above the Playground he introduced alpines; planting walls with rock plants was an idea he shared with Miss Jekyll. To the east of the Playground he put a belt of yew trees and built a summerhouse.

In March 1886 he laid out the Formal Garden (the West Garden) with lawn and corner flower beds. Here he planted his beloved tea roses; these were fragrant but not very hardy roses that, though very pretty, were bound to go out of fashion once the sturdier hybrid teas came in; he underplanted them with small rock plants such as *Sedum*. Also here, and in the South Garden, he grew border carnations and his so-called Tufted Pansies (crosses between the native *Viola tricolor* and the alpine species like *cornuta*). These had much more charm for him than the larger

florists' varieties. In 1902 he redesigned the beds in the West Garden, making 46 rectangular ones, which, from his photographs, look unnecessarily small. The present owner has simplified the design, replacing many of the beds with lawn, which is what Robinson conceived originally, flanked by flower-borders in an integrated colour-scheme. On the north side of this garden, he built a formal tank where he grew Marliac's water-lilies (see Chapter 14).

Amongst the rhododendrons in the terrace above the West Garden he planted Michaelmas daisies, which he called Starworts, and whose popularity he did much to promote. His philosophy of wild gardening found expression there and in the Alpine Meadow, below the West Garden, leading down to the Lakes, where thousands of spring bulbs were naturalised: fritillaries, *Narcissus*, wild tulips, snowflakes, scillas, grape hyacinths, dog tooth violets (*Erythronium*), Star of Bethlehem and, of course, *Anemone appenina* and *Anemone robinsoniana*. The meadow was cut for hay when the bulbs had died down.

The Upper Lake was drained after a gardener committed suicide or was accidentally drowned, the stories vary, and Robinson planted the

Figure 1.5 William Robinson lying amongst Tufted Pansies, Gravetye

Figure 1.6 View across West Garden, Gravetye, 'After my beds were completed'

Figure 1.7 'Colony of Starworts among Rhododendrons' by H.G. Moon

boggy ground with moisture-loving trees. In the last few years the lake has been filled once more.

Between 1898 and 1900, he developed a kitchen-garden of more than one acre outside the garden proper, which, because of the way the land lay, was set out in a broad oval. The wall was made of stone quarried on the estate and is a most impressive sight, especially where an old mulberry tree leans over the wall from the wood above to form a bower. Here, typically, there is a plaque with the date and Robinson's initials. (There are plaques all over the estate with legends such as '1888 Corsicans' [pines] and the house itself is dotted with inscriptions, in one case two in the same room. No one can be in any doubt as to whose legacy this is.) He called this his Fruit Garden and for 15 years employed a French fruit expert to work there.

Robinson's lasting and monumental achievement was the planting of hundreds of thousands of ornamental trees, which now set Gravetye apart from the surrounding countryside by the range of autumn colour against a constant background of evergreen trees. He used maples, hickories and willows, Austrian and Corsican pines and cedars. In one year alone he planted 120,000 trees. Left by Robinson to the nation, the woodlands are now managed by the Forestry Commission. He undoubtedly had a good eye for landscape possibilities, removing fences where possible and planting belts and masses of trees and hedges rather than dotting them about. Now, some hundred years later, the effect at any time of the year is spectacular.

He was fortunate in having considerable and experienced help, for in the case of making the upper drive to the house much moving of earth was necessary to make the approach simple but attractive. To the east of the courtyard is the East Garden, a large slope bisected by grass paths. Here are planted rhododendrons and many other shrubs left, as he would have liked, to look after themselves. There is also a fine stand of mature Scots Pines, which he discovered when he came, and to which he gave prominence and space by felling the surrounding trees.

In Robinson's time there were many pergolas but only two original ones remain, the others being victims of the dead hand of time and decay. The one from the forecourt to the Alpine Meadow, from which hangs a venerable wisteria, is particularly effective as a frame to the view.

Robinson's great strength as a gardener lay in his considerable knowledge of hardy plants and their requirements and his confidence which led him to carry out his plans with conviction. By the time he came to own a garden his views had matured and, though occasionally he found it necessary to modify them in the face of practical considerations, Gravetye exists today as a fitting memorial to his foresight and sensitivity to beauty.

Notes

1. W. Robinson, *Gleanings from French Gardens*, 2nd edn (Frederick Warne, 1869), p. 2.

2. Quoted in G. Taylor, *Some Nineteenth Century Gardeners*, 1st edn (Skeffington, 1951), p. 87.

3. Quoted in M. Allan, *William Robinson*, 1st edn (Faber and Faber, 1982), p. 205.

4. Quoted in ibid., p. 223.

Gertrude Jekyll

1843-1932

Figure 2.1 Gertrude Jekyll by Sir William Nicholson (1920)

It would no doubt astonish Gertrude Jekyll, who despite her prodigious talents was not unduly boastful, to know that her ideas have influenced more gardeners in the last hundred years than any other person, before or since. But it is so. Through her writings, and through the example of the gardens that she designed, especially those for Lutyens' houses, she has touched and caught the imagination of millions. There are few good gardens, even today, that do not exhibit some feature or colour grouping that she advocated. She was fortunate to see her influence spread in her own lifetime; she was a prophet with honour in her own country. Agnes Jekyll commented, in the Introduction to Francis Jekyll's Memoir, published soon after Gertrude's death, 'It has been said recently and with truth, that no one except the Creator has done more to beautify the face of England than did Miss Jekyll ...'[1]

Born on 29 November 1843, of well-to-do parents, Gertrude Jekyll spent the first five years of her life in London, before the family moved to Bramley House near Guildford in Surrey. Here she roamed freely in a countryside distinctive for its sandy acid soil, but as yet hardly built over or spoiled. She quickly learned to recognise wild flowers, and to understand their ways, and the foundation was laid of a deep love of the Surrey landscape.

The atmosphere in which she grew to womanhood was cultured and intellectual. Her early artistic leanings, especially in the fields of music and painting, were fostered and in 1861 she took the bold step (in those days, for a young gentlewoman), of becoming a student at the

Kensington School of Art. Mrs Earle, of *Pot-Pourri from a Surrey Garden* fame, studied there at the same time. The impression one derives is that Miss Jekyll was independent-minded, bordering even on the politely rebellious. This course of study and the travels she was encouraged to undertake in Europe and the eastern Mediterranean in order to study art, show to what a tolerant and emancipated family she had the good fortune to belong.

Her qualifications as an artist were acknowledged by the Royal Academy when they accepted one of her pictures to be hung in Burlington House when she was only 23. At about the same time she met John Ruskin whose paintings and writings she had long admired. He, of course, was deeply impressed by the works of J.M.W. Turner, and so was Hercules Brabazon Brabazon to whom she was introduced in the late 1860s; his ideas on colour, which he was keen to share with his young friend, were profoundly to influence her paintings and later her designs for gardens.

The fact that she lived a metropolitan and cultivated existence at this time, is very much at variance with the received wisdom that all young unmarried Victorian ladies of good family stayed at home, living cloistered and cramped lives. She met William Morris in 1869, and it is likely that he encouraged her interest in the Arts and Crafts movement, of which he was the doyen, for at this time she not only painted but was a highly skilled worker of embroideries, a silversmith and a woodcarver, and was already showing an interest in gardening.

Her skills were recognised by, amongst others, the Duke of Westminster who commissioned her, in the 1870s, to advise on the decorations to his recently extensively altered Eaton Hall in Cheshire. About this time George Leslie, the artist, described her as 'Clever and witty in conversation, active and energetic in mind and body, and possessed of artistic talents of no common order, she would at all times have shone conspicuously bright among other ladies'.[2]

In 1868 her father inherited a house in Berkshire called Wargrave Hill and the family moved there and stayed till his death in 1876. Homesickness for Surrey then brought Gertrude and her mother back, this time to Munstead Heath near Godalming, where Mrs Jekyll had a house built for which Gertrude designed a garden. Her knowledge and interest in garden-

ing increased to such an extent that she became a contributor to William Robinson's journal, *The Garden*, from 1875. She became acquainted with his ideas on natural and wild gardening, and the good growing of hardy plants. Like Robinson, she was impressed by the ideas of Ruskin, Morris and the Pre-Raphaelite Brotherhood. She also became acquainted with the foremost amateur gardeners of the day, amongst them that triumvirate of exceptional clergymen, Canon Ellacombe, Dean Hole and the Reverend C. Wolley-Dod. In 1880, Robinson, accompanied by Dean Hole, visited Munstead Heath and he helped with the design of Mrs Jekyll's garden.

As the years went by, and Mrs Jekyll grew old and less able to cope with her daughter's stream of visitors, it was decided that Miss Jekyll should build a house nearby. To that end, in 1883, 15 acres of felled wood were bought, on soil 'excessively poor and sandy', across the road in Munstead Wood.

In 1889 came an event of considerable importance to Miss Jekyll and also, it must be said, for the direction taken by domestic architecture in this country. At a tea party at a house nearby called Littleworth, she met a young architect called Edwin Lutyens. It was soon agreed that he should collaborate with her on the design of her house at Munstead Wood, where she had already established a garden of great beauty. First he built 'the Hut' for her to live in while the main house was being constructed. This was finished in 1894. It was more of a cottage than a hut, and in later years she used it as a guest-house. In 1896, the house was begun. The stone was the local Bargate stone and the roof tiles were hand-made; the use of local and finely crafted materials was essential to their outlook. The doors and window frames were of well-seasoned oak, and the windows were small so that not too much light would enter to hurt her ailing eyes. At the west end of the large sitting-room was a large stone-hooded fireplace, and next to it a handsome staircase leading to a long, oak-beamed gallery above. The gallery overhung the house on the north side of the house, so that there was somewhere protected to sit in the courtyard outside. There are upstairs galleries in other Lutyens houses, notably Lindisfarne and the Deanery Garden, Sonning. His client and her requirements were at the centre of Lutyens' vision, and Miss Jekyll in her turn closely supervised the building of the house with him, deriv-

Figure 2.2 South Front of Munstead Wood with Scotch Briars. On the grass may be seen one of her much-loved cats. (From First Edition of A Gardener's Testament, *by Gertrude Jekyll)*

ing immense pleasure from seeing the craftsmen at work. There were one or two disagreements on policy, but both were very well satisfied with the result.

If there is ever such a thing as a distinct watershed in anyone's life, then so this meeting proved to be for Miss Jekyll. For the striking up of a friendship and association with Lutyens came at the same time as a rapid deterioration in her eyesight which, never good, had become a cause of grave concern. She visited a German eye specialist of terrifying eminence in 1891, who advised her most strongly to abandon close work such as embroidery and painting, and so she turned to gardening as the only realistic outlet left for her artistic and creative impulses. She did not give up her craftwork entirely, but she did feel constrained to curtail it.

The friendship forged between Edwin Lutyens and Gertrude Jekyll, despite an age difference of 25 years, was to be crucial to them both. Miss Jekyll had already completed several garden design commissions for friends, and it was not long before she was planning gardens for Lutyens' new houses, the first being Wood-

side at Chenies in Buckinghamshire. By 1900 they had collaborated on 27 projects and, by 1914, over a hundred. Theirs was a harmonious relationship, only occasionally marred by sharp divergence of opinion. This accord resulted from an understanding of each other's task. She brought to the partnership immense knowledge of local materials and craftwork, which chimed well with his unerring sense of place. He brought a depth of vision and wide creative imagination that she could well appreciate and to which she could respond. As Robert Lutyens wrote, Miss Jekyll found in his father, 'the ideal interpreter who eventually exalted her limited conception on to the plane of creative formal design'.[3] Both saw the house and garden as the two independent and inseparable halves of a mutually benefiting whole and the care Lutyens took over the design of garden steps, paths and pergolas was as complete as for any feature of his houses.

Although the houses remain, many of the gardens of this partnership have fallen into ruin. Some have been restored and, of these, the most notable is Hestercombe in Somerset, a garden of

Figure 2.3 The Circular Water-Court, Hestercombe, Somerset. (From Fifth Edition of Wall and Water Gardens, *by Gertrude Jekyll)*

three terraces, laid out between 1904 and 1909. The bottom terrace is a sunken 'plat' and beyond it, forming the southern boundary to the garden is a pergola spanning the width of the garden, with alternate square and round pillars in characteristic Lutyens style. Above the plat on the east and west sides are two rills (formal narrow and shallow canals), which run into square water tanks. Beyond the two pools are breaks in the pergola, through which there are spectacular views of Taunton Vale. In contrast to the house, which had been much altered to its detriment in the 1870s, Lutyens built a classically proportioned Orangery. Miss Jekyll filled the beds, terrace walls and rills with plants. Hestercombe represents the best ideal of informal planting within a strictly regulated and geometrical framework.

There is also Millmead in Surrey, which only extends to half an acre, and demonstrated what could be done in a relatively small space; Folly Farm, Sulhampstead, Berkshire, where the present owners have endeavoured to retain the Jekyll atmosphere, even where the original plantings have disappeared; and the Deanery Garden, Sonning, in Berkshire.

The architect and gardener, 'Ned' and 'Aunt Bumps', became fast friends, sharing as well as a complementary artistic sympathy, a sense of humour and of the absurd, and wide intellectual interests. While Miss Jekyll was still living in the Hut, Lady Emily Lytton, soon to be married to Lutyens, wrote:

> She is the most enchanting person and lives in the most fascinating cottage you ever saw. Mr. Lutyens calls her Bumps, and it is a very good name. She is fat and stumpy, dresses rather like a man, little tiny eyes, very nearly blind, and big spectacles. She is simply fascinating.[4]

Miss Jekyll sounds, from this description, like a

storybook portrait of a kindly mole.

In 1897, Edward Hudson, a friend and kindred spirit, founded *Country Life*. From 1901, Country Life published all her books with the exception of *Old English Household Life*. In 1897, on the day before she moved into the house at Munstead Wood she was the recipient of the highest award given by the Royal Horticultural Society, the Victoria Medal of Honour, of which there are now always 63, one for every year of Queen Victoria's reign.

In 1898, she was prevailed upon by Longmans to publish, in book form, a series of articles she had written in *The Guardian*, together with 71 of her own photographs, under the name of *Wood and Garden*. She had taken up photography in 1885, and was serious and professional in her approach. This book contained most of her deeply-held gardening beliefs. She was, like Robinson, a champion of the cause of 'natural' gardening, which was a far cry from the mid-Victorian diversion into the ways of garish and regimented bedding schemes. For such is all it was—a diversion, a temporary aberration from what the Europeans called 'English gardening'. The precepts that she sought to teach her readers in a gently assertive way were: the importance of striving for harmonious colour schemes; growing plants for their own sake and beauty; the importance of scented plants and foliage effects; and seeking to achieve simplicity and informality of planting within a formal framework.

These years saw a tremendous outpouring of creative energy. In 1900 the complementary volume, *Home and Garden* appeared, although she was already apologising for her lack of strength; in 1901, *Lilies for English Gardens* and *Wall and Water Gardens*; and the following year *Roses for English Gardens*. In 1904, her encyclopaedic knowledge of the old ways of Surrey life was set down in *Old West Surrey* enlarged in 1925 as *Old English Household Life*. For 40 years from 1891 she wrote prolifically in periodicals and national newspapers.

In 1904, *Some English Gardens* was published, and it was in that year that Miss Jekyll made her last trip to London. In 1907, *Flower Decoration in the House* came out, published by Country Life. 1908 saw the publication of the delightfully down-to-earth and amusing *Children and Gardens*. Although, or perhaps because, she was a maiden lady, she had a keen sympathy with children and, having lived a full and happy if rather solitary childhood, she wished to pass on

her youthful pleasures to others. It is marvellously illuminating, uncondescending and most informative, with drawings of loaves, penny buns and pumpkins to show what 'plan', 'elevation' and 'section' are. There is even a chapter on cats of which she was very fond.

Incredibly, considering how busy she was with design commissions that year, 1908 also saw the publication of *Colour in the Flower Garden*, later renamed *Colour Schemes for the Flower Garden*. This was probably the most considered and influential of all her books. For this work, her early training as an artist proved to be most valuable.

Of all her books, this is perhaps the one which contains the quintessence of her personal contribution to gardening *as a fine art*—the translation into terms of floral colour of a painter's vision and technique.[5]

And:

A precarious art, it may be objected, since the failure of one flower to bloom at a given moment may impair or destroy the balance of the whole composition . . . and somewhat out of fashion at a moment [1930s] when the trend of serious gardening has become botanical rather than pictorial—the collection and culture of new species rather than the production of new effects from familiar materials.[6]

Certainly the import of so many new plants from abroad in the early years of the century encouraged the collection-minded, but Miss Sackville-West has shown that the painting of garden pictures was by no means everywhere abandoned.

By 1910, Miss Jekyll was confined almost entirely to Munstead; however, even when active, she had rarely visited the sites for which she was devising planting schemes. She preferred working from plans and eliciting information from letters. In all she accomplished about 260 plans on her own account as well as the 100 or so on which she collaborated with Lutyens. Her eyesight was bad, she tired more easily, and she was very busy with her writing and gardening. This pattern of life continued almost till her death. Her friendship with Lutyens endured, although she did less landscape design with him and he had embarked on ambitious projects, which took him abroad, like the Government buildings of New Delhi from 1912 and war memorials in France after the Great War.

Gardens for Small Country Houses appeared in 1912 and describes several of the gardens that she had planned with Lutyens, including Millmead and Munstead Wood. To modern eyes the 'smallness' of the country houses seems rather relative.

Garden Ornament, which came out in 1918, contained less criticism of earlier fashions. Indeed, there are even pictures in it of parterres and bedding-out schemes.

Her writings were the rich, ripe fruits of years of practical experience and close observation and show an integrity of vision which is lacking in Robinson's work. The sales were considerable, not only in Britain but also in the United States, where American gardeners avidly followed Miss Jekyll's advice, even though rather different conditions often obtained. Mrs Francis King, one of the founders of the Garden Club of America, and herself an influential garden writer, was a friend and correspondent.

In 1920, Lutyens persuaded the most reluctant Miss Jekyll to sit for the portraitist, William Nicholson. Because she required the daylight hours for work, she sat for him only in the evening and, while she was otherwise engaged, he painted a picture of her old gardening boots, and created a painting as accomplished as the portrait and, if anything, more famous. It now hangs in the Tate Gallery.

She died on 8 December 1932, aged 89. She was buried in the churchyard at nearby Busbridge and was mourned by a wide circle of friends, as well as by a mighty company of keen gardeners.

Her appeal for her friends lay in her sharp intellect that never failed her, her sense of humour, easy wit and tolerant disposition, and her love of a good argument. Although fat and dumpy and frankly plain (Logan Pearsall Smith, a good friend, described her face as like 'some ancient, incredibly aristocratic denizen of a river jungle, gazing gravely out from the tangled reeds'[7]), she exerted a wonderful charm. The word often used to describe her is 'serene'. She could be acerbic with visitors, especially if she sensed she was being patronised, or her efforts under-rated, although the sharpness was often tempered by a twinkling humour, but she would go to great pains for anyone who was genuinely interested, like the factory boy from the north who advertised for advice on how to plant a window-box. People found her kindly but she could be formidable and even a little frightening. Her innocent snobbishness seems unattractive to us now; she wished for people to know their place and she laughed at poor people who tried, as she thought, to ape their betters. In this respect she was entirely of her time. Allied to this was her desire to hark back to an idealised earlier age, before the Industrial Revolution spelled the end, as she saw it, of honest craftsmanship. She even wrote a novel, about an England without iron, which was never published.

She was quietly but steadfastly religious; her last words are reported to have been 'Peace, perfect peace, in the arms of Jesus Christ'. From this conviction must have stemmed her courage, on which many people commented, especially in accepting the challenge of changed and undesired circumstances. Her partial blindness was a bitter blow and an intense sadness to her but, always observant, she learned to make the best of what sight she had. 'The will and power to observe' she wrote, 'does not depend on the possession of keen sight ... I often find that I have observed things that have escaped strong and long-sighted people'.[8] Her other senses were developed too. She wrote a great deal about scent, for even as a child she had a highly developed sense of smell and this became most important to her as she gradually ceased to be able to discern colour; her hearing also was acute. 'As if by way of compensation I have very keen hearing ... I can nearly always tell what trees I am near by the sound of wind in their leaves ...'[9]

She was an excellent practical gardener. She maintained, I am sure truthfully, that she had never written a line that had not been accounted for by her own work and experience. For example, in *Wood and Garden* she told her readers that: 'I have built and planted a good many hundred yards of dry walling with my own hands ...'[10]

She took so much care over everything she did. The secret of her success is to be found in this methodical working and also in her dislike of 'pure idleness' which seemed to her 'akin to folly, or even worse'. She described in the same book an incident, when 'half-lazily, and yet with a faint prick of the moral spur that urges me against complete idleness, I picked a leaf [of *Alchemilla alpina*] to have a good look at it ...'[11]

To her immense following of readers what set her apart from the common run of gardening writers was that intense power of observation, her unfeigned humility and childlike sense of wonder and a flowing, mellifluous, often humorous prose-style that was never patronising or obscure.

Of the five gardeners represented in this book, Miss Jekyll was incomparably the greatest. She was a genius and the enormous influence her work continues to exert over successive generations of gardeners is evidence of that. Her legacy endures in the few gardens she planned that survive; in those like Sissinghurst, Hidcote, Nymans and Great Dixter where her style has been consciously imitated; and in the countless private gardens, large and small, where her influence, often unconsciously absorbed, pervades.

Munstead Wood

Many years after the event, in 1927, Miss Jekyll recalled the year when Munstead Wood was acquired.

In the early eighties I became possessed of the fifteen acres in south-west Surrey where I have made my home. It is roughly triangular in shape, widest to the south, and slopes down to the north-west. There had been a close wood of Scotch Pine lately felled in the upper nine acres, then a wide strip of Chestnut coppice, and at the narrow end a small field of poor sandy soil. The sandy field is now a profitable kitchen garden, the middle space [i.e. the chestnut coppice] is the site of the house and surrounding lawn and shrubs and flowers, and the upper wild part, where the Scotch Pines were cleared, soon became filled with young trees of natural growth; seedling Pines, Birch, Holly, Oak, Mountain Ash and Spanish Chestnut. They all grew up together and my first care was to keep the kinds a little apart in order to get natural pictures of one kind of a tree at a time. A space near the middle was cleared for Azaleas and for a bit of Heath garden. Now, after forty years, it has

Figure 2.4 The Garden Court, Munstead Wood. (From Gardens for Small Country Houses, *by Gertrude Jekyll)*

all grown up into a state of satisfactory maturity.[12]

Her house was not begun till 1896 and the so-called 'Hut' nearby, where she lived till the house was finished, was not built till 1894; all the intervening years, while her mother was still alive, were spent, when time allowed, laying out the garden and especially the wild garden. She admitted frankly in *Gardens for Small Country Houses* that the fact that she designed and planted so much of it before she knew where the house was to be placed meant that awkward bits had somehow to be united.

In fact [she went on to say] there was no definite planning at the beginning. Various parts were taken in hand at different times and treated on their individual merits, and the whole afterwards reconciled as might most suitably be contrived.[13]

Most people will sympathise with her predicament, but though the development of Munstead Wood was piecemeal and gradual, it was nevertheless extremely important for the direction taken by the Lutyens and Jekyll partnership in later garden designs. She tried out so many of her ideas here.

At the same time as the house was built, the north court was laid out. Being shaded it was suitable for the growing of hostas, ferns and lilies, and these were separated from the sandstone paving, laid in circles, by box hedges. She grew hydrangeas in pots that stood on the paving. The felicitous connection of house with garden by way of an inviting paved courtyard was an idea developed to a high point by Lutyens.

Steps led down from here past a small water-tank to the Nut Walk of filberts (*Corylus maxima*), underplanted with her strain of primroses and also hellebores, anemones and daffodils; then on to a pergola which bisected this path more or less at right angles. East of the Nut Walk was the Michaelmas Daisy garden and beyond the pergola the Kalmia border. This garden was partly enclosed by a yew hedge, which was the continuation of the long garden wall that backed the main flower border; this was therefore at right angles to the Nut Walk. Between the Kalmia garden and the main borders was a yew hedge and in front of it 'The Cenotaph of Sigismunda', a stone seat whose title is thought to

have inspired Edwin Lutyens when naming his memorial in Whitehall to the British dead of the First World War. It literally means an empty tomb or monument to someone buried elsewhere.

The main flower border was 18 feet wide and 180 feet long. At the back there was a narrow path to make the gardeners' work of maintenance easier and, behind that, a bed of climbers under the tall sandstone wall. About one-third of the way along its length this border was divided by a broad path that led to a door in the wall and then on to the Spring Garden. The main border, designed to flower from July to October had a colour scheme, such as is described by her in Chapter seven, of cool blues, whites and yellows with grey foliage at one end and whites, purples and pinks with grey foliage at the other, gradually becoming warmer and stronger through the yellows and oranges to the middle where bright red predominated. Yuccas, at both ends and where the path crossed, provided an element to tie the scheme together.

The large Spring Garden, into which the door led and which also could be reached through a gate from the pergola, was at its best till early May and depended heavily, though not entirely,

Figure 2.5 Part of a Border at Munstead Wood, with Lilies, Yuccas, Euphorbia, *and* Eryngium

Figure 2.6 Munstead Bunch Primroses in the Nut Walk. (From First Edition of A Gardener's Testament, *by Gertrude Jekyll)*

on bulbs. Substance was provided by the striking leaves of Sweet Cicely (*Myrrhis odorata*), *Euphorbia wulfenii*, bergenias and *Veratrum nigrum*. There were tree paeonies to carry the interest on in early summer. Nearby was a special border with a grey, white, purple and pink colour scheme.

Beyond the Spring Garden and another wall was the kitchen garden, the potting sheds and, at the northern apex of the garden's triangle, the Thunderhouse built by Lutyens. She called it a 'raised gazebo'. Open to three sides it was ideal for watching a storm pass overhead. It was also almost the only place from where she had a good view of open country.

Near the Hut and to the east of the Rose Garden and shrub borders was the Rock Garden and the Hidden Garden, a private enclosure of shade-loving plants completely surrounded by 'unclipped yew, holly and *Quercus ilex*'.

Around the Hut was the June Garden, full of her cottage favourites, which many thought touchingly quaint and old-fashioned then: old shrub roses, lupins, white columbines, double paeonies, rosemary clipped into neat hedges and one of her best-loved roses, 'The Garland'.

> Of these useful garden Roses none is more beautiful than the Garland, with its masses of pretty blush-white bloom. It is well worth getting up at 4 A.M. on a mid-June morning to see the tender loveliness of the newly opening buds; for, beautiful though they are at noon, they are better still when just awaking after the refreshing influence of the short summer night.[14]

To the south-east of the house lay Miss Jekyll's great pride, the ten-acre Woodland Garden. Here her ideas on wild gardening were demonstrated as well as anywhere. On a thin, acid sandy soil she created a natural looking woodland, full of native trees, in four main groups, which merged at their edges: silver birch and hollies; oak; beech; and Scots pine. Five paths radiated from the lawn. The central one, opposite the sitting-room windows and the door of the house, was the broadest walk, where rhododendrons, grouped in compatible colours, were underplanted with ferns in the shade and British native heathers on the other side. She referred to it as her 'most precious possession'. Behind the rhododendrons could be seen the white trunks of the birches, in effective contrast.

Figure 2.7 Approach to the House, through the Wood

At the end of the vista was a double-trunked Scots pine, so handsome that it was preserved when its neighbours were felled.

The other paths were narrower and given up to particular sorts of plants. In one, ferns predominated, by another daffodils were naturalised amongst oaks and birches, another had large lumps of sandstone placed to create a rock-garden effect, where were planted alpine rhododendrons, gaultheria and pieris. 'At the beginning of all these paths I took some pains to make the Garden melt imperceptibly into the wood, and in each case to do it in a different way.'[15]

In the oak wood, the floor was covered with yellow and white Munstead polyanthus and, in a sunny clearing, she grew cistuses, which she had loved since her first visits as a young woman to the Mediterranean.

In the Woodland Garden she could indulge her passion for what she called 'flowery incidents', that is, placing a few plants in very particular situations in order to create a specific effect. One good example of this was the planting of white foxgloves where they would catch the light through the trees. She was careful to see that only one feature prevailed at any given time, lest the simplicity which she sought would be lost. When she planned the woodland and thin-

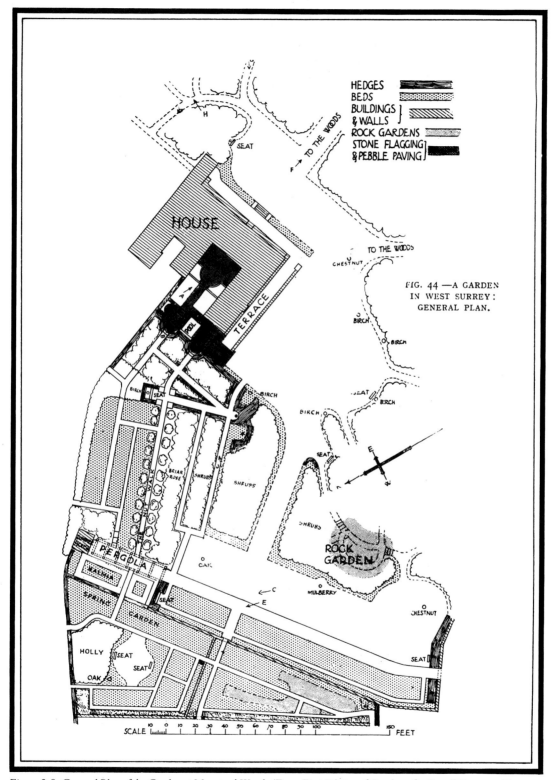

HEDGES
BEDS
BUILDINGS
& WALLS
ROCK GARDENS
STONE FLAGGING
& PEBBLE PAVING

FIG. 44 — A GARDEN
IN WEST SURREY:
GENERAL PLAN.

HOUSE

TERRACE

TO THE WOODS

TO THE WOODS

CHESTNUT

BIRCH

BIRCH

SEAT

BIRCH

BIRCH

BIRCH

SEAT

BIRCH

SEAT

BRIAR
ROSE

SHRUBS

SHRUBS

SHRUBS

PERGOLA

WALMA

SPRING
GARDEN

HOLLY

SEAT

SEAT

OAK

OAK

ROCK
GARDEN

SHRUBS

C

E

MULBERRY

CHESTNUT

SEAT

SEAT

SCALE 10 0 10 20 30 40 50 60 70 80 90 100 150 FEET

Figure 2.8 General Plan of the Garden at Munstead Wood. (From First Edition of Gardens for Small Country Houses,
by Gertrude Jekyll)

ned the seedling trees, she did so in order that striking groups would emerge. 'Now,' she wrote in 1908, 'after twenty years, the saplings have become trees, and the preponderance of one kind of tree at a time has given a feeling of repose and dignity'.[16]

The separation of the garden at Munstead Wood into smaller, and almost discrete, ele-ments required a unity of purpose that was quite out of the common way and a guiding spirit as able to encompass the larger vision as deal in the minutiae of garden planning. The passing of that spirit, coupled with the garden's requirement for 17 gardeners in Miss Jekyll's lifetime, tolled the death-knell for its intact survival after her death.

Notes

1. F. Jekyll, *Gertrude Jekyll*, 1st edn (Jonathan Cape, 1934), p. 12.

2. Ibid., p. 83.

3. R. Lutyens, *Sir Edwin Lutyens: An Appreciation in Perspective* (Country Life), quoted in B. Massingham, *Miss Jekyll*, 1st edn (Country Life, 1966), p. 92.

4. Lady Emily Lutyens, *A Blessed Girl* (Rupert Hart-Davis, 1953), p. 297.

5. Jekyll, *Gertrude Jekyll*, p. 150.

6. Ibid., p. 151.

7. Logan Pearsall Smith, *Life and Letters*, quoted in Jekyll, *Gertrude Jekyll*, p. 199.

8. G. Jekyll, *Home and Garden*, facsimile of 1st edn (Antique Collectors' Club, 1982), p. 349.

9. Ibid., pp. 349–50.

10. G. Jekyll, *Wood and Garden*, facsimile of 1st edn (Antique Collectors' Club, 1981), p. 168.

11. Jekyll, *Home and Garden*, p. 152.

12. G. Jekyll, *A Gardener's Testament*, F. Jekyll and G.C. Taylor (eds.), facsimile of 1937 edn (Antique Collectors' Club, 1982), pp. 13–14.

13. G. Jekyll and L. Weaver, *Gardens for Small Country Houses*, facsimile of 1st edn (Antique Collectors' Club, 1981), p. 36.

14. G. Jekyll and E. Mawley, *Roses for English Gardens*, facsimile of 1st edn (Antique Collectors' Club, 1982), p. 163.

15. G. Jekyll, *Colour Schemes for the Flower Garden*, facsimile of 1936 edn (Antique Collectors' Club, 1982), p. 43.

16. Ibid., p. 40.

CHAPTER
৯ 3 ৯
E. A. Bowles
1865-1954

Figure 3.1 E.A. Bowles with his dog, Kip

Bulls Cross, near Enfield, is a quiet collection of houses, surprisingly rural even now considering its proximity to London. In 1865, Myddelton House, through whose grounds flowed the New River bringing clean water to London, was the home of the Bowles family and in that year, on 14 May, Edward Augustus Bowles, their third surviving child, was born. The house is of white Suffolk brick and stands on the site of an Elizabethan red-brick house which was pulled down by his grandfather, H.C. Bowles, in 1818. It had been in the family's hands since 1724 when Michael Garnault bought it. He was of a Huguenot family which had fled from France in the late seventeenth century and made their money from acquiring a majority share in the New River Company. Bowles' father was the last Governor of the company; it provided the family's largest source of income. Despite their exalted social position in the district, they were not substantial landowners. Myddelton House was not vast by the standards of the day, but it did have 25 family rooms as well as the usual offices and servants' quarters. Bowles' father and mother were amiable, public-spirited and full of Christian charity; they believed that there should be no privilege without obligation so they did what they could for the poor of the district. This worthy attitude was inherited by their children.

Bowles' childhood was happy but dogged with illness. He had asthma, which persisted into middle life, and at the age of eight caught an eye infection which permanently affected the sight in his right eye. A great deal of sport was thus denied him, but he was always keen on animals and flowers and created a garden of his own in the kitchen-garden.

His eldest brother, Henry Ferryman, was called to the Bar and later became an MP. He was subsequently created a baronet. His second brother, John, joined the Army and Gussie, as Bowles was called, was destined for the Church for which he undoubtedly had a strong calling. After three years at Jesus College, Cambridge, where he read theology and pursued his interest in entomology, he was being tutored for ordination when his brother, home from the Sudan campaign, died of tuberculosis in October 1887, and his younger sister, Medora, paid the penalty of devoted nursing by contracting the disease, and dying before the end of the year. This was an unimaginable tragedy for the Bowles family; Gussie rushed home to be with his parents and made the important decision to give up all idea of taking Holy Orders and to stay at home with them. Whether he originally intended it or not, with the exception of foreign travel and visits to friends every year, he remained at Myddelton House for the rest of his long life. The following year he founded a Night School for the poor boys of the area, called the Turkey Street School. With that, his Sunday School teaching, lay reading and a burgeoning interest in gardening, he kept himself well occupied. In 1889, after travelling to Italy, he brought back plants for the first time to put in his parents' garden.

The weekly meetings of the New River Company were held at Myddelton House, and one of the shareholders who attended was Canon Henry Ellacombe of Bitton in Gloucestershire. A scholarly, kindly and generous man, who had created in the space of only one-and-a-half acres one of the best and widest collections of plants in the country, he encouraged the young Bowles not only with the gift of many plants but with good advice about building up a library of botanical and horticultural books. They were firm friends until Ellacombe's death in 1916. Ellacombe's book, *In a Gloucestershire Garden*, is an enduring classic of horticultural observation and enthusiasm.

Bowles began, with his father's qualified approval, to take over the planting of the garden. It had, he tells us, been a very dull affair, of evergreen shrubs mainly, but there were some very old trees to provide a framework for his plans. The New River flowed through the garden but, unfortunately, its banks were made so well that none of the water seeped through to the

Figure 3.2 Canon Henry N. Ellacombe, Rector of Bitton, Gloucestershire

garden, which consisted of a thin layer of soil over gravel, and dried out rapidly in summer. At first his changes were modest so as not to alarm his parents. In 1895, he started to develop an interest in crocuses which he grew in open frames in the kitchen-garden; he had more than 60 sorts by 1896, and 135 by 1901. Reginald Farrer's *Among the Hills* was dedicated to him— 'Ave crocorum rex imperator paterculus Augustus' ('Hail to thee, King and Emperor of all Crocuses, Little Father Augustus'). He knew that bulbs and corms would do well in his free-draining soil and he grew many kinds of snowdrop, Narcissus and tulip too. Never trained formally, as Miss Jekyll was, though with the same problem of poor eyesight, he began to paint his crocuses and his talent for accurate botanical drawing was considerable.

In 1900 he was elected to the Scientific Committee of the Royal Horticultural Society which, for a man who had only been gardening for a few years, was an immense tribute. Thorough and observant, he had by then a good knowledge of botany and his entomological interests must also have helped him. So good was he with bulbs that he began to exchange Crocus corms with the Royal Botanic Gardens, Kew. At the same time he developed a notable collection of hardy and half-hardy cacti. In 1908 came the ultimate accolade; he was elected to the Council, that is the governing body, of the RHS, and he served on it, despite the infirmities that come with old age, till the end of his life.

While his horticultural interests were developing, he was fully and actively engaged in good works for the poor of Enfield and district. He was especially interested in the welfare of young boys and, as well as the Night School and Sunday School, he dedicated his Sunday afternoons to them. They spent that time at Myddelton House, hearing stories, going for walks, playing games and skating on the pond in the winter. His influence for the good on many whose own backgrounds promised little, can scarcely be overestimated. Every year on his birthday there was the Tulip Tea, there were Bank Holiday treats, and the annual flower show and Church fête were held in the grounds of Myddelton House. Alongside his work for boys, he was a benefactor of the Church and closely concerned with parish affairs.

He became well known in the horticultural world, through his connection with the RHS and his plant-hunting trips. A martyr to hay-fever, he had the perfect excuse for spending June in the alpine regions of Europe. He continued to do this till 1936. His plant-hunting colleagues included Reginald Farrer, with whom he went to Mont Cenis in 1910 and 1911 when they found *Primula bowlesii* and *Eritrichium nanum*. In 1912 they travelled to the Tirol and the North Italian Lakes, which trip gave rise to Farrer's *The Dolomites*, and in 1913, hunting in the area around St Martin le Vésubie they found *Primula crucis* 'Bowles'. He numbered also Dick Trotter, the Garnett-Botfields and Lady Beatrix Stanley amongst his plant-hunting friends. He knew Gertrude Jekyll and William Robinson quite well, and indeed he was staying with the latter the day of his fateful fall.

In 1912, the editor of *The Gardeners' Chronicle* asked him to write a book about his garden; the result was *My Garden in Spring* and *My Garden in Summer*, both published in 1914. The trilogy was completed by *My Garden in Autumn and Winter* in 1915. These delightful books, quoted extensively in this anthology, amount to a gardening autobiography, with Bowles adopting the device of conducting the reader around his garden, as Farrer did in *In a Yorkshire Garden*. It was for *My Garden in Spring* that Farrer wrote a

Preface which caused a row with Sir Frank Crisp, who believed his rock garden was being ridiculed. Crisp wrote a furious pamphlet in reply, in which he blamed Bowles, quite unfairly, for the contents of the Preface (see Chapter 10). Farrer read the first two volumes in Sining-Fu, in China, even putting away his Jane Austen for 'four days of pure unalloyed and ever-increasing delight ... Your two vols. are about as nearly perfect of their kind as anything could be'.[1] The trilogy was, on the whole, very well-received by the gardening public, though curiously its discursive style was criticised in a review in the *Times Literary Supplement*. In it, sound practical advice was coupled felicitously with an artistic sensibility and a very ready sense of humour.

He was awarded the Victoria Medal of Honour in 1917, as Miss Jekyll was 20 years before. The following year his father died and he was left quite well-off and with a life interest in the house. Nothing changed; the house remained as it had been, without gas, electricity or heating, and with all the Victorian ornaments and furnishings that his mother had liked. All that did change was that the boys had even readier access to him.

The only young girl he ever really encouraged was Frances Everett who, as Frances Perry, has become a very well-known horticulturist, interested especially in water plants, and who owed her start in large part to his advice and help.

Of his publications, after the Trilogy, and apart from a great many contributions to journals, his most influential botanical work, *A Handbook of Crocus and Colchicum for Gardeners* came out in 1923. In 1934, *A Handbook of Narcissus* was published. Both of these contain marvellous drawings by him, which was particularly an achievement in the second case because the sight in his good eye was by then deteriorating. Although he began to collaborate with W.T. Stearn on a work on anemones in 1925, the results of their labours were never made into book form. Towards the end of his life he worked with Sir Frederick Stern on a monograph on snowdrops, but for Bowles it was unsatisfactory, being too exclusively botanical for his taste. In effect his acknowledged contribution was restricted to one chapter only, that on growing snowdrops in the garden.

During the Second World War, Myddelton House was an alarming place in which to live,

Figure 3.3 E.A. Bowles at 88

for it lay on the flightpath for V1 and V2 bombs. Bowles' health was gradually failing although, even when over eighty, he was still cleaning out the pond in his bathing costume. What finally put a stop to that was an allergy he developed to Sagittaria which made his skin turn purple.

In 1951 he was very ill, having strained his heart, but he recovered and, though he was ill again in 1953, he still managed to sit on a committee of the RHS in April 1954. Two weeks later he suffered a heart attack and died on 7 May. The garden was acquired by the School of Pharmacy at the University of London, and they still have the kitchen-garden for growing medicinal plants. The rest of the garden and the house are owned by the Lea Valley Regional Park Authority and although the Rock Garden has been lost, probably for ever, commendable efforts are being made to renovate the rest and give increasing access to visitors.

It is hard not to let any account of his life and personality degenerate into hagiography, for there is universal agreement that Bowles was a very good man, who was deeply and sincerely loved by many people: by his friends, by professional and amateur gardeners, by his servants, the people in the parish, and of course his boys, as well as by the large readership of his books, many of whom felt a personal sense of loss when he died. He was loved for his humanity, his wisdom, his kindness and generosity, his energy, his abiding sense of fun, and patience with all human failings except sloppiness and shoddiness. He was modest, for there is hardly any boasting in the Trilogy, and what passes for such is always qualified; he was unostentatious, and he had none of the irritability which Farrer could show for less gifted mortals. He saw no point or profit in avenging his good name when it was impugned in the course of the row with Sir Frank Crisp, Miss Ellen Willmott and others, indeed he contented himself with a firm but mild letter to William Robinson when the hurtful pamphlet was published in *Gardening Illustrated*. He was also loyal and unreproachful, attributes which were necessary for any friend of Farrer's.

His judgement was good, his purpose firm and he possessed a sense of honour and fair play that was exemplary. He was fortunate to have been born into comfortable circumstances with a sufficient private income to make work unnecessary but, though that did release him to pursue his horticultural career to greatness, one feels that he was already a man of considerable, if diffuse, talents, who would have succeeded in most circumstances. He was perhaps a little unworldly and unambitious, preferring a peaceful congenial existence at Myddelton to the necessarily harsher world of law and politics that his brother Henry knew. We can envy his Victorian certainties, his steadfast belief in God and in Man's fundamental goodness. We envy, too, his keen powers of observation, self-taught despite the adversity of bad sight, coupled with an unquenchable curiosity in the natural world.

He was, I believe, one of those men who are natural bachelors. Although no hater of women, having many as gardening friends, he obviously saw no need to fill the house with wife and children. There may well have been a romantic attachment in Biarritz in 1894 but we know little and it does not seem he was ever in much danger. Marriage, delightful as it can be, is a great dissipater of energies and it is not a coincidence that four of the authors in this anthology never married and the exception, Miss Sackville-West, used gardening partly as an escape from emotional tensions.

It would be misleading to give the impression that because Bowles did not earn his living he was not active on a wider stage. His work for the RHS, serving tirelessly and conscientiously on many of its committees through the period when the Society was increasing enormously in stature and influence, was crucial to its continuing success. His scientific monographs and articles on Narcissus, Crocus and Colchicum, Galanthus and Anemone were widely respected by botanists and are still referred to today. His unworldliness did ensure, however, that he never drove hard bargains with publishers, and it is certain he never made much money out of writing.

He was a very good gardener, who could often be seen on his hands and knees weeding, even on some occasions while in his best clothes on his way back from Church or a day in London. He was an immense enthusiast for outdoor plants, especially alpines and bulbs, and this enthusiasm was coupled with astonishing powers of observation and a natural gift for communicating the pleasure, and even joy, that he derived from flowers. It is the combination of botanical expertise and affection for gardening that makes his writing so persuasive and readable. If his prose lacked the colour that Farrer could bring to description it was mercifully free of archness and affectation too. The freshness of it will not stale.

Myddelton House

We are fortunate to know a great deal about Bowles' garden, for its state in the years before the First World War is clearly explained to us in the Trilogy. It changed over the years, of course, but he continued to write 'Notes from Myddelton House' in *The Garden* and there are the botanical monographs, too, which described plants in his garden.

In 1909, the Reverend Joseph Jacob, a great grower of daffodils, wrote about the garden at Myddelton House:

> To begin with, the garden is Mr. Bowles' father's ... Although he has very nearly a free hand, there are, I fancy, just one or two little restrictions which he has to observe. For example, he may not take in all the nice meadow land, some of which is so temptingly near the rockery, nor may he fill all the hedgerows with his untidy plants, or if he does they will have to take their 'luck' when the stern decree goes forth that the hedges must be cleaned, [but] Practically he has a free hand, and the result of the wisdom of the father and the skill and taste of the son is a most interesting and varied garden.[2]

Bowles' idea was that gardens were places for growing plants rather than for making colour effects, although he made efforts with his bedding schemes of tulips, his rose garden where he planted roses of complementary colours, and he took care with the colours and flowering times of his irises. In this respect he and Farrer are in a different tradition from the other three, a tradition that persists to this day in the gardens of what are known as 'plantsmen'. Bowles ruefully admitted:

> Many find the garden too museumy to please them. I plead guilty to the charge, knowing there is more of the botanist and lover of

Figure 3.4 The Morning-Room at Myddelton House in May. (From First Edition of My Garden in Spring, *by E.A. Bowles)*

Figure 3.5 The Tulip Beds by the New River in the Garden of Myddelton House

Figure 3.6 The Iris Beds by the New River

species and natural forms in me than there is of the florist or fine cultivator.[3]

In this he was too modest, for there was plenty of the fine cultivator in him.

I have already commented on the dryness of the garden which was, very often, the despair of Bowles' gardening life. The New River was no use to him, the water so alkaline (hard) as he said that it 'would be scarcely a miracle to walk on it',[4] but such a curve of running water was a highly ornamental feature, which sadly, since his death, has been emptied, filled in and is now a broad grass path. On one side of the river he grew the only bedding in his garden, 22 beds of his favourite tulips, usually at their best around his birthday, hence his annual Tulip Tea. These Darwin tulips, planted together with Miss Willmott's dark blue Myosotis, flowered in beds behind miniature box hedges; the display was followed in the summer by echeverias, heliotrope and pelargoniums and a dark pink penstemon called 'Myddelton Gem'. Such was the care taken with the colour-scheme that even Robinson could not have found anything to offend him.

Where the New River disappeared under the iron-railed bridge next to the boundary wall, a pair of lead ostriches stood sentinel. Over this bridge grew, and grows, a very fine *Wisteria floribunda* var. *macrobotrys*.

> ... this has covered about 25 yards of the wall by which it was planted and has climbed to the top of an old Yew to a height of 40 feet and festoons the south-eastern side of it with lilac tassels. That side of the Yew is next to the wall along the road, so the show is free and gratis to those who pass by, and most of them stop to gaze. One was heard to say, 'My! Whatever sort of tree is that?' and was told, 'It's what people call a Blueburnum'.[5]

Quite close to the bridge was a triangular bed that had become, by 1909, the 'Lunatic Asylum'. Very much a scholarly descendant of Parkinson, Gerard and Ray, Bowles was fascinated by the frankly curious as well as the beautiful. He grubbed up some dull evergreen shrubs that were there, planted a *Magnolia lennei* as 'keeper', and put in a variety of peculiar plants. There was the twisted hazel, a twisted hawthorn, an upright form of the common elder and a dwarf one that was evergreen. There was an oak-

Figure 3.7 The Market-Cross in the Rose Garden at Myddelton

leaved laburnum and all sorts of eccentric plantains and strawberries (see Chapter 11).

Close by, where the river made a bend, there were some extremely venerable yews. In his father's time laurels and *Viburnum tinus* grew in front of them but he replaced these with bed upon bed of bearded irises. He would, undoubtedly, have seen and admired the Iris Walk at Bitton.

Away from the river, behind the Iris beds, was Bowles' Rose Garden. This garden, on the face of it, was a poor place to grow roses, for the soil was light and very quick-draining, but by dint of much hard work, it was successful. In the centre was the old Market Cross from Enfield which, having been abandoned in favour of an Edward VII Coronation memorial, was found, extraordinarily enough, by Bowles.

After a year or two of unhonoured repose in a builder's yard it came here for a quiet time among the roses, and makes a splendid support and background for that lovely single-flowered climber *Rosa laevigata Anemone*.[6]

Close to this was the Pergola Garden for climbers.

Nearby was his wall, built to give a south aspect for climbers, facing the Rose Garden and river. There is a charming story about the building of the wall. When his father was pulling down the house that he owned at Gough Park nearby, Bowles rescued many items from it, such as the leaden ostriches already mentioned. Amongst these was a fine old brick pillar, diamond-shaped in section, which he caused to be cut in half and brought to Myddelton. He then persuaded his father that a wall was necessary to go with the pillar. He wrote in *My Garden in Summer* that it reminded him of the story of the Irishman who took a button to a charitable lady and asked if she would sew a shirt on to it, so he called the wall 'the Irishman's shirt'. They put a round stone ball on the top of the pillar's capstone, only to find, as one still does today, that the ball looks as if it is about to fall off on one's head—from whichever angle one views it. Nearby was his 'Tom Tiddler's Ground' of variegated and coloured-leaved plants and, to the west, the pond, which he cleared out every year with the help of his boys, wearing an old-fashioned blue-and-white bathing costume and boater.

Undoubtedly Bowles' Rock Garden, along with his crocus beds, gave him the most pleasure. The making of it was, I feel sure, partly influenced by Farrer's *My Rock Garden* and the man himself, after they had become friends. Farrer certainly thought it most successful, so presumably it accorded well with his own ideas.

Come straight from the high hills into this garden of Mr. Bowles, and it is not by any difference in the look of the ground or its plants that you will know you are not still there: here are no precious plants pining for company in a grim and tidy isolation ... But here only the noxious is removed, the plants are given free scope for enjoying themselves in the company they love, and rare difficult treasures are jostled into health and happiness again by the rough-and-tumble of life as they lived it on the hills; ... There is one special corner of which I know that he will not choose adequately to talk, but of which I, therefore, must, seeing that it has long appeared to me quite the finest piece of real gardening that I know. It is a roughly triangular piece of ground, and is filled with the Dwarf Almond,

Figure 3.8 The Rock-Garden at Myddelton

a blaze of pink and white in spring. But in spring, too, all its ground is surfaced and crammed and overflowing with rare Crocus and Primrose and Bland Anemone, and every vernal bulb that is usually looked after and cleansed and cossetted, but here left alone to make itself a wild plant and seed and establish in perfect naturalness under the eye of the gardener who knows and loves each one as a shepherd knows his lambs. So much for early spring; and then barrenness? Or else digging and fussing and planting? Not a spade touches that holy ground . . . but as the Anemones and the Crocus fade, up spring Daffodils and rare Tulips and difficult Fritillaries that are everybody else's despair and have to be treated as annuals, but here look as if they had just been poked in casually and forgotten by our late sovereign lady Queen Elizabeth, so that the whole patch, under the light trellis of the Almonds growing green, becomes anew, or continues, a dancing sea of light and colour.[7]

After his father died in 1918, Bowles made an Alpine meadow of the patch of field below the

Figure 3.9 A Crocus Frame in the Kitchen Garden at Myddelton House

43

Rock Garden that ran down to a stream at the bottom, just as he must have told the Rev. Mr Jacob he would like to do. Because of its slope it was ideal and he grew snowflakes (*Leucojum*), followed by masses of dwarf narcissi, snake's head fritillaries and crocuses, and later the 'Pheasant-eye' daffodils, camassias and hardy geraniums.

Bowles was an acknowledged expert on the genus *Crocus* long before the First World War. Indeed he grew nearly all the known crocus species as well as many hybrids that he had raised in the garden. He was undoubtedly helped by the sharply-draining soil, but it was his methodical and painstaking approach that ensured the real success. The frames are gone now, for nothing so utterly personal could survive.

Combining, as he did, a passion for crossing good garden plants to produce worthy children that he could name and send out into the world, with a first-rate eye for a curiosity or original, it is not surprising that the name Bowles should be well known to gardeners as a byword for excellence. Many of the 'Bowles plants' were actually named after him by others, either out of affection for him, or because the seedling arose in his garden, or as a tribute to his most unusual gifts. There are others that we associate with him, or Myddelton, even though they do not bear the name. Amongst the best known are *Viola* 'Bowles's Black'; *Cheiranthus* 'Bowles's Mauve'; *Milium effusum* 'Aureum'; *Crocus chrysanthus* 'Snow Bunting' and 'Yellowhammer', *Crocus sieberi* 'Hubert Edelsten', *Crocus tomasinianus* var. *pictus*; and *Iris reticulata* 'Cantab'.

Bowles ended *My Garden in Autumn and Winter* with the words:

I conclude with the wish that they [i.e. other gardeners] may find as much joy in bright and happy days, and as much relaxation and consolation in periods of pain and anxiety as I have derived from this my garden, in Spring, Summer, Autumn and Winter.[8]

Notes

1. Quoted in M. Allan, *E.A. Bowles*, 1st edn (Faber and Faber, 1973), p. 125.

2. Rev. J. Jacob, 'Myddelton House: its Garden and its Gardener', *The Garden*, vol. 53, 1909, p. 315.

3. E.A. Bowles, *My Garden in Spring*, 1st edn (T.C. and E.C. Jack, 1914), p. 17.

4. Ibid., p. 13.

5. E.A. Bowles, 'Features of My Garden—VI. Reminiscences of Myddelton House, Enfield', *Journal of the Royal Horticultural Society*, vol. 66, part 7, p. 229.

6. Bowles, *My Garden in Spring*, p. 291.

7. Ibid., pp. xii–xiii.

8. E.A. Bowles, *My Garden in Autumn and Winter*, 1st edn (T.C. and E.C. Jack, 1915), p. 263.

CHAPTER
❧ 4 ❧

Reginald Farrer

1880~1920

Figure 4.1 Reginald John Farrer

Reginald John Farrer poses problems for any biographer, not only because he left instructions in his Will that his diaries should be burned but also because he was a paradox. Ridiculous in appearance with a high piercing voice, hare lip and cleft palate, he was nevertheless highly valued by many as a most attractive individual, whose physical shortcomings were soon forgotten. The son of narrowly Anglican parents he became a Buddhist and, in doing so, forfeited much of his family's sympathy. Wishing always to shine in company, he could spend weeks on end alone, except for his servants, in isolated and perilous regions and be blithely happy. Educated at home and always a gentleman amateur he was at the same time a botanist, plant-hunter and gardener of distinction and lasting influence. The paradox extended to attitudes towards him. For one he was 'a malevolent gnome',[1] for another 'a cad, but an amusing one',[2] and yet for others still he proved a delightful and fascinating companion, who was sincerely mourned upon his early and unexpected death.

He was born in February 1880, into a rich and respected county family, who lived at Ingleborough House in Clapham, West Yorkshire, in the shadow of Ingleborough mountain. His father was several times a Liberal MP. Not being sent away to school freed the young Reginald to pursue his interest in wild flowers and when he was only 14 he made his first rock-garden in a disued quarry in the garden. In the same year he contributed to the *Journal of Botany* a piece on the finding of *Arenaria gothica*, the Yorkshire sandwort, on Ingleborough.

Figure 4.2 Ingleborough House, Clapham, West Yorkshire

In 1897 he went up to Balliol College, Oxford, to read Greats. He derived considerable pleasure from helping to cultivate the delightful, and still existing, rock-garden at St John's College and in being part of the gilded circle that included Raymond Asquith, John Buchan and Aubrey Herbert. He came down in 1902 having gained a not very distinguished degree.

The next year he spent in Tokyo and travelling around Japan, Korea and China, which provided the material for *The Garden of Asia*, a book of his experiences, published in 1904. At that time he had plans to be a playwright and novelist, and several plays and novels were published in the succeeding years, amongst them *The Sundered Streams, The Anne-Queen's Chronicle* and *The Dowager of Jerusalem*. They are neither read nor performed today because of their ridiculous plots, odd characterisation and dreadful overwriting. If his reputation depended on them alone no one now would know his name. Fortunately, however, he had the sense to realise that his future might lie more in collecting plants and writing about them.

In 1907, he published what was to be his most influential book, *My Rock Garden*. It stayed in print for more than 40 years, and had gone into an eighth impression by 1930. The same year he

went to Ceylon and became a Buddhist; about this trip he wrote another travel book, *In Old Ceylon*. His conversion proved a source of great difficulty in the family, according to his cousin, Osbert Sitwell. They found it incomprehensible and distressing.

An indignant shudder passed through every gathering of relatives for prayer when, with an accompanying tremble in their voices, they besought the Lord that the heathen be permitted to see the true light.[3]

The following year, the companion volume to *My Rock Garden, Alpines and Bog Plants*, came out, and in 1909 *In a Yorkshire Garden*. This did not find universal favour, although it contains very useful descriptions of his garden as well as some interesting biographical sidelights. In it he played a practical joke on his readers by dedicating it to Alice, who was in fact a dog.

For the next three years he made some efforts, though not wholehearted ones it must be said, to enter politics. But he was not a committed party man and may well have entered the lists solely to please his father. He fought the Ashford Division for the Liberals in 1911 but lost. He is supposed to have spent most of the £1,000 that his father gave him for political expenses, on orchids. There ended his parliamentary ambitions although he was elected a county councillor for Yorkshire and also became a Justice of the Peace. It is unlikely that he took his local duties as seriously as did Bowles.

Every year after Oxford, except when he was in the Far East, he travelled to the European Alps looking for wild flowers and became a considerable expert on the flora, both of the limestone and the granite mountains. In 1910, his summer trip to the Graian, Cottian and Maritime Alps, accompanied for part of the time by Bowles, was described in a charming book, *Among the Hills.* He claimed to dislike walking, although I do not know how much credence we should give to that.

I regard the British craze for exercise as a superstition, and, of all Mr. [Joseph] Chamberlain's ideas, am proud only to share one, in our common prejudice against unnecessary exertion.[4]

In 1912, writing a quite unexceptional book called *The Rock Garden* he thoroughly angered William Robinson whose review of it in *Gardening Illustrated* was forthright in its disapproval. The ostensible reason was the bad quality of the illustrations, a subject about which Robinson was most particular, but probably stemmed as much from Farrer not being able to resist a dig at the 'detestable affectation of finding English names to replace Latin ones for plants'. (I might add that in this Farrer, too, was a culprit, referring, as he did, to *Meconopsis quintuplinervia* as 'the Harebell Poppy'; *Primula farinosa* as 'Pretty Bird E'en' and *Eritrichium nanum* as 'Woolly-Hair the Dwarf'.) He particularly disliked Rockfoil for Saxifrage, which was a name Robinson copied from John Ruskin.

Calm was restored and the next year saw, after another trip with Bowles looking for primulas, the publication of *The Dolomites.* However, worse was to come in 1914 when Farrer's Preface to Bowles' *My Garden in Spring* stirred up a hornet's nest of protest in what has become known as the Crispian Row (this dispute is explained in Chapter 10). Farrer was like a small terrier who starts a fight involving slower, bigger dogs and then gets out of the way to watch the fun. By the time the storm broke he was safe in western China, where he intended, with his new friend and assistant, William Pur-

Figure 4.3 William Purdom dressed as a Coolie. (From First Edition of On the Eaves of the World *Vol. II, by Reginald Farrer)*

dom, to spend the next two years looking for plants in the mountainous marches between Kansu and Tibet. Purdom, a man trained at Kew and an excellent photographer, had travelled in the area before as a plant collector for Veitch's nursery and spoke Chinese.

The first year of this expedition, particularly, was a great success and Farrer recorded it in what he called a 'succinct and laconic work', *On The Eaves of the World*, in two large volumes. They searched in a region, up to 10,000 feet high and rich in alpines, which, apart from one nineteenth-century Russian collector, had never been visited by plant-hunters. Purdom was indispensable as he was popular with the Chinese. The work was difficult and dangerous because that part of China was subject to constant local strife and insurrection and the natives, especially the priests, were not always friendly. At one point, in order to collect seed of a particularly beautiful dipelta and *Buddleia farreri* (the 'flannel buddleia') they had seen earlier across the Tibetan border, Purdom crossed disguised as a coolie. Farrer recalled that he could not go because his gold teeth would have given him away. Amongst the great finds of the first year were *Rosa farreri* (the Threepenny-bit Rose), *Potentilla fruticosa, Daphne tangutica, Buddleia*

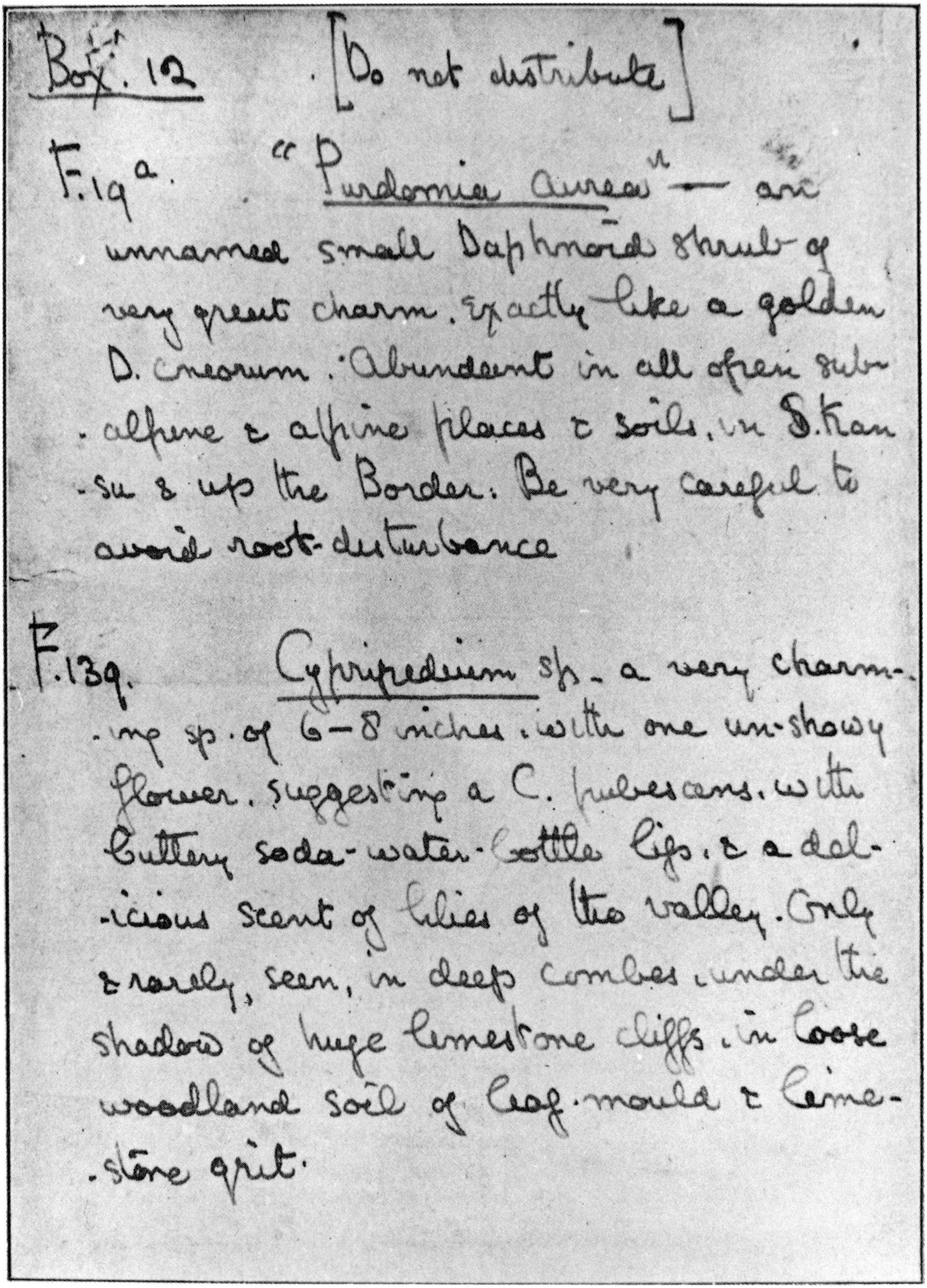

Box. 12 . [Do not distribute]

F.19ª . "Purdomia aurea" — an
unnamed small Daphnoid shrub of
very great charm. Exactly like a golden
D. cneorum. Abundant in all open sub
. alpine & alpine places & soils. in S.Kan
-su & up the Border. Be very careful to
avoid root-disturbance

F.139. Cypripedium sp. a very charm-
.ing sp. of 6—8 inches. with one un-showy
flower. suggesting a C. pubescens. with
buttery soda-water-bottle lips. & a del-
-icious scent of lilies of the valley. Only
& rarely, seen, in deep combes. under the
shadow of huge limestone cliffs. in loose
woodland soil of leaf-mould & lime-
.stone grit.

Figure 4.4 Facsimile of a Page of Farrer's Field Notes for the Expedition to Western China in 1914. (From Bulletin of the Alpine Garden Society, *Vol. 1, No. 10)*

1. Gravetye Manor – the West Garden in flower (see Ch. 1)

2. Gravetye Manor – the Alpine Meadow (see Ch. 1)

3. A cottage garden (see Ch. 12)

alternifolia, the white *Paeonia suffruticosa*, *Geranium farreri* and *Viburnum farreri*, still often called *V. fragrans*.

That winter of 1914 Farrer spent in Lanchow, correcting the proofs of his *The English Rock Garden*, written in 1913, but not published till after the War. He was under some pressure from people he knew in England to return as there was a war on but he did not and continued to look for plants the following year in the Da-Tung Alps to the north-west of Lanchow. Disappointing though this region was as far as finds were concerned, except for *Gentiana farreri*, and despite some difficulties with the Tibetans, he nevertheless loved it. About this second year's travel, he wrote *The Rainbow Bridge*, published in 1921. He also wrote many articles for *The Gardeners' Chronicle* from China and later from Burma. He was a more than competent artist and painted the flowers of his Kansu expedition; an exhibition of these pictures was held in London in 1917.

Home he went in the spring of 1916. Turned down for military service on medical grounds, as he presumably knew he would be, he found a job in the Ministry of Information. He spent some time in France as a civilian, sending letters of his personal impressions home to his superior, and old friend since Oxford days, John Buchan. These letters also saw the light of day in 1918 under the title *The Void of War*, but the book did not sell, perhaps because it failed to catch the mood of a disillusioned reading public.

In 1919 *The English Rock Garden* in two volumes, his *magnum opus*, was finally published. He wrote it to clear up confusions, especially relating to naming, in an area that had become very popular with amateur and professional gardeners. It is an astonishing achievement, being both a botanical and a horticultural work, witty and cultured as well as observant and knowledgeable. His descriptions were always aimed at the intelligent amateur, and were never wearisome or obscure.

It owes its existence [he wrote] . . . to my own craving for guidance across the uncharted seas of catalogues.[5]

To me at least it is already a dictionary of real succour. It contains at least a thousand times as much knowledge as I myself possess, or can ever hope to attain.[6]

In 1919, anxious to be travelling again after an operation for appendicitis, he agreed with Euan Cox, a rhododendron enthusiast, that they should explore the jungles of Upper Burma. It was not really from choice but his first hope, Yunnan in China, was being systematically combed by George Forrest, who disliked his territory being invaded by other collectors and his other choices, Nepal and Sechuan, were closed to foreigners. In many ways this trip was a disappointment to them, for they discovered that few of the plants they found would survive the drier colder climate of Great Britain and there were too many woody plants for Farrer's liking.

As Cox wrote later:

The sad truth is that these Burmese hills do not breed species of Alpines that give any return for care or kindness at the hands of the gardener.[7]

Of their collections, the most garden-worthy were *Rhododendron calostratum*, *Primula sonchifolia*, *Jasminum farreri* and the 'Coffin' juniper *Juniperus coxii*.

At the end of the first season, Cox came back, parting amicably with Farrer who stayed on to explore the frontier ranges between Burma and China. He was further from civilisation than ever, he was alone except for his native servants, and that year was particularly wet even for such a wet region. For weeks on end visibility in the mountains, because of the mist and rain, was just a few yards. It must have been physically debilitating and mentally dispiriting. Nevertheless, between January and October 1920 he travelled over a thousand miles, much of it on foot or on pony, collected 400 plant specimens and wrote his field notes, despatches for *The Gardeners' Chronicle*, his diary, many letters home, a full-length novel and another book of 'historical fantasies'. For more than half that time the weather was terrible.

On 1 October 1920, he fell ill at Nyitadi, possibly from bronchial pneumonia. Jange Bhaju, his most loyal servant, made a brave attempt to get help by running without stopping for just under four days, to fetch medical supplies, but he arrived back only a short while before Farrer died. Bhaju told Cox what happened in a letter afterwards.

. . . from 14th October 1920 he discontinued to take his food except soda water, wiskly [sic] and medicines for his benefit but it has been unsuccessful at least and without giving any pain and trouble to us he breathe [sic] his last on the morning of the 17th October . . . [8]

They carried the body of 'Burra Sahab Bahadur' in a coffin to Konglu which was a military outpost and he was buried there. They salvaged his equipment and also some herbarium specimens but the seeds were lost.

The memorial erected in the garden at Ingleborough by his parents refers to him as 'author, traveller, botanist and flower-painter'. He was all that and gardener too. In 1931, Cox remembered his friend in a book about Farrer's plant introductions:

Even after the lapse of eleven years I have a vivid memory of Farrer in the hills, his stocky figure clad in khaki shorts and shirt, tieless and collarless, a faded topee on his head, old boots, and stockings that gradually slipped down and clung about his ankles as the day wore on. The bustle of the early start; the constant use of the field-glasses which always hung around his neck; the discussions, very one-sided owing to my ignorance, about the value and relationship of the various plants; his intense satisfaction when a plant was once in the collecting tin and was found worthy; his grunt of disapproval when it was worthless; the luncheon interval with its attendant cold goat rissole and slab chocolate; his enjoyment of our evening tot of rum, a necessity in the rains; and, above all, his indomitable energy that never spared a frame which was hardly built for long days of searching and climbing.[9]

His contemporaries either disliked him intensely or they loved him, as Bowles did, and mourned his loss, so far away and terribly alone. Pacific personalities, such as those possessed by Bowles and Purdom, brought out the best in his more mercurial nature.

He was certainly a complicated man and one cannot escape the conclusion that he was often unhappy and that this unhappiness could show itself in biting irony and bitter derision. Highly intelligent, he had an elephantine memory, which served him well when he had to correct the proofs of *The English Rock Garden* in Lanchow, thousands of miles from the nearest useful botanical institution, but meant he remembered all too well his friends' and enemies'

slights, real or imagined. His dogmatic nature and dislike of opposition caused him to row with other botanists. His trouble-making propensities are obvious in the deliberately controversial Preface to *My Garden in Spring*.

It may be that he was a suppressed homosexual, we do not know. If it were so, it contributed to the unsatisfactory nature of his personal relationships. His hero-worshipping of Aubrey Herbert, and his distress at Herbert's casual neglect of him, was stiflingly intense even for that time of close and unselfconscious masculine friendships. Gardening, and especially planthunting, must have been a necessary and welcome escape and relief from any personal difficulty at home. An extrovert show-off who could be conceited, selfish and thoughtless, he was also romantic, cerebral, poetic and cultured. His favourite author, about whom he was an authority, was Jane Austen. He never went on his travels without a set of her novels. Once when ill in China,

only quinine could lug me so far out of coma as to be capable of even Pride and Prejudice—a drug of itself which I had always hitherto believed could cope with the highest temperature and the deepest lethargy.[10]

He declared, and there is no reason to disbelieve him, that

a fanaticsm for beauty has always been the real key of my life, and all its happinesses and hindrances.[11]

He had an immensely charming side to him, which comes out clearly in his books, especially an aptitude for self-mockery which is most attractive, for he obviously recognised that, fat, moustachioed and macrocephalic, he cut a faintly ludicrous figure. He was also highly sensitive, both to landscape and human suffering. It is a pity that there is no place in this anthology for his moving and eloquent account in *The Rainbow Bridge* of the battlefield at Ypres.

He was unusually energetic and enthusiastic. Happiest when plant-hunting in high places, it brought out his best qualities of courage and strength, wit and humanity. Cox wrote of him:

He had as many facets as a diamond. When he was engaged on anything to do with plants he was like a being transformed. Then he was direct in his emotions ... and words flowed off his tongue or from his pen with a vigour and directness that left no doubt of his meaning. But remove him from his plants, and everything was clothed and lighted in the habit and reflection of his immediate mood. [12]

Even when conditions were very bad in Burma in 1920 he continued to send cheerful letters home. A lover of fine things and also of creature comforts, he could do well without them and was steadfast in adversity. Although not perhaps such an obviously sympathetic personality to Orientals as Purdom, it is apparent that he inspired enormous devotion in his servants.

He introduced hundreds of new species and varieties and although many were known about, like *Viburnum farreri*, he was the first to introduce them. It is now a valued and easy garden plant. Amongst his triumphs were *Saxifraga aeizoon* 'Rex', *Gentiana farreri* and *Buddleia alternifolia*. If he had a fault it was to underrate the difficulties with which many of his favourite plants could be cultivated. *Saxifraga florulenta* ('The Ancient King'), *Isopyrum farreri*, *Primula farreriana*, *Primula reginella* and *Farreria pretiosa* proved more or less impossible to keep in healthy cultivation for very long.

As a botanist he was most observant and methodical though not quite in the same class as the professionals, Forrest and Kingdon-Ward. But then he was a gentleman plant-hunter, who to a large extent paid for his own expeditions, and his heart was not in the collection of dried specimens for their sake alone. He did not, for example, always collect a plant in fruit as well as in flower, which could make the botanical naming problematical. Nor did he love rarities, just because they were rarities. He knew a good garden plant when he saw it.

As a rock-gardener, Farrer's claim to the notice of posterity is three-fold. First, though Robinson did much to popularise the idea of the 'natural' rock-garden in the years after 1870, grandness and a baleful competitiveness in size and expense had crept in, to the detriment of simplicity. Farrer in 1907 and again in 1914 sought to bring the sheep back into the natural and unostentatious fold once more, where they remained until rock-gardens became less fashionable because of cost after the Second World War and raised beds and peat banks largely took their place.

Secondly, though he did not actually invent the 'scree' or 'moraine' bed as a method of growing difficult high alpines in our very different climate, the tribute for disseminating the idea must be his. He made them so fashionable that, according to Bowles, moraines became part of accepted dinner-party conversation.

Thirdly, he was an excellent cultivator, sending out from his Craven Nursery at Clapham some first-rate plants. He took endless pains and he had the great advantage of having seen so many of the 'wee people' of the hills growing in their native rocks.

His writing was fluent, wide-ranging and scholarly and above all interesting and funny. In *The Rainbow Bridge* he reminded his readers that:

> I am writing this book for the relief and release of one person only in the world. I am strenuously re-living, in fact, the dead years, in order to win free for a while from the present; and, out of my own memories and stored emotions, spinning a rainbow bridge, far-flung over black depths, towards the golden irrecoverable past. [13]

If that were really so we are indeed fortunate that he was persuaded to publish it.

I have always enjoyed the extravagant similes, the unfair comparisons, the often exaggerated digs at rivals (the great and good Henri Correvon of Geneva came in for especial criticism), the setting up on pedestals of sometimes unworthy plants. It is true that he overwrote shockingly at times, but it was indicative of his flamboyant and ebullient nature and done to entertain his readership. His capacity for working up a small, but potentially amusing, incident gives a good idea of what a delightful companion he must have been. At times his style was affected and irritating and he could be painfully arch; it is hard, for example, to take seriously the talk of fairies. The archaic words and prose forms, of which he was so fond, are less and less accessible to the reader as the years go by. But these small lapses only serve to highlight the heights, both of description and anecdote, to which he could aspire. More than any other plant-collector, with the exception of Kingdon-Ward, he could transport the reader to the high and lonely places.

It is easy to dismiss his lasting impact as a poet and novelist, but as a writer of immensely readable, informative, individual and scholarly gardening books he is without better. The achievement of *The English Rock Garden* is especially awesome and humbling, not only because it was written when he was only 33, but also because of its minute accuracy of observation, the breadth of its conception and the sheer industry needed to complete it. His descriptive powers, if sometimes misleading, were considerable; many a plant was rescued from a just oblivion by a kind word from Farrer.

As far as influence on the gardening public is concerned, *My Rock Garden*, published in 1907 was his most successful book. By the force of his personality and will, he turned every future generation of gardeners into alpine enthusiasts. The founding of the Alpine Garden Society in 1929 owed a great deal to Farrer's posthumous but benign and pervasive influence. His lasting legacy is his promotion of the Alpine as a worthwhile garden plant.

Ingleborough

For an account of the garden at Ingleborough House we must rely on Farrer himself for, apart from scattered references by obituarists, there is little written down and now the sad passage of years and changes of ownership make it difficult to see what there once was. Ponies graze in the remains of his first rock-garden. The big house is owned by Bradford Metropolitan Council as an educational centre for children, and no more than general maintenance of the garden is possible. What the descendants of Farrer's family still own, the Lake and the Cliff, they look after as well as possible, but the Cliff now reveals only the successive generations of a few ferns and ramondas as pale reminders of what once was. Farrer's last travelling companion, E. H. M. Cox, could find little there by 1927, although he spoke admiringly of how well the rest of the garden, including the labour-intensive rock-garden, was still being maintained. Alice's Garden is wild beyond Farrer's dream of a 'wild garden'. However, at the top of the Lake is a narrow belt of acid Silurian rock which made the growing of rhododendrons possible and they still flower, lending the glen a Himalayan appearance.

What we do know is gleaned, sometimes through the distorting glass of Farrer's ego, from *In a Yorkshire Garden*, and also *My Rock Garden*, but he was often maddeningly vague about topography. Like Bowles he had the problem of gardening in someone else's garden and,

though one imagines that his father was quite tolerant, Farrer must always have come up against the restraints of the available labour being needed elsewhere.

Farrer maintained with some justification that:

I have a sad, ungracious climate, a sad, ungracious soil, a struggling garden without any advantages of art or nature.[14]

It is true Ingleborough House was set on a hill, and that the climate was difficult and the soil unattractive, but there was plenty of space and no garden is hopeless. Heavy rainfall would be very unpopular with his woolly-leaved mountain rock plants but would encourage the rhododendrons. Obviously he exaggerated his problems, the more to exaggerate his achievements, but it is a marvel what choosy alpine treasures he could grow there and it is a tribute to the care taken in the preparation of the ground.

By the time of the publication of *My Rock Garden* he had two rock-gardens. The Old he made with the help of the gardeners when he was 14, and in later years he always had difficulty with it.

My own rock-gardens are two in number and two in nature. The one is ill-built, ill-soiled, and a perpetual worry. Nothing except the commonest things will live or thrive, except with endless bother. There is some fatal canker in the soil, I fear, and besides, I made the garden many years ago, when, like Cleopatra, I was exceedingly green in judgment. Its situation is the best thing about it; being a big semi-circle in a sunny slope, whence, at one time, sand was quarried for the repairing of the house. That is to say, the whole bank is rubble and dust of an old moraine, absolutely devoid of nutriment, so that I have had to bring all the soil I needed from afar. On either side are shelving banks, and through one a gorge. In the centre lies a big pool, so shallow and ineffectually done—the result of many makeshifts—that, after years of worry, I am now renouncing it, and having it turned into a bed for *Iris Kaempferi*. [This is a plant which likes moisture. It appears from *In a Yorkshire Garden* that the pond was remade in 1907 or 1908]. The rest of the space is taken up by masses of rock-work, with two deep glens—one sunny, the other shady—running on each side of a big mountain-mass.[15]

It certainly sounds like a well-planned and sophisticated rock-garden, especially considering his age when he made it. The Old Garden had the Great Moraine at the bottom of it which was triumphantly successful despite its being at ground-level and not raised up.

Of the much later New Rock-Garden, on the other hand, he was more than proud. It was on the site of an old kitchen-garden, next to his Craven Nursery, and plants thrived in it. Rich in soil but very sharply-drained, thanks to the care he took with the foundations, this garden was bounded on three sides by a wall, but he disguised the formality of that by building banks of rock against the walls until they were effectively hidden. This rock-garden had a large flat bog-garden and a pool which gave a home for his precious water-lilies. Beyond the pond were the two main ranges of rockery, which he referred to as 'stately mountain piles, separated by a narrow gorge'.[16] On the sunny aspect he grew, before he colonised the Cliff, his saxifrages. His

primulas and ramondas grew on the shadier sides. This rock garden was, needless to say, made of the Craven limestone, such as he always maintained was the best of all for rock-garden construction.

The Craven Nursery was a venture started by Farrer early in the 1900s, presumably to try to offset the high costs of his gardening and his trips abroad and to sell and disseminate surplus plants. It was windy, although sheltered to the west by a high wall. Here he made his first moraine, called the Old Moraine.

Further up the garden, outside the nursery, were the kitchen-garden, peach and vine houses, and the Orchid house, where lived the plants for which Farrer felt a 'guilty' passion, or so he said. All this was very much under the control of what he referred to as 'the Powers that ruled', by which he presumably meant the Head Gardener. Up the hill, round the corner from the Orchid house, the path led on to the Upper Garden and House. The Upper Garden consisted of shrub borders and rose beds and, on one side of a large lawn to the east of the House, the south-facing Terrace wall where grew plants inclined to be

Figure 4.5 The Craven Nursery, Ingleborough

Figure 4.6 The Terrace at Ingleborough House

tender. He was allowed some say in the design of this part of the Upper Garden. Above this wall was the long and large herbaceous border, in the middle of which his parents erected a pillar memorial to their son after his death, and planted some of his best and most famous introductions such as the harebell poppy, *Meconopsis quintuplinervia* and *Lilium farreri*. This memorial garden was enclosed by a hedge of *Viburnum farreri* (syn. *fragrans*).

High above the House, reached by a long steep walk, is Ingleborough Lake. It had been made by an ancestor of Farrer's who dammed Clap Beck as it flowed down a valley from the mountain. On the eastern side of the Lake was the great 60-foot limestone cliff. For a long while he could only admire it from afar as there was no path along or below it; however, one day in 1907, 'the Powers that rule' made a Cliff-walk.

... the very first time I wandered along that path I saw at once that the whole cliff was riddled with deep cracks and crevices and fissures, the very place of all places that heart could desire, for the making of a really genuinely wild rock-garden. And so, immediately, as a preliminary experiment, did I spend that autumn wadding up the chinks with little bits of *Saxifraga lingulata* and *Saxifraga aeizoon*. And they took to their places so heartily that from that hour to this the Cliff-Garden has been an ever-increasing success ...[17]

At the north end of the lake was the Valley Garden, where were, and are, rhododendrons, bamboos and flowering shrubs, and nearby Alice's Garden, which he made as a wild garden, full of herbaceous plants too vigorous for the garden proper.

Notes

1. Quoted in M. Fitzherbert, *The Man who was Greenmantle*, 1st edn (John Murray, 1983), p. 100.
2. Quoted in ibid., p. 49.
3. O. Sitwell, *Noble Essences*, 1st edn (Macmillan, 1950), p. 15.
4. R. J. Farrer, *My Rock Garden*, facsimile of 1st edn (Theophrastus, 1971), p. 252.
5. R. J. Farrer, *The English Rock Garden*, 4th impression (2 vols., T.C. and E.C. Jack, 1928), vol. 1, p. xi.
6. Ibid., p. lxiv.
7. F. H. Fisher, 'Reginald Farrer', *Alpine Garden Society Bulletin*, vol. 1, no. 10 (1933), p. 3.
8. E.H.M. Cox, *Farrer's Last Journey*, 1st edn (Dulau and Co., 1926), p. 209.
9. E.H.M. Cox (ed.), *The Plant Introductions of Reginald Farrer*, 1st edn (New Flora and Silva, 1930), pp. 10–11.
10. R. J. Farrer, *The Rainbow Bridge*, 3rd impression (Edward Arnold, 1926), p. 273.
11. Ibid., p. 335.
12. Cox, *Farrer's Last Journey*, pp. 211–12.
13. Farrer, *The Rainbow Bridge*, p. 95.
14. R. J. Farrer, *In a Yorkshire Garden*, 1st edn (Edward Arnold, 1909), p. 11.
15. Farrer, *My Rock Garden*, pp. 10–11.
16. Ibid., p. 13.
17. Farrer, *Yorkshire Garden*, pp. 269–70.

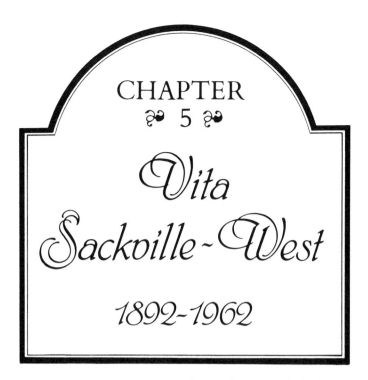

CHAPTER
ࣟ 5 ࣟ

Vita Sackville-West

1892-1962

Figure 5.1 Studio Portrait of Vita Sackville-West, 1934

The story of Vita Sackville-West's life is an extraordinary one. Familiarity with it may dull one's sense of its peculiarity and one may forget how striking it must be for anyone who hears it

for the first time. It is, however, a story worth knowing for the bearing it had on her ability and inclination to garden.

She was born on 9 March 1892, the only child of Lionel, Lord Sackville and his wife, Victoria. Her parents were first cousins, for Victoria was one of the products of a liaison between Sackville's uncle, also called Lionel, when he was a diplomat in Paris, and a married Spanish dancer called Pepita, about whom Miss Sackville-West was to write a book. Pepita died later in childbirth, Sackville came back to the family seat of Knole, near Sevenoaks in Kent, when he inherited the title and Victoria went with him. She married her cousin, who was to inherit from her father, and it was at Knole that their only child Victoria, known as Vita, was born.

Knole is a fascinating house. Built by Thomas Sackville, one of Queen Elizabeth I's courtiers, it is reputed to have 365 rooms, 52 staircases and seven acres of roof. It was a vast, unique and magical place for a young and solitary girl, full of stirring notions of blood and ancestry, to grow up in. Her love for Knole bordered on an obsession. She never quite got over the tragedy, as she saw it, of not being born a boy. Her mother was, by all accounts, an attractive and charming but tricky woman, selfish, wilful and, in her last years, subject to bouts of insanity; with whom Vita always had a close, but sometimes humiliating, relationship. Her parents were not faithful to each other and eventually separated. She was bookish and, so she maintained, plain. While she was growing up she wrote dozens of novels and plays of a highly coloured historical kind. Though she did cultivate some friendships as a girl, like the intense one that she enjoyed with Rosamund Grosvenor, she developed an essentially secretive and self-contained personality.

As she grew to womanhood, and came out as a debutante, she made friends with Violet Keppel, the daughter of King Edward VII's mistress, whom she first met in 1904. At the same time she was much sought after by men, even to the extent of being followed across Europe by one infatuated Italian count. She was most attractive, being tall and statuesque, with dark Latin looks and an aloofness that set her apart.

On 1 October 1913, after a long and rather troubled courtship and engagement, she married, at Knole, Harold Nicolson, son of Sir Arthur Nicolson (later Lord Carnock). The son of a diplomat, he had followed in his father's footsteps, and his first posting, after their wedding, was Constantinople. For six months they lived at Cospoloi where they made a garden and took their first steps towards acquiring skill and knowledge.

1914 saw the birth of their son, Ben, but the following year a second boy was born dead. This was a source of great sorrow to them, but in 1917 a third son, Nigel, was safely delivered. In that year something occurred to mar their happiness. Harold contracted a form of venereal disease from a homosexual encounter. In April 1918 Violet Keppel started an affair with Miss Sackville-West. This led to the most serious crisis in their entire married life and caused a considerable stir in polite circles, for the lovers went off together for long periods at a time; to Cornwall, to Paris, and again to France after Miss Keppel had married a glamorous Army officer, Denys Trefusis. The drama came to its climax when the two husbands flew in a small aeroplane to Amiens where the lovers were staying. In the end, after a great deal of unpleasantness, Nicolson succeeded in getting his wife back.

Set down baldly in this way, it is hard to communicate the distress, anguish and fury that this elopement engendered. Even after the affair fizzled out in 1921 the Nicolsons were left bruised by the experience. So much so that, in an attempt at catharsis, she wrote a secret account of the affair, which was found by her son, Nigel, after her death and published in his book, *Portrait of a Marriage*. Harold Nicolson's behaviour seems to have been heroic, but it is likely that his monumental tolerance and forbearance stemmed from his guilt about his own affairs and his desire at all costs to save his marriage. In a curious way, when the storm had abated, they had gained a closeness, understanding and need for each other which lasted all their lives. This is certainly what they maintained to each other in their voluminous correspondence. This most unconventional marriage seems to have satisfied them at least, even if it leaves the rest of us staring a little. As she wrote once to Nicolson, 'We are sure of each other, in this odd, strange, detached, intimate, mystical relationship which we could never explain to any outside person'.[1] She was consistently unfaithful to him over the years, the most serious affair being with Virginia Woolf, but there is no sign that her 'muddles', as he called them, profoundly discomposed him thereafter.

There is no evidence that she considered her bisexuality as anything wrong or undesirable. What she does not seem to have taken into account properly is that although her personality was equal to the pressures and high-pitched emotions, there were those around her who found the tense and charged atmosphere and the infidelity most upsetting. There were other casualties of her cavalier attitude, besides Nicolson and Trefusis, who felt confused and let down.

Two years after the Nicolsons married, they acquired a house in the country near Sevenoaks as a weekend retreat. Miss Sackville-West spent increasing amounts of time there, especially after 1925 when their London house was sold. It was called Long Barn. A fourteenth-century house, with supposed connections with Caxton, it required extensive renovation, both of the house and garden. The Nicolsons' interest and expertise in gardening burgeoned. His part was to design the garden, while she did the lion's share of the planting; this partnership was to reach its apotheosis at Sissinghurst. In August 1917, her mother, who was a great friend of Edwin Lutyens, took her to Munstead Wood to meet Miss Jekyll. Of this meeting she wrote, 'Miss Jekyll rather fat, and rather grumbly; garden not at its best, but can see it must be lovely.'[2] After this she and Nicolson worked at designing a white and yellow garden at Long Barn. It is my belief that Miss Jekyll, or rather her writing, had a profound influence on Miss Sackville-West's ideas.

In 1929, after considerable heart-searching, Nicolson left the Diplomatic Service to become a journalist, and to give himself more time for his writing. (He was an inspired diarist and reviewer and wrote the official biography of George V.) His wife had never been interested in his work, indeed in later years she did not even join him *en poste* abroad, although she did visit him twice in Tehran in 1926 and 1927, about which she wrote *Passenger to Teheran* and *Twelve Days*. Nicolson became the writer of 'The Londoner's Diary' in the *Evening Standard*. In 1931 he edited Oswald Mosley's paper *Action*, and in 1935 he was elected the National Labour MP for West Leicester which he held till the 'Khaki' election of 1945. His wife was not interested in politics, either.

She was a born writer, both of prose and poetry, and saw writing as her work in life. These days she is best remembered for two of her novels published in the early 1930s, *The Edwardians* and *All Passion Spent*, and for her long poem *The Land* which came out in 1926 and won the Hawthornden prize the following year. Its sequel, *The Garden*, which was awarded the Heinemann prize, was published 20 years later.

In 1930, chased out of Long Barn by the threat of a nearby development, the Nicolsons bought a ramshackle collection of farm buildings and a tall Tudor tower, near Cranbrook in Kent, called Sissinghurst Castle. An ancestor of her's had lived there, which was some compensation to her romantic soul for the loss of Knole. This house was a gamble, however, for it had not been continuously inhabited for a very long time and although, with a farmhouse and five hundred acres as well, it only cost £12,000, Nicolson estimated that to put it right would cost another £15,000. The garden of seven acres was derelict. As she wrote:

The amount of old bedsteads, old plough-shares, old Cabbage stalks, old broken-down earth closets, old matted wire, and mountains of sardine tins, all muddled up in a tangle of Bindweed, Nettles and Ground elder, should have sufficed to daunt anybody. Yet the place, when I first saw it on a spring day in 1930, caught instantly at my heart and my imagination. I fell in love at first sight. I saw what might be made of it. It was Sleeping Beauty's

Castle; ... a garden crying out for rescue. It was easy to foresee, even then, what a struggle we should have to redeem it.[3]

It was nearly two years before the house was fully habitable but they began immediately to plan and plant up the garden. Gardening, and the design of the garden, were never more than leisure-time hobbies, bringing peace and respite from their fraught and difficult work, and emotional entanglements. This makes their achievement the more remarkable. Despite the lack of time available, however, gardening was very important to them and their happy collaboration in the garden undoubtedly contributed to their marital stability and security. They were unashamed letter writers and there are hundreds of letters extant in which every fine point of planting or placing is discussed and shared. Even when separated by hundreds of miles, neither ever made major alterations in the garden without the other's consent and approval.

Miss Sackville-West's first article on gardening matters was published in the *Evening Standard* in 1924, she began to give talks on gardening on the wireless in 1933, but her word was established as authoritative when she was asked to write a weekly column in the *Observer*, which she did from 1946 till 1961. The best of these was later published in four books; *In Your Garden*, followed by *In Your Garden Again, More For Your Garden* and finally *Even More For Your Garden*. The *Observer* articles made her a household name in a way that her other writings had not. She was read and enjoyed by many who had never read a line of her poetry. There is an irony here, for she dismissed them as 'beastly little ... articles'[4] and she was surprised and taken aback, although also rather pleased, when she was awarded the Veitch Memorial Medal by the RHS in 1954, in great part because of her work as a journalist. The influence of these articles on gardening in post-war Britain has been enormous if incalculable. The Sissinghurst style of gardening is firmly established and no one since has suggested any radical departure from it.

She was a romantic, firmly embedded in an idealised past, but with the seductive ability sometimes to put her feet firmly in other people's shoes. This she did to good effect in her gardening writing, which is lively, sophisticated, much influenced by her travels, but at the same time practical, sympathetic and honest, and where her love of the good earth comes

Figure 5.2 Vita Sackville-West, photographed by Cecil Beaton

through strongly. She rarely dwelt on plants she did not care for—except for the unfortunate Rose 'American Pillar'—for her attitude was positive and, for a serious nostalgic, she took the trouble to learn about post-war technological innovations. The secret of her enduring success lies in the fact that, although the canvas on which she worked was large, she painted pictures with small groups of plants so that her ideas could be translated into fact in the smallest of gardens. Her writings opened up an almost fantastical world to her readers, where they were invited to imagine and consider ideas that had never come

their way before, all written in a light and excited and, at times, charmingly diffident manner. Very much the amateur, she appeared to understand completely the problems her readers experienced, while at the same time lifting their eyes towards horizons they may well not have known existed.

Although she never mentioned the name of her garden, she wrote most clearly about it. It must have fascinated visitors in the 1940s and 1950s to see the model that they knew so well from the weekly articles. She displayed a considerable depth of feeling for her garden, and its plants, and her knowledge of their individual ways was as profound as Miss Jekyll's. At the same time it must be said that the column was of uneven quality. A uniform standard in a weekly essay is hard to maintain, and it is possible to discern the feeling that she sometimes found her Sunday morning task a chore.

The layout of the garden at Sissinghurst was finished by 1939, except for the White Garden which came into being in 1949 to 1950, and the Thyme Lawn the same year. The Nicolsons were not well off in the early years, and so had, perforce, to go slowly. They were helped financially, however, by a legacy from her mother when she died in 1936.

The garden was open to the public for the first time in 1938, and from 1941 this meant every day in the growing season. The cost of entry was a shilling, and the Nicolsons often referred to their visitors as 'shillingses'. Miss Sackville-West found them rather easier to get on with than her own acquaintances. She could often be seen gardening, or talking to strangers, dressed in a pair of men's breeches which gave point to Noel Coward's unkind remark that she was Lady Chatterley above the waist, and the gamekeeper below.

Figure 5.3 The Tower and Tower Lawn in 1942

During the war she rather unwillingly organised the Women's Land Army in the area and in 1949 she was elected to the National Trust Gardens Committee. She was also a local magistrate. But it was her writing and gardening that really absorbed her, and after the war she rarely strayed far from Sissinghurst. Like Miss Jekyll she became more reclusive as the years went by, and, like her, felt that too much contact with people sapped her energies. Nicolson would commute to London on Sunday evenings and come back on Friday nights. He had his own study in the South Cottage and they slept there, she worked in the Tower and the children were housed with their nannies in the Priest's House and later in the gatehouse block. They met for meals in the Priest's House just as if they were living a collegiate existence. It did not seem a strange arrangement to them; they had established a similar pattern of living at Long Barn.

In 1961 Miss Sackville-West developed cancer and she died at Sissinghurst on 2 June 1962. Sissinghurst was inherited by her son, Nigel, and was given over to the National Trust in 1967, in lieu of death duties. Harold was seriously undermined by her death and he died in 1968, having been ailing for some years. There have inevitably been changes made in the garden since the Nicolsons' death, and its translation into the hands of the National Trust, for some concession has had to be made to the influx of many thousands of visitors every year. The Trust has preserved, as far as possible, the personality and atmosphere of the garden. In this they have been vastly helped by the two present head gardeners who worked for the Nicolsons from the year before Miss Sackville-West died.

Miss Sackville-West was a complex woman who defies simplistic analysis. She was genuinely loved by her friends, who may have found the ménage unconventional but who were attracted by the Nicolsons' style and energy. She was courteous, dignified and amusing, with a natural ability to make her friends feel they really mattered to her. So much so that, by the end of her life, there existed a string of so-called 'emotional pensioners'. Many of these were one-time lovers with whom she could not cut her ties completely, even if she had the ability firmly, even ruthlessly, to terminate affairs. She looked down upon ordinary domestic happiness, being a strange mixture—though hardly strange when one thinks of her parentage—of patrician and Bohemian. She would have dismissed conven-

Figure 5.4 The Rose Garden, 1942

tional domesticity as middle class and therefore to be faintly despised. In her youth she was devil-may-care, although she shrank from exposing her behaviour to the public gaze. Hers was essentially a secretive nature.

Her poetic temperament, for she saw herself as writer and poet rather than as gardener, led her to compose *The Land* and *The Garden*, whereas the more down-to-earth Miss Jekyll wrote *Old West Surrey*. All are deep-felt celebrations of English rural life.

She was an immensely hard worker. Sissinghurst is as much the product of careful preparation and planning as it is of inspiration, or rather the two strands are intertwined. As a gardener her outlook, as she freely admitted, was 'romantic' as a counterpoint to Harold's 'classical' view. It was a felicitous partnership, as fruitful, on a more limited scale, as that between Lutyens and Miss Jekyll. She was thoroughly imbued with the ideas of William Robinson, whom she knew, and who advocated all those features that have come to be associated with Sissinghurst: clim-

bers through old trees and clothing walls, cottage gardens, the mixed shrub and perennial border, and roses underplanted with violas. She also liked a certain natural 'wildness' in the garden. From Miss Jekyll she drew the idea of seasonal gardens and one-colour gardens, and developed them to a degree never known at Munstead. A carpet of polyanthus, à la Munstead, was laid under the canopy of Kentish cobnuts in the Nuttery. She believed, like Robinson and Miss Jekyll, in informality within a formal setting. The hallmark of Sissinghurst was the generosity and profusion with which everything grew, fostered by someone who loved opulence. That is why she enjoyed Old Roses so much; for that and their historical associations. Their fortunes she succeeded in turning round, almost single-handedly.

Like the other writers she had an excellent eye for a garden-worthy plant and was careful to discard the second-rate. She had a colour sense which was highly developed and a taste that was sophisticated without being narrow: her lapses in taste were even fewer than Miss Jekyll's although Nicolson chaffed her for her weakness for 'beastly red-hot pokers'. Many of her preferences will become apparent in the anthology, but it is helpful to mention here that she enjoyed subtle colours. As Nicolson put it, 'Vita only likes flowers which are brown and difficult to grow'.[5] That is, of course, very unfair but it does point to her love for green flowers, which were not fashionable at the time. She did much to enhance the reputations of *Helleborus* and *Euphorbia* particularly. Nicolson liked bright colours, as could, and can, be seen in the parts of the garden where he had most influence, namely the Spring Garden and the Cottage Garden. She loved plant species, rather than nurseryman's hybrids; single rather than double flowers, though not exclusively as witness her admiration for the Cabbage Rose, *Rosa centifolia*; she encouraged the planting of winter flowers, and half-hardy plants, and she believed in always growing the best kinds if she could and letting desirable plants seed about if they would. A little controlled disorder was acceptable, even desirable to her; in that respect her garden-making mirrored her life.

Sissinghurst is seductive in a subtle way; nothing is brash or overdone, although there is plenty of life and colour. She set out to create, around an ancient cluster of buildings, a suitably timeless setting. The garden is the achievement of someone seeking contentment and peace away from a chaotic and ultimately unsatisfactory world. Sissinghurst is the reward.

Sissinghurst

When creating the garden at Sissinghurst, the Nicolsons were fortunate to have had Long Barn as a 'dummy run', so to speak, for many of their ideas. Even at Sissinghurst, however, as they freely admitted, mistakes were made that later had to be rectified. In the main, however, their sureness of touch and of eye was remarkable.

Nicolson was determined that the outline should be orderly and coherent. It was he that saw the necessity of designing the garden on a north/south and east/west axis, in order to create a series of enclosures. He must have absorbed, during his time as a diplomat in Persia, a sense of the symmetry which is a hallmark of Mughal gardens, and the Nicolsons had visited Italian gardens too. His talent for garden-design was stretched, however, to its limit by the difficulties of the ground that they had acquired. As Miss Sackville-West explained:

The walls ... were not all at right-angles to one another: the courtyard was not rectangular but coffin-shaped; the Tower was not opposite the main entrance; the moat-walk, with its supporting wall, ran away on so queer a bias that the statue we placed on the bank behind the moat stood opposite both to the Tower and to the seat at the upper end of the moat walk. All this was disconcerting, and there were also minor crookednesses which had somehow to be camouflaged. I do not think that you would notice them from ground-level now ...

I could never have done it myself.

Fortunately I had acquired, through marriage, the ideal collaborator. Harold Nicolson should have been a garden-architect in another life. He has a natural taste for symmetry, and an ingenuity for forcing focal points or long-distance views where everything seemed against him, a capacity I totally lacked. After weeks of paper struggle he would come home to discover that I had stuck some tree or shrub bang in the middle of his projected path or gateway. We did, however, agree entirely on what was to be the main principle of the garden: a combination of long axial walks, running north and south, east and west, usually with terminal points such as a statue or an archway or a pair of sentinel poplars, and the more intimate surprise of small geometrical gardens opening off them, rather as the rooms of an enormous house would open off the arterial corridors. There should be the strictest formality of design, with the maximum informality in planting. This is what we aimed at, and is, I hope, what we have achieved.[6]

They had the idea, which Major Lawrence Johnston had perfected at Hidcote, of private enclosures, or what he had called 'garden rooms', where particular sorts of plants or a season of interest could be accommodated. Major Johnston, in his turn, may have been influenced by Miss Jekyll. But whether the Nicolsons arrived at their plans independently or whether they faithfully followed in the footsteps of others is not very important. What matters is that they created something unique, by reason of geography and circumstance and the mixture of their own individual interests and personalities. Eclectic in origin, Sissinghurst is highly original in outcome.

In October 1948, Nicolson wrote,

Sissinghurst has a quality of mellowness, of retirement, of un-flaunting dignity, which is just what we wanted to achieve and which in some ways we have achieved by chance. I think it is mainly due to the succession of privacies: the forecourt, the first arch, the main court, the tower arch, the lawn, the orchard. All a series of escapes from the world, giving the impression of cumulative escape.[7]

The use of the word escape is revealing.

In the Front Courtyard, in front of the Tower, is the Purple border, and all the walls are clothed with climbers, amongst them *Actinidia*, *Ceanothus*, *Hydrangea*, vines and clematis. To the north is the celebrated White Garden, where in small beds surrounded by miniature box hedges, white flowers are grown amongst grey and green foliage; the predominant feature is a fine *Pyrus salicifolia* 'Pendula', and in summer the garden is scented by regale lilies and cardiocrinums (see Chapter 12 for her description of it).

Close by is the so-called Delos Garden, which was apparently never very satisfactory in the Nicolsons' lifetime, but now has magnolias in spring, and in the autumn, gentians and the hardy *Cyclamen hederifolium*. To the east of the Tower Lawn is the Rose Garden, where her love of exuberance and generous profusion was

Figure 5.6 The Tower at Sissinghurst

Figure 5.5 Vita Sackville-West and Harold Nicolson, by Cecil Beaton

allowed full rein (see Chapter 11). In the centre is the circular Rondel of yew which serves to divide the Rose Garden into compartments. The Rose Garden is best in June and July because she grew so many old-fashioned varieties, many of which have only one, single, glorious flush of flower. The roses were underplanted with *Alchemilla*, catmint, pansies, *Allium albopilosum*, foxgloves and hardy geraniums. How William Robinson would have admired it. At one end of the Rose Garden is the famous wall designed by the architect, Albert R. Powys, with its large semi-circular bay. Sissinghurst is well-served with old walls as well; these provided excellent opportunities for sheltering tenderish climbers.

To the south of the Rose Garden runs the Lime Walk, or Spring Garden, which was Harold's preserve. He called it 'Unter den Linden', a memory of his time in Berlin, or 'My Life's Work'. Here pleached limes are underplanted with bulbs and primroses and pul-

4. A modern bedding-out scheme (see Ch. 7)

5. *Gentiana verna* (see Ch. 6)

6. Hellebores and anemones in light woodland (see Ch. 9)

Figure 5.7 The Gate onto the Tower Lawn, Sissinghurst, 1942

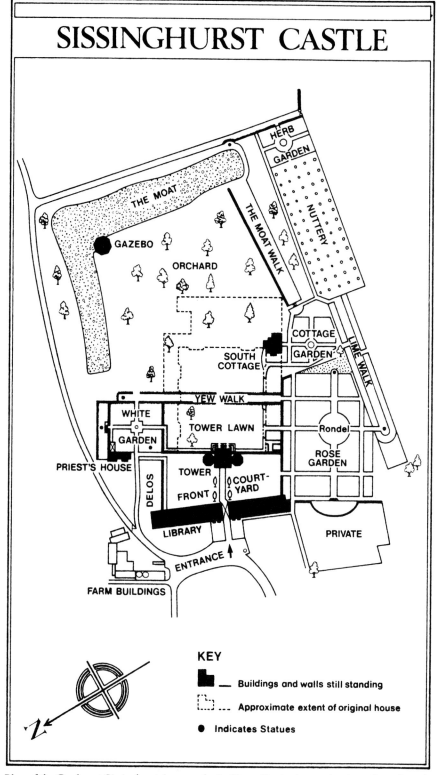

Figure 5.8 Plan of the Garden at Sissinghurst (present-day). (From Sissinghurst, *by Anne Scott-James)*

monarias. The planting was as carefully thought out as anywhere else in the garden. Towards the end of the Lime Walk an opening to the left leads to the Cottage Garden. Best in midsummer, the colour scheme here is yellow, orange and bright red, and the accent is on old cottage favourites, such as Miss Jekyll had recommended and, in some cases, rescued from obscurity. Here are day lilies, pansies, columbines, paeonies and snapdragons and, later in the summer, dahlias and red hot pokers, and on the wall of the Cottage is a very fine specimen of the noisette rose, white with the faintest blush of pink, 'Madame Alfred Carrière'.

The extension of the Lime Walk is the Nuttery and, at the far end of that, the Herb Garden, enclosed by yew hedges. In the middle of the Herb Garden is a marble bowl which they brought back from their first garden at Cospoloi and, outside it, the Thyme Lawn, which was a brilliant invention of her own. In this lawn she grew *Thymus serpyllum*, which has purple flowers, and also those forms of it that are bright red or white. She planted dwarf narcissi and hardy cyclamen too, and succeeded in creating the effect that she desired, that of a Persian carpet laid out-of-doors.

Steps in the Cottage Garden lead to the Moat Walk, where scented azaleas flower in late spring, and *Aster frikartii* 'Mönch' in the autumn. A bank separates this walk from the Nuttery. The Walk leads to the Moat, which is L-shaped and, in the elbow, is a gazebo of Kentish oast-house appearance, erected as a memorial to Nicolson by his two sons in 1969. Here grows *Rosa* 'Sissinghurst Castle' which Miss Sackville-West was most excited to find growing amongst the rubbish in the garden when the house was acquired; for some time it was thought to be *Rosa gallica* 'Rose des Maures' but the name has since been changed. Between the Moat Walk and the Moat is the Orchard, which had existed before, and up whose apple-trees Vita could grow vigorous roses like *Rosa filipes* 'Kiftsgate', just as William Robinson would have liked. Here grow thickets of shrub roses too and, naturalised in the grass, bulbs such as *Narcissus* and the autumn-flowering *Colchicum*.

Notes

1. Quoted in N. Nicolson, *Portrait of a Marriage*, 1st edn (Weidenfeld and Nicolson, 1973), p. 188.

2. V. Glendinning, *Vita*, 1st edn (Weidenfeld and Nicolson, 1983), p. 85.

3. V. Sackville-West, 'The Garden at Sissinghurst Castle, Cranbrook, Kent', *Journal of the Royal Horticultural Society*, vol. 78, part 11 (1953), p. 402.

4. Quoted in J. Brown, *Vita's Other World*, 1st edn (Viking, 1985), p. 203.

5. Quoted in A. Scott-James, *Sissinghurst. The Making of a Garden*, 6th impression (Michael Joseph, 1983), p. 84.

6. Sackville-West, 'The Garden at Sissinghurst', p. 403.

7. Quoted in A. Scott-James, *Sissinghurst*, 6th impression (Michael Joseph, 1983), p. 111.

CHAPTER
❧ 6 ❧

Plant—hunting

I make no apology for including a chapter on plant-hunting in an anthology of garden writing, for Farrer wrote five books specifically about it and his experiences came into his other more horticultural books, so that the picture of him that emerged would not be complete, and indeed would be positively misleading, without some account of his travels and collections. All the others, in particular Bowles, collected abroad at one time or another in their lives.

From the 1830s onwards, interest in British botanical and commercial horticultural circles centred on the introduction of new plants from abroad. Gardeners like Robert Fortune, nurserymen like John Veitch, his nursery's employees the Lobb brothers, and botanists such as Joseph Hooker, set off east and west looking for plants, both for scientific purposes and to satisfy the desire for novelty in the garden and especially in the greenhouse. This movement continued with Forrest, Farrer and Kingdon-Ward, but has slackened in pace since the last world war. Farrer and Bowles represented one of the two types of twentieth-century plant-hunter, the gifted and knowledgeable amateur who financed his expeditions mainly out of his own pocket but with some help from gardeners who required plants and seeds in return.

It is perhaps a little misleading to call Farrer an amateur, of course, because he did have his own nursery for which to provide plants, but commerce or no commerce, he would have gone anyway, for the excitement of the 'lonely places', and the exultation at finding new, previously undiscovered, plants.

The second type was a professional collector, of which Frank Kingdon-Ward, E.H. Wilson and George Forrest were prominent examples, who were sent by nursery or botanical institutions to find good garden plants, no matter how adverse the conditions or circumstances.

Amateur or professional, there appears to have been little difference, however, in how systematic and unflagging they were. The gentleman amateur has disappeared almost completely, deterred by the ruinous expense and by stricter conservation policies abroad. Paid professionals have been replaced in large part by scientists, from the botanic gardens, working in small groups and very often looking for particular plants to aid research.

Large-scale horticultural collecting, therefore, where the most important considerations are the beauty and garden-worthiness of plants, is no longer possible. Only botanical collecting is practised, although in the process beautiful plants are introduced. These days the conservation of plants is foremost in everyone's minds, but even in 1911 Farrer could write:

I am not more horrified than astounded to find that scandal, like a worm in the bud, has recently been preying on my damask reputation ... For strange, stray women ... have gone about accusing me of 'devastating' regions and valleys of the Alps on which ... I have never yet set foot. Is this legend worth the pains of scotching? Come, come let us reason. On a given range a given species dwells. But that range, remember, is many miles long, in and out, up and down, incalculably vast and high; and the populating species can only be counted by the million and the very many million. What a mighty void shall I then leave in even half a mile of slope, if I pluck thence a hundred plants or so![1]

There are now so many intrepid tourists that his point no longer holds good, if in fact it ever did. In his day, though he was always complaining of the crowded nature of the hills, the numbers of walkers and climbers were just not of the same magnitude, but there were serious depredations of rare alpines, nevertheless. For us plant-hunting, on the scale that Farrer and Bowles enjoyed, is not practicable, but it is still possible to derive a strong vicarious pleasure from reading about it. The fun of it for Bowles comes through strongly when he describes a trip with Farrer to northern Italy:

> ... how I should like a magic carpet to take me there to grub out more Cyclamens, and after gathering enough ... to go down among the hemp crops at dusk and inhale the sweetness of vine blossoms, and listen to the racket of the tree-frogs ... That is the reward for going out to gather one's own plants—first happy hours in quaint and picturesque places, full of good sights, sounds, and scents, to be enjoyed then and remembered afterwards, when the unpleasant ones can be forgotten, and then in after years to have your treasures recall it all again as you look at them.[2]

Gathering one's own plants, especially a rarely found species like the high alpine Eritrichium or, as in this case, a long-sought yellow form of *Saxifraga aeizoön*, was a joy to be savoured slowly.

For what can equal the delicious moments while one sits down in glory at the side of one's discovery, and finds the moments far too holy and precious to be cut short by the premature introduction of the trowel upon the scene? The thing is there, for us to deal with at our reverent pleasure; meanwhile we must adore every detail of our find, lovingly touch the upturned petals, mark the growth, the health, the beauty, the whole delight of the plant. There is no hurry about precipitating the end.[3]

This pleasure was intensified if the search had been arduous.

> I cursed my folly in the whole expedition, and swore that when I reached a group of three big blocks about ten yards further on I would positively not go one step beyond them, whether I found them barren or no. Through the blizzard I drearily toiled towards them. Two of them were like frozen versions of Mrs. Hubbard's cupboard. But the third was full of *Eritrichium nanum*.
>
> Full—brimming, crowded with cosy clusters of Eritrichium. I could hardly dare believe my eyes; but there is never any mistaking those silken rosettes of silver fluff. It was Eritrichium this, all right, although it was only just beginning to stir from its long sleep, and the sleet stood out in dense jewel-work of diamond over its furry cushions. And for a further tempering of the wind to the shorn lamb ... that rock was rotten with ruin ... By this time I was so cold that sensation had wholly fled from my fingers and to work with them was like using so many chunks of wood. However with these lifeless implements I toiled and tugged until I had a decent sufficiency of plants, without sacrilegiously denuding that boulder.[4]

What was all the fuss about?

> There is no colour that I know exactly like that of *Eritrichium*. It is blue—the absolute blue. And yet there is a softness about it which sets it far apart from the terrifying brilliance of *Gentiana verna*, or the almost vicious blatancy of *Scilla sibirica* ... As for the Forget-me-nots—well, I can only say that their otherwise lovely blues become harsh, thin and mean beside that of their tiny cousin ... I find that in *Eritrichium* a dash of Chinese white is mixed with the azure and thus the softer tone is produced; there is also—and now I must be read with caution—the minutest, minutest touch

of crimson,—oh, so little that the very suggestion seems ridiculous, and yet the cobalt-laden brush, after a lick of white, must make the merest feinting flirt across the cake of crimson, if the rich, clear, gentle, perfect blue of the flower is to be finally divorced from any suspicion of yellow.[5]

Anyone who has visited the Alps will find that the plants that come to mind above all others as the archetypal mountain flowers are the gentians. That was certainly what Robinson thought.

The vernal Gentian is known to many as the type of all that is charming in alpine vegetation: its vivid colour and peerless beauty stamp themselves on the mind of the dullest traveller that crosses the Alps as deeply as the vast and death-like wastes of snow, ever-darting silvery waterfalls, or the high dark, plumy ridges of pines, though it be but a diminutive speck compared to any of these. It is there a hardy little gem-like triumph of life in the midst of death, buried under the deep all-shrouding snow for four, six, or even eight months out of the twelve, and blooming during the brightest summer days near the margin of the wide glaciers, and within the sound of the little snow cataracts that tumble off the high Alps in summer.[6]

Gentians are not of course confined only to the European Alps, indeed the finest of all the genus was found by Farrer at the end of the second year of his Chinese trip.

And hardly had I started when, in the fine turf that crowned the top of a sloping boulder, there stared at me a new Gentian, a Gentian that instantly obliterates all others of its race, and sinks even G. *verna* and G. *Gentianella* into a common depth of dullness. When the first awe was over, I gave tongue for Bill [Purdom], and together, in reverend silence, we contemplated that marvel of luminous loveliness. Not the faintest hope possessed me that this glaring miracle could be a new species. Had not Przewalsky crossed this range? How then could he possibly have missed a splendour so assaulting as this? I forgot the chances of the season, and the complete and abject insignificance of *Gentiana Farreri* when not in flower . . .

The collector's dream is to have some illustrious plant to bear his name immortal through the gardens of future generations, long after he himself shall have become dust of their paths. Mere beauty will not do it; for the plant may fail and fade in cultivation, and his name be no more known, except to the learned, as attached to a dead dry sliver on the sheets of a herbarium. To become vividly immortal in the Valhalla of gardeners, one must own a species as vigorous as it is glorious, a thing capable of becoming, and remaining, a household word among English enthusiasts [which was not the case with many others of his introduction] . . . A fine frail tuft-like grass radiating some half a dozen fine flapping stems—that is G. *Farreri*, quite inconspicuous and obscure in all the high lawns of the Da-Tung . . . Until it flowers; and every day in early September brings a fresh crashing explosion of colour in the folds of the lawns. For each of these weakly stems concludes in one enormous upturned trumpet, more gorgeous than anything attained by G. *Gentianella*, but in the same general style and form. But the outline is different, with a more subtle swell to the chalice, and that is freaked outside in heavy lines of black-purple that divide long vandykes of dim periwinkle blue with panels of Nankeen buff between; inside the tube and throat are white, but the mouth and the wide bold flanges are of so luminous and intense a light azure that one blossom of it will blaze out at you among the grass on the other side of the valley. In no other plant, except perhaps, *Ipomoea Learii*, or *Nemophila*, do I know such a shattering acuteness of colour: it is like a clear sky soon after sunrise, shrill and translucent, as if it had a light inside. It literally burns in the alpine turf like an electric jewel, an incandescent turquoise.[7]

There is a picturesque story attached to this plant, one of the very best of Farrer's introductions. He found it in flower at the end of the season, could not wait for the seed harvest, and sent home whole plants which all duly died on the long journey home on the Trans-Siberian Railway. Farrer was bitterly disappointed. From the same trip, the seed of *Gentiana hexaphylla* was sent to the Botanic Gardens in Edinburgh, and when it germinated some was found to be *Gentiana farreri*. It had been unknowingly collected during the first year of the Chinese expedition.

One of his most glorious discoveries in China was *Meconopsis quintuplinervia*. On alpine lawns, much like those in Europe, he and Purdom found the Harebell Poppy.

It was everywhere, flickering and dancing in millions upon millions of pale purple butterflies, as far as eye could see, over all the enormous slopes and braes of the grass. The sun was now coming up, and its earliest rays slanted upon the upland in shafts of gold dust; in the young fresh light the whole alp was a glistering jewel-work with dew in a powdered haze of diamond, with the innumerable soft blue laughter of the Poppies rippling universally above a floor of pale Alpine Asters, interspersed with here and there the complacent pinkness of the Welcome Primula. In the far-off memory of that scene I have to rein myself in, for fear a flux of words should ensue ... Stupid with a blank delight, I wandered spellbound over those unharvested lawns, agonizing with the effort to contain without breaking the infinite flood of glory they were so mercilessly pouring into so frail and finite a vessel. One did not dare speak ... And at my side walked Bill, silent as I. What was he~thinking then? How was this sight striking home to him? ... We continued together, voiceless and smitten.

And then at last he turned to me, and in the awe-striken whisper of one overwhelmed by a divine presence, he said 'Doesn't it make your very soul ache?'[8]

Farrer's soul must have ached on many occasions at the awesomely impressive surroundings that formed the backcloth to his search for little plants. He described climbing, in a snowstorm, up to the top of a mountain in the Da-Tung Alps in Kansu province when suddenly the snow ceased and the sun came out.

My heart thumped, agonising with height and ecstasy as I toiled up the remaining yards, and stood on the actual crest, some 13,600 ft. above the sea, delirious in the vista of marvellous peaks all round me, swimming among silvery vapours, and blinding in the unmitigated glory of virgin snow.

Looking back the way they had come he saw,

the curves of the gorge, deep under the crags

and pinnacles of wet blue and violet, gleaming in the sun; and out beyond, beneath straight heavy layers of purple cloud and golden horizon, lay the plains and rivers, very remote and sullen. It was a vision of crystal fairyland, a transformation scene in some Olympian pantomime—cruelly vast in scale, cruelly blue above, and cruelly white all round in the glare, with only here and there rock shadows as black as jet, and dark fantastic pinnacles of dolomite jetting up from the slopes in phallic towers with streaming flanks of wetness in the sunshine.[9]

He had a very strong feeling for mountains; sought them out, remembered their names, described their fissures and crags and faces.

Robinson too was profoundly impressed by the Alps, and the variety of conditions that existed there.

In no part of the earth are they so wondrously varied, severe, and even terrible. Valleys that would tempt young goddesses to gather flowers, and valleys planted with cliffs fit to guard the River of Death; beautiful forest shade for woodland flowers, and vast prairies without a tree, yet paved with Gentians; sunburnt slopes and chilly gorges; mountain copses with shade and shelter for the taller plants, and uplands with large areas of plants withered up, owing to the snow lying more than a year. Plants rooted deep in prime river-carried soil, and others living and thriving in little depressions in the earthless rock. Lakes and pools at every elevation, torrents, streams splashing from snowy peaks; pools, bogs, and spring-fed rills at every altitude; long melting snow-fields, giving the plants imprisoned below them their freedom at different times, and so leading to a succession of alpine flower life.[10]

Foul weather was very much the rule, not only in Burma as would be expected, but also in the mountainous regions of western China and of Europe. Bad conditions mattered very much indeed, not only because they made walking always unpleasant and often dangerous or even impossible, but also because they affected the drying of plant material to make herbarium specimens. In the Marches of Tibet, the difficulties were compounded by the natives believing that any natural disaster was a direct result of the mountain gods' displeasure. According to them, any odd and suspicious activity by foreigners on the heights, searching after what they considered to be worthless weeds, was bound to anger these gods, who would mete out their revenge on the poor, unfortunate peasants. In 1914, Farrer's little party was threatened at one point by an army 3,000 strong 'intent, in simple piety, on nothing less than the immediate extermination of our whole party once and for all'[11] as a result of their crops being ruined by a hailstorm. In the same year, Farrer described, as if he believed the cause himself, what terrible weather ensued because they climbed the highest mountain outside Siku.

But Thundercrown [highest of the peaks round Siku, east of Min S'an, and in China] as the peasants of the valley had warned us, is a mountain of no easy temper, and soon he left us no doubt that he was affronted at our intrusion. Grim wafts of icy wind drove down from the summit, and grey wraiths of clouds gathered more and more heavily round the enveloping peaks and precipes overhead, and the air of Thundercrown grew ever colder and colder towards us, till we were chilled to the bone and retired to the shelter of the tents. Having failed to dislodge us by these comparatively civil and lenient hints, the mountain then lost his temper, and began to cry with rage, in long, icy flaws of rain that swept down in steady torrents, lashed into spattering special furies every now and then by violent gales and hysterical sobs of tempest that the infuriate spirit would from time to time send in a wild whirlwind round our tents, which flapped and fluttered and bowed their heads beneath the tearing strokes of the wind and the innumerable sudden slappings of the squalls, but stood bravely firm against the outmost efforts of the air. And now at last the full anger of the mountain was roused to make itself heard. Thundercrown lifted up his voice and howled aloud in volleys of bellowing thunder, announcing to all his brothers and sisters of Tibet this outrage he was suffering, this microscopic intrusion that he was powerless to repel. Awfully his utterance resounded from the crags and precipices, black in the darkness of the storm, except when the lightnings lit them in a ghastly glare and was gone. It was a grim welcome into regions notoriously haunted of demons, nor was there any secret

made of it to the world. Far down in Siku they would certainly be knowing what Thundercrown thought about our invasion of his sanctity, and I agonised over the vicarious vengeance he was probably taking below in the way of rice and millet ruined by hail.[12]

Just occasionally would come a really lovely day. On Mont Cenis in the Alps:

The whole air was full of a majestic peace, leisurely and tranquil, warm with the little breezes of summer among the high hills. Clouds, white and innocuous, now and then came curling over the foreground of the picture, obliterating all the low-lands. Now and then their films would rise to where we were, close round the base of the huge red precipice, eddy about it gently upward, until, like a mist of oblivion, they caused the whole solid world to grow transparent and dissolve through ghostliness into nonentity; then, in a little, russet shadows would pierce the greyness, ebb and flow as the vapours shifted; gradually widen and grow into hard glimpses of precipice, until at length the veil would all ravel slowly and part again, floating away to nothingness above and below in wrack and wreath of vapour. And always the vast sunlight slumbered over the earth: through thinning gauzes which turned it to silver, the constant illumination could still be felt. Then silver dusk would become golden afternoon once more.[13]

It must have been a strange procession of servants, soldiers, donkeymen and donkeys that wended its way on mountain tracks through western China and even into lawless, priest-ridden Tibet in 1914 and 1915. Farrer lovingly described Mafu, his head servant.

The Mafu proved, indeed, our stay and stand-by, a man of many qualities and of their many defects. His very appearance was enough to daunt the most hostile village; for he was of a hideousness rare and special among men. Imagine a bandy-legged rhomboidal gorilla, gap-toothed and rubicund, capable of blossoming into a demoniac frenzy of yells and leaps and howls that might well affright a fiend. I have certainly never in my life seen anything so ugly. [That was till he employed this man's younger brother,

Go-go.] From that moment I vacillated uneasily all the time as to which deserved the palm of absolute ugliness.[14]

Farrer was most impressed by the meticulous and methodical care his servants took over the pressing of his plant specimens, even though it was quite outside their usual experience. The Mafu

took them from me with a calm firm hand, and dealt with them himself in such a way as cured me for ever of the fancy that I could dry flowers, an art on which, in former days, I had rather piqued myself. But nothing can compare with the untiring expert neatness of the Chinese, and after I had once seen the Mafu at his task I left the business wholly in his hands from that time forth. [After a while Go-go took over.] It used to be my unfailing joy to watch him exquisitely toiling at his art, with a patient minute care of which no European botanist has any notion, taking the frail poppy-blooms, for instance, and arranging little tabs of blotting paper under each several petal, so that each should dry separately and keep its shape and colour perfectly, and combine to present one in the end with a flower as living and lovely as if it still were flaunting in the field.[15]

It is not always appreciated by those who have never been plant-hunting just how difficult some plants are to get out of the ground. Particularly tiresome for Farrer were *Daphne rupestris, Saxifraga florulenta* and *Phyteuma comosum. Anemone alpina* was apparently a 'fiend'.

Let no mild maiden sally forth upon the mountains to get it, armed with her reticule and a penknife. Pickaxes and mattocks, to say nothing of dynamite itself, seem necessary before you can get to the end of its woody trunk. I have never got there yet; and it is only when you have reached the end of the stock that the real roots begin. I have employed men for whole days upon the mountain, I have delved in the sweat of my brow for hours, and my manager has toiled on bended knees till the shadows grew long upon the slopes; never yet, I think, have any of us really reached the end of an anemone's root.[16]

Here lay the secret of the success of those

mountain plants, hanging on for dear life on seemingly dead and infertile rock.

Apart from the dried specimens collected on expeditions, and the live plants that were sent home to gardens, private or botanic, the main feature of a large-scale expedition was the collecting of the seed at the end of the season. Especially from the Far East, seed was much more likely to survive the hazards of the posts home than living, green and potentially rotting plants. The seed harvest, however, was a mammoth and profoundly risky business.

Packets of seed look dear in lists at a shilling each; I know now that they would be cheap at sixty, so much will they assuredly have cost their collector in anxiety and trouble and nerve-strain before he has acquired them.

For seed-gathering is simply the most harrowing form of gambling as yet invented by humanity. All the gods are against you, all men, all beasts, all elements combined, with the changes and chances of posts to complicate matters, and wars and rumours of wars; to say nothing of what the raiser at home may make of your results . . . In fine such are the grim and glorious uncertainties of seed-collecting that, to financiers bored with the staleness of the Stock Exchange, to lovers and gamblers sickened with the monotony of their respective sports, I recommend a season of seed-collecting in Tibet as a sure stimulant to their jaded capacities for excitement.[17]

Of course, in Europe, much less dependence need be put on the seed harvest, for most plants in flower would survive the short journey home, if wrapped up properly in suitable receptacles. Farrer and Bowles favoured biscuit boxes for this. From Mont Cenis each had sent four large biscuit boxes full of plants, including *Eritrichium* and *Saxifraga bellardii*, down to Susa, from whence, they had been told, they were safely despatched to England. When they arrived at Susa on the way to collect *Daphne rupestris* on Rocca Longa, they found the eight boxes still waiting at the Post Office. There was no alternative but to take the boxes on with them to Turin, and send the plants themselves.

Have you ever lugged four very large and very heavy square biscuit-boxes for a quarter of a mile? Until you have done so, you can have no notion how many corners a square box manages to have, nor how sharp they are. [Somehow they got them onto the train for Turin.] Halfway to Turin we had a change; out they had to come, one after another. It seemed as if the procession would never end. They stood piled on the platform like a pyramid, looking like bricks from a child-giant's building box.

When the express arrived, it was very full, and each of the boxes had to be handed through the carriage-window into the arms of patient fellow-passengers.

These were as good as gold, and much kinder. They lent a hand to our labour. But their eyes grew wider and wider as biscuit-box succeeded biscuit-box in an unrelenting string: they thought us quite mad. We, meanwhile, were crushed to the earth with shame, and red as Monte Rosa in the sunset. We hated those eight boxes passionately, and felt apologetic even for our existence.

At least they thought they would be rid of them at Turin, but it was not to be. The train they needed for the last leg of their journey was on the point of departure, so that they had to run for it.

By now we moved as if in a bad dream . . . the procession moved in precipitate state down the platform of Turin, through wondering crowds. Eight porters advanced, in single file, each carrying a biscuit-box. We followed in the rear with our own baggage. The cortège must have had an imposing and even oriental look to the spectators; it was like a picture of the Queen of Sheba going to see Solomon, with propitiatory presents . . . It was after midnight when two blighted beings, crushed now into meekness by the tyranny of the biscuit boxes, crawled out of the station at Basilea. With one accord we fell upon the hall-porter, and insisted that he should despatch the confounded things next morning, without saying another word to us about them on any account. We were almost too desperate to care whether he discharged the commission or not . . . really we felt that death would be preferable to another day in their company; to say nothing of the fact that after fermenting thus long in the tropical heats of Lombardy, there could be no reasonable

doubt that both *Eritrichium* and *Bellardii* were by now an indistinguishable jam of rottenness.[18]

They need not have worried; the boxes arrived safely and the plants were unharmed. That experience may have been discomfiting, but there were times in every plant-hunter's life when danger itself came much too close. Farrer at one point in 1914 in Tibet was forced to cross a river on his pony by way of a rickety bridge.

It was a typical Tibetan bridge of poor class, arching high over the stream at the narrow point of a combe, and in no very good repair, with the rails all gone and half the planks also . . . Spotted Fat sniffed at the bridge for a moment, and then began solemnly to advance step by step, picking his way delicately from rickety pole to pole. Beneath me, far down between the gaps of the planks, I could see the boiling, ice-grey water of the churned torrent, and in my ear there was a general roar. And suddenly I became aware that Spotted Fat was sidling out towards the unprotected edge, in evident disapproval of the vacancies between his feet. A paralysis possessed me as I felt his hind-quarters swinging out more and more perilously. Purdom's frozen face of horror advancing to meet me remains photographed on my mind as the last thing I remember ere, incredulous to the last, I was conscious of a stumbling subsidence behind me, a splintering crash, and there was barely time to release my feet from the stirrups in a spasm of instinctive prudence before Spotted Fat and I, no longer one, but two, were falling, falling through twenty feet of emptiness, and down into the glacial abysses of the river.

Down and down into the icy water we sank, and as I slowly mounted through the depths of grey glare it seemed as if I should never emerge again to the light of day. When I did so I was already below the bridge, being rapidly borne down stream towards that engaging gorge, whose charms I now envisaged from quite a different standpoint. There was no swimming possible, and no struggling. Heavy mountain boots held me so deep and upright in the water that only in intervals could I get my mouth above the current, and a heavy macintosh encumbered all my movements. From this, in a spasm of rage, however, I immediately released myself, and away ahead it sailed toward the ghyll, precursor of my own doom; while I myself impotently floundered and bubbled in the tide, being smoothly and quite passionlessly swept onwards at the pace of a rapid train. Desperately I struck out at each rocky headland as it raced into sight, and raced away behind me again out of reach. They came and passed with the uncanny quick elusiveness of nightmares, seeming to be held out only to be withdrawn again at once, like things slid in and out on the wings of a theatre . . .

My latter end was already plainly in sight, but no high and holy thoughts possessed me, as would have been proper, nor any panoramic vistas of memory. Instead I was consumed only with rage over so ignominious a conclusion, a rage that even extended to Purdom, who meanwhile was hopping along from promontory to promontory with cheerful smiles and shouts of encouragement. The least he could have done, I felt, was to jump in and perish also, as the dramatic exigencies of the moment demanded; or else what is the use of Victoria Crosses? Yet there he was, still on terra firma, grinning like a grig, if grigs do grin. Spuming and burbling I drove onwards to my solitary death, each instant lower and lower in the water, each instant lower and lower in spirits, as each of Purdom's futile attempts to stretch me out a hand from the flying promontories fell short. Spluttering my indignation to the high gods, I was whirled straight towards the race, and abandoned hope; when suddenly I felt the point of a rock beneath my toe. Frantically I sought lodgment on it, but could not stand against the flood, and in an instant was torn onwards, only immediately after to come to rest as ignominiously as any dead Tepo, [a member of a local tribe] on a long wide shallow where not so much as a kitten could easily have drowned.

Purdom of course could see what was going to happen from the beginning.

There was nothing for it but to waddle tamely ashore like a duck, in fits of laughter, with my breeches bellying out in tight balloons of water.[19]

Spotted Fat had swum to safety with no difficulty, and Farrer would have been quite safe if he had simply clung onto his tail. But, as always with Farrer, it made a good story.

Robinson had a rather alarming time in the Alps. In wet and unpleasant weather, and with a long way to go before he and his companion could rest for the night:

With rapid pace and eyes fixed on the stony footway, on we went, the valley becoming narrower as we progressed, and in some parts dangerous-looking from almost perpendicularly rising hills of loose stone. Presently a little rough weather-beaten wooden cross was passed beside the footway. 'Why a cross here?' said I to the guide. 'That great stone or rock you see, killed, in its way down, a man returning with his marketings from the valley', he replies. Poor fellow! he must have formed but a small obstacle to the ponderous mass—hard as iron and big as a small cottage—which fell from its bed with such impetuosity that it leaped from point to point, and at last right over the torrent-bed, resting on a little lawn of rich grass and bright flowers on the other side.

Ten minutes afterwards we came to a group of three more rough wooden crosses, almost projecting into the pathway, and loosely fixed in the stones at its sides. They marked the spot where three human beings, two women and a man, had been buried by an avalanche. 'And how,' said I, 'do you recover people's bodies who are thus overwhelmed?' 'We wait till the snow melts in spring, and then find and bury them' . . . It is no exaggeration to state that in many places along this valley these wooden crosses . . . occurred so thickly as to remind one of a cemetery. I should not have minded seeing one or two instances, but to meet them within view of each other was highly suggestive. A railway collision would seem to offer capital chances of escape compared to what one would have in case of being in the way of any crumbling matter in these parts.[20]

In the end we may ask whether it was all worth while; the discomfort, that is, and the dangers and the loneliness, in order to bring back plants for the garden, many of which turned out to be moderate in their appeal and fugitive of long culture. While Farrer lay dying, in Burma, of his body's inability to cope with the monstrous climate, he may perhaps have wondered. But he had no such doubts at the end of the first year of his Chinese expedition.

Perhaps there is nothing quite comparable to the intense and glorious fatigue that settles down on the successful seed-collector at the end of his season. All the year he has been working, undergoing an incessant course of diverse strains and anxieties, climbing for his flowers, travelling to far districts and back again for their pods. He has been on the go the whole time in arduous conditions, never resting, never able to rest even if circumstances allowed, harried like Io across the world, with the gadflies of successive inquietudes as to his seeds and their stage of maturity; and tormented to supererogatory efforts by the awful feeling that the one rock or gully that he does not visit may prove against every probability to be the one place where a novelty is to be met, or capsules still lingering of some plant that everywhere else has scattered its germs long since. And then in a rush, as the climax of the summer's stresses comes the wild crisis of the autumn, whirling him to and fro like one of its leaves, leaving him no peace by day, and no quiet of soul neither by day or night, in the culmination and final concentration of all his energies and anxieties.

And then, after the furious fitful fever, suddenly he sleeps well, and slack go all the limbs of his soul in the relaxation of that exquisite absolute fatigue that follows on achievement. The work is done, and big boxes of bulging packets surround him on every side; the last remembered treasure has been harvested, and what is more difficult, even the last of the second-rate useful species has been swept into the net. With what rapture does he now let himself go flat, and savour the redoubled sweetness of all the bygone beauties of the summer, redoubled in sweetness by the fact that they all now are, empacketed in envelopes and bags, infinite possibilities of beauty renewed in a far strange land for generations to come, at the price of toils and ardours that give yet added sweetness to their memories of the past, the realisation of the present and the hopes of the future. It is a very good weariness, indeed, that follows on the close of such a year's good work as ours had been.[21]

Notes

1. R. J. Farrer, *Among the Hills*, 1st edn (Headley Brothers, 1911), Afterword.

2. E.A. Bowles, *My Garden in Summer*, 1st edn (T.C. and E.C. Jack, 1914), pp. 213–14.

3. R. J. Farrer, *Alpines and Bog Plants*, 1st edn (Edward Arnold, 1908), pp. 82–3.

4. Farrer, *Among the Hills*, p. 49.

5. R.J. Farrer, *My Rock Garden*, reprint of fourth impression (Theophrastus, 1971), pp. 259–60.

6. W. Robinson, *Alpine Flowers for English Gardens*, 1st edn (John Murray, 1870), p. 83.

7. R. J. Farrer, *The Rainbow Bridge*, 3rd impression (Edward Arnold, 1926), pp. 281–3.

8. Ibid., pp. 222–3.

9. Ibid., pp. 81–2.

10. W. Robinson, *Alpine Flowers for Gardens*, 3rd edn (John Murray, 1903), p. xiv.

11. R. J. Farrer, *On the Eaves of the World*, 1st edn (2 vols., Edward Arnold, 1917), vol. 1, p. 231.

12. Farrer, *On the Eaves of the World*, vol. 2, pp. 20–1.

13. Farrer, *Among the Hills*, pp. 65–6.

14. Farrer, *On the Eaves of the World*, vol. 1, p. 31.

15. Ibid., pp. 99–101.

16. Farrer, *Among the Hills*, pp. 25–6.

17. Farrer, *On the Eaves of the World*, vol. 2, pp. 204–6.

18. Farrer, *Among the Hills*, pp. 284–7.

19. Farrer, *On the Eaves of the World*, vol. 2, pp. 143–5.

20. Robinson, *Alpine Flowers for English Gardens*, pp. 89–90.

21. Farrer, *On the Eaves of the World*, vol. 2, pp. 299–300.

CHAPTER ❧ 7 ❧

Garden Design

In order to understand fully the impact that Robinson and Miss Jekyll made on the design of gardens after 1870, it is helpful to give some account of the fashion that prevailed at the time amongst the well-to-do. The craze, for it was nothing less, consisted of making geometrically rigid gardens, often Italianate in appearance, with a 'parterre' close to the house, of elaborately curled beds, which were filled with brightly-coloured tender annuals for the brief summer months, and then were very often left bare for the rest of the year. Though not the originator of this trend, nor alone in promoting it, this fashion of bedding-out has come to be linked with the name of Joseph Paxton, the energetic head gardener at Chatsworth, Derbyshire from 1826 to 1858, and architect of the Crystal Palace, built for the Great Exhibition of 1851. His public standing was so enormous that his weakness for the grand and ostentatious had a widespread and baleful effect on the larger gardens of the day. For many garden-owners, bedding-out was a heaven-sent opportunity to show off, requiring, as it did, considerable labour and the provision of heated glasshouses. Glasshouses, as we know them, were only possible when the technique of curving cast-iron became widely known in the early nineteenth century. The fashion for bedding-out was also given tremendous impetus when the glass-tax was abolished in 1845.

About a generation ago, [Robinson wrote in 1870] a taste began to be shown for placing numbers of tender plants in the open air in summer, to produce showy masses of colour. The plants were mostly from sub-tropical lands; placed annually in the open air of our summer, and in fresh earth, every year they grew and flowered abundantly until cut down by the first frosts. The showy colour of this system was very attractive, and since its introduction there has been a gradual rooting out of all the old favourites in favour of this 'bedding' system. This was carried to such an extent that it was not uncommon, indeed it was the rule, to find the largest gardens in the country without a single hardy flower, all energies being devoted to the few exotics for the summer decoration. It should be borne in mind that the expense for this system is an annual one; that no matter what may be spent in this way, or how many years may be devoted to perfecting it, the first sharp frost of November announces yet further labours . . .

I will not here enter into the question of the merits of this system; it is enough to state that even on its votaries it is beginning to pall. Some are looking back with regret to the old mixed-border gardens; others are endeavouring to soften the harshness of the bedding system by the introduction of fine-leaved plants, [something he advocated in *The Sub-*

Figure 7.1 'Bed of alpine succulents, crested with dwarf Agave'. (From First Edition of Alpine Flowers for English Gardens, *by William Robinson)*

tropical Garden] but all are agreed that a mistake has been made in destroying all our old flowers, from Lilies to Hepaticas, though few have a fair idea of the numbers of beautiful hardy plants which we may gather from every northern and temperate clime to grace our gardens under a more artistic system.[1]

Also immensely popular was the practice of carpet-bedding, when plants were placed to make a pattern or even spell out words. This next passage is from the first edition of *Alpine Flowers* (1870). I cannot imagine what Robinson was thinking of to give his approval to such an unnatural practice. (For all students of Robinson's inconsistencies, it is very interesting to note that his attitude towards carpet-bedding hardened as the years went by.) It is not given to many of us to be constant in outlook all through our lives, but this passage must have caused Robinson considerable embarrassment in later life and, not surprisingly, it does not appear in later editions of the same book.

The dwarfer and succulent alpine plants are capable of affording beautiful and distinct effects from their neat foliage and habit alone, and the introduction of them is one of the most rapidly growing improvements now taking place in our flower-gardens ... [The examples he mentioned were succulents like the hardy sempervivums, but also tender echeverias that needed greenhouse treatment in the winter. He went on to say:]

The way in which these plants have hitherto been found most useful in flower-gardens is in the making of edgings, borders etc; but when people begin to be more familiar with their curiously chiselled forms, they will use them abundantly for making small mosaic beds ...

The ways of arranging these plants so as to secure the most satisfactory effects vary much. They make the most exquisite little geometrical gardens yet seen, and have also been used with charming effect in the English or natural style of garden on a miniature scale. For several years past they have been much used in Battersea Park, on a series of irregular mounds ranging from two to twelve feet high—a Lilliputian imitation of a hilly country—the whole simply formed by throwing up earth. These little hills had very dwarf

7. The Pergola – Hestercombe, Somerset (see Ch. 2)

8. The 'Plat' – Hestercombe, Somerset (see Ch. 2)

9. *Crocus chrysanthus* 'E.A. Bowles' (see Ch. 3)

10. *Iris unguicularis* (see Ch. 12)

alpine plants for turf, and neat specimen plants, hardy and tender, from six inches to three feet high, for 'trees'. Two hills were covered with what is no exaggeration to say appeared like molten silver, and that was *Antennaria tomentosa*.[2]

By 1898, his mind had changed.

Unhappily, our gardeners for ages have suffered at the hands of the decorative artist, when applying his 'designs' to the garden, and designs which may be quite right on a surface like a carpet or panel have been applied a thousand times to the surface of the much enduring earth. It is this adapting of absurd 'knots' and patterns from old books to any surface where a flower garden has to be made that leads to bad and frivolous design—wrong in plan and hopeless for the life of plants ...

For ages the flower-garden has been marred by absurdities of this kind of work as regards plan, though the flowers were in simple and natural ways. But in our own time the same 'decorative' idea has come to be carried out in the planting of the flowers under the name of 'bedding out', 'carpet bedding', or 'mosaic culture'. In this the beautiful forms of flowers are degraded to the level of crude colour to make a design, and without reference to the natural form or beauty of plants, clipping being freely done to get the carpets or patterns 'true'.[3]

He went on to say that these gardens were difficult to plant and so the use of broken brick, white sand and painted stone, had come into fashion and, in this connection, he mentioned Nesfield's work at the Horticultural Society's gardens in South Kensington and Sir Charles Barry's at Shrubland. Shrubland Park in Suffolk, according to Robinson, illustrated most clearly the recent history of English-flower gardening as it was the bedding-out garden *par excellence*.

The great terrace garden in front of the house was laid out in scrolls and intricate beds, all filled with yellow, white, red, and blue, and edged with box. In every spot in this garden the same rigid system of set beds was followed, and not a creeper was permitted to ramble over the masonry and stone work of the various terraces. Every bit of Ivy that tried to creep up the walls and cover the stonework had to be removed, to leave the stone in its first bareness. Where some particular colour was wanted in a certain spot, coloured stones were freely used—yellow, red and blue—and in the summer, when the hedgerows and meadows are full of flowers, there were no flowers in this large garden to cut for the house![4]

All that changed when the house passed into the hands of the Hon. James Saumarez and Robinson was employed by him to redesign the garden. When that happened, he tells us, the terrace-garden was planted with roses, carnations and lavender and climbers 'clothed the walls'. Elsewhere in the garden he replaced ribbon borders with bamboos and lilies, hostas and *Macleya cordata*. Although he very likely exaggerated in order to make his point, Robinson stressed how all-pervasive the fashion of bedding-out had become.

... the process which is commonly called 'bedding-out' presents to us simply the best possible appliance for stealing from nature every grace of form, beauty of colour, and vital interest. The genius of cretinism itself could hardly delight in anything more tasteless or ignoble than the absurd daubs of colour that every summer flare in the neighbourhood of nearly every country-house in Western Europe. Enter the garden of a rich amateur, who spends a small fortune on his flowers, say in the neighbourhood of Lyons. You find orchids from Mexico and the Eastern Archipelago; the beauties of the flora of New Holland as healthy as ever they were in their native homes; tropical fruits perfect in flavour and size, ferns gathered from every clime, and exotics from all parts of the world; but mention the name of some long-discovered native of North Europe or Siberia, hardy as Ivy and beautiful as numbers of highly popular exotics, and in all but extremely rare cases the owner will never even have heard of it! ... Even our great botanic gardens, which ought beyond all others to show us the capabilities of the plants of our own climes, do not exhibit anything better than the gaudiness of great masses of flowers of the same colour on one hand, and the repulsive formality resulting from scientific arrangements of plants on the other.[5]

For Robinson,

> There is nothing whatever used in bedding-out to be compared in colour, form, or fragrance with many families of hardy plants. There is no beauty among bedding plants at all comparable with that of Irises, Lilies, Delphiniums, Evening Primroses, Paeonies, Carnations, Narcissi and a host of others.[6]

Annual bedding was thoroughly disapproved of by Miss Jekyll as well. In 1899 she wrote:

> It is curious to look back at the old days of bedding-out, when that and that only meant gardening to most people, and to remember how the fashion, beginning in the larger gardens, made its way like a great inundating wave, submerging the lesser ones, and almost drowning out the beauties of the many little flowery cottage plots of our English waysides. And one wonders how it all came about, and why the bedding system, admirable for its own purpose, [that Robinson would not have admitted] should have thus outstepped its bounds, and have been allowed to run riot among gardens great and small throughout the land. But so it was, and for many years the fashion, for it was scarcely anything better, reigned supreme.[7]

In 1924 she reflected,

> In the old days of sixty years ago, [i.e. in the 1860s] it was simply the most garish effects that were sought for; the brightest colourings that could be obtained in red, blue, and yellow were put close together, often in rings like a target, and there would be meandering lines, wriggling along for no reason, of Golden Feather Feverfew, edged with a companion wriggle of Lobelia and an inner line of scarlet Geraniums, the only excuse being that such a ribbon border was then in fashion. It was at a time when endless invention and ingenuity, time and labour, were wasted in what was known as carpet-bedding; elaborate and intricate patterns worked out in succulents and a variety of dwarf plants. When the ingenious monstrosity was completed the chief impression it gave was that it must have taken a long time to do ...[8]

In 1914, Bowles wrote:

> I remember a garden of twenty years ago that was the most bedded out I ever saw. Thousands of bedding plants were prepared for planting out in Summer, but always in straight lines in long, straight borders. It all began at the stable gates, and ran round three sides of the house, and continued in unbroken sequence, like Macbeth's vision of kings, for two sides of a croquet lawn, and then rushed up one side and down the other of a long path starting at right angles from the middle of the lawn, and if you began at the gates with blue lobelia, Mrs. Pollock Pelargonium, Perilla, Yellow Calceolaria, and some Scarlet Pelargoniums in ranks according to their relative stature, so you continued for yards, poles, perches, furlongs, or whatever it was ... and so you ended up when the border brought you back again to the lawn. I once suggested 'Why not paint the ground in stripes and have the effect all the year round, even if snow had to be swept off sometimes?'.[9]

Robinson's tireless work in promoting the virtues of hardy flowers earned him the following tribute from Miss Jekyll in 1899.

> It was well for all real lovers of flowers when some quarter of a century ago a strong champion of the good old flowers arose, and fought strenuously to stay the devastating tide, and to restore the healthy liking for the good old garden flowers. Many soon followed, and now one may say that all England has flocked to the standard. Bedding as an all-prevailing fashion is now dead; the old garden-flowers are again honoured and loved, and every encouragement is freely offered to those who will improve old kinds and bring forward others.[10]

Having said that she could not resist suggesting instances when bedding would be appropriate.

> And when bedding as a fashion was dead, when this false god had been toppled off his pedestal, and his worshippers had been converted to better beliefs, in turning and rending him they often went too far, and did injustice to the innocent by professing a dislike to many a good plant, and renouncing its use. It was not the fault of the Geranium or of the Cal-

ceolaria that they had been grievously mis-used and made to usurp too large a share of our garden spaces. Not once but many a time my visitors have expressed unbounded sur-prise when they saw these plants in my gar-den, saying, 'I should have thought that you would have despised Geraniums'. On the con-trary, I love Geraniums. There are no plants to come near them for pot, or box, or stone basket, or for massing in any sheltered place in hottest sunshine ...[11]

It would be wrong to suppose that bedding-out disappeared completely from gardens when it went out of fashion. Far from it. In 1914, Bowles could write of dwarf spring bulbs that

all are quite unsuitable for the modern mil-lionaire's made-by-contract, opulent style of gardening—a thing I hate rather than envy ... the filling of so many square yards of prepared soil with so many thousands of expensive bulbs, to yield a certain shade of colour for a fortnight and then be pulled up to make place for another massing, gives me a sort of gar-dening bilious attack and a feeling of pity for the plants and contempt for the gardening skill that relies upon Bank of England notes for manure.[12]

Like Miss Jekyll he liked the individual bed-ding plants, having a particular penchant, and one that I confess I do not share, for the scarlet salvia.

We have tried many things [in beds near the New River] but nothing is so satisfying to the eye as *Salvia splendens* 'Pride of Zurich', which goes out in June as nice bushy little plants with fiery scarlet heads, and flares away in ever-increasing, red-hot refulgence until a sharp October frost throws a pailful of cold water on its glowing cinders and puts out their glory.[13]

Robinson, implicitly at least, took the credit for the change in fashion away from wholesale bedding-out. In the sixth edition of *The English Flower Garden* (1898), he said:

... I saw the flower-gardener meanly trying to rival the tile or wallpaper men, and throwing aside with contempt all the lovely things that through their height or form did not conform

to this idea ... [He went on that] I began to see clearly that the common way was a great error and was the greatest obstacle to true garden-ing or artistic effects of any kind in the flower-garden or home landscape, and then, made up my mind to fight the thing out in any way open to me ...[14]

He listed the papers and books in which he had propounded this view, ending with *The English Flower Garden*.

This dislike for bedding was part of a wider movement towards a freer form of gardening, less hidebound by the constraints of pattern and rectangle. It manifested itself in a desire for per-manence using hardy flowers, and restrained freedom, as in the case of the wild garden, and for the much wider use of trees and flowering shrubs which would be left, more-or-less unpruned, to establish their own individual shapes. Wildernesses, beyond the formal gar-den, had been popular in the seventeenth cen-tury, but Robinson wished to see something less stylised than that; a garden not full of weeds but which would, in the main, look after itself. What exactly did the term 'Wild Garden' mean to him?

It is applied essentially to the placing of perfectly hardy exotic plants under conditions where they will thrive without further care. It has nothing to do with the old idea of the 'Wilderness'. It does not mean the picturesque garden, for a garden may be highly pictures-que and yet in every part the result of ceaseless care.

What it does mean is best explained by the winter Aconite flowering under a grove of naked trees in February; by the Snowflake, tall and numerous in meadows by the Thames side; by the blue Lupine dyeing an islet with its purple in a Scotch river; and by the blue Appenine Anemone staining an English wood blue before the coming of our blue bells. Mul-tiply these instances a thousandfold, given by many types of plants, from countries colder than ours, and one may get a just idea of the 'Wild Garden'. Some have thought of it as a garden run wild, or sowing annuals in a mud-dle; whereas it does not interfere with the regulation flower garden at all.[15]

Among reasons for thinking wild gardening worth practising ... are ...

First, because hundreds of the finest hardy flowers will thrive much better in rough places than ever they did in the old-fashioned border ...

Secondly, because they will look infinitely better than they ever did in formal beds, in consequence of fine-leaved plant, fern, and flower, and climber, grass and trailing shrub, relieving each other in delightful ways ...

Thirdly, because no disagreeable effects result from decay. The raggedness of the old mixed border after the first flush of spring and early summer bloom had passed was intolerable to many, with its bundles of decayed stems tied to sticks ... When Lilies are sparsely dotted through masses of shrubs, their flowers are admired more than if they were in isolated showy masses; when they pass out of bloom they are unnoticed amidst the vegetation, and not eyesores, as when in rigid unrelieved tufts in borders ...

Fourthly, because it will enable us to grow many plants that have never yet obtained a place in our 'trim gardens'.[16]

Amongst these he numbered golden rod and other large members of the daisy family which are coarse and rampant and overrun other choicer plants. He also strongly advised keeping the winter heliotrope and the giant polygonums for the wild garden, a view with which I would cheerfully agree. He did also suggest Michaelmas daisies and Japanese anemones which are perfectly fine in the border, but will also survive and thrive in a rougher situation.

Fifthly, because we may in this way settle the question of the spring flower-garden ...

Sixthly, because there can be few more agreeable phases of communion with Nature than naturalising the natives of countries in which we are infinitely more interested than in those of which greenhouse or stove plants are native.[17]

That is certainly not a consideration which would weigh with the modern gardener. He did go on, however, sensibly to underline the advantage that this form of gardening was a permanent one, not subject to digging up twice a year. He was always careful to say that the wild garden was for the outer reaches of the garden and not for ground near the house. He expounded the theory of planting bulbs in grass to create a spring garden, an idea called 'naturalising' which we have now wholeheartedly adopted.

Ten years ago I planted many thousands of Narcissi in the grass, never doubting that I should succeed with them, but not expecting I should succeed nearly so well. They have thriven admirably, bloomed well and regularly; the flowers are large and handsome, and in most cases have not diminished in size. In open rich, heavy bottoms, along hedgerows, banks, in quiet open loamy fields, in every position they have been tried, the leaves ripen, disappear before mowing time, and do not in any way interfere with the farming.[18]

Miss Jekyll wrote:

Just as wild gardening should never look like garden gardening, or, as it so sadly often does, like garden plants gone astray, and quite out of place, so wood paths should never look like garden paths. There must be no hard edges, no obvious boundaries. The wood path is merely an easy way that the eye just perceives and the foot follows. It dies away imperceptibly on either side into the floor of the wood and is of exactly the same nature, only that it is smooth and easy and is not encumbered by projecting tree-roots, Bracken or Bramble, these being all removed when the path is made.[19]

She also had the felicitous idea of extending the rose garden into a woodland clearing, using vigorous shrub roses to form 'brakes', and with here and there one climbing into a tall tree.

Miss Jekyll practised 'wild gardening' at Munstead as we know, but with her usual commonsense she was careful to avoid the obvious pitfalls.

Because it has in some measure become fashionable, and because it is understood to mean the planting of exotics in wild places, unthinking people rush to the conclusion that they can put any garden plants into any wild places, and that that is wild gardening. I have seen woody places that were already perfect with their own simple charm just muddled and spoilt by a reckless planting of garden refuse, and heathy hillsides already sufficiently and beautifully clothed with native vegetation made to look lamentably silly by the planting of a nurseryman's mixed lot of exotic Conifers.

In my own case, I have always devoted the

most careful consideration to any bit of wild gardening I thought of doing, never allowing myself to decide upon it till I felt thoroughly assured that the place seemed to ask for the planting in contemplation, and that it would be distinctly a gain in pictorial value; so there are stretches of Daffodils in one part of the copse, while another is carpeted with Lily of the Valley. A cool bank is covered with Gaultheria, and just where I thought they would look well as little jewels of beauty, are spreading patches of Trillium and the great yellow dog-tooth violet [*Erythronium tuolumnense*]. Besides these there are only some groups of the Giant Lily [*Cardiocrinum giganteum*]. Many other exotic plants could have been made to grow in the wooded ground, but they did not seem to be wanted; I thought where the copse looked well and complete in itself it was better left alone.[20]

Robinson's philosophy of 'natural' planting was not a licence for anarchy. He was not advocating the rejection of a strong and logical framework of paths and walls, especially near the house. What he was against was geometrical patterns of planting, unnecessary terracing and stonework, and the ridiculous excesses of topiary, as exemplified by the importations of nurserymen, like the aptly named Herbert Cutbush, from Holland—tables, chairs, cocked hats and other fripperies.

The union between the house beautiful and the ground near it—happy marriage it should be—is worthy of more thought than it has had in the past, and the best way of effecting that union artistically should interest men more and more as our cities grow larger and our lovely English landscape shrinks back from them. We have never yet got from the garden and the home landscape half the beauty which we might get by abolishing the needless patterns which disfigure so many gardens. Formality is often essential to the plan of the garden but never to the arrangement of its flowers or shrubs, and to array these in rigid lines, circles, or patterns can only be ugly wherever it may be!

After we have settled the essential approaches and levels around a house, the natural form or lines of the earth itself are in nearly all cases the best to follow, and it is often well to face any labour to get the ground back into its natural grade where it is disfigured by ugly or needless banks, lines, or angles. But in the true Italian garden *on the hills* we have to alter the natural line of the earth, or 'terrace it', because we cannot otherwise cultivate the ground or stand at ease upon it, and in such ground the strictly formal is as right as the lawn is in a garden in the Thames valley. But the lawn is the heart of the true English garden, and as essential to it as the terrace to the gardens on the steep hills and English lawns have been too often destroyed for plans ruinous both to the garden and the home landscape. Sometimes on level ground the terrace walls cut off the landscape from the house, and, on the other hand, the house from the landscape![21]

Restraint and good taste are obviously necessary, something that the Crystal Palace can never be said to have exhibited. Robinson was critical of it and in the process revealed his contemptuous attitude towards a great deal of garden ornament.

There are positions where stonework is necessary; but the beautiful terrace gardens are those that are built where the nature of the ground required them; and there is nothing more melancholy than the walls, fountain basins, clipped trees, and long canals of places like the Crystal Palace, not only because they fail to satisfy the desire for beauty, but because they tell of wasted effort, riches worse than lost ... This has been called a work of genius, but it is the fruit of a poor ambition to outdo another ugly extravagance—Versailles.[22]

He growled about unnecessary statuary too:

In a northern country like ours a statue of any high merit as a work of art deserves to be protected by a building of some kind. The effect of frost and rain in our climate on statuary out-of-doors is very destructive ... the scattering of numerous statues of a low order of merit, or of no merit at all, which we see in some Italian gardens, often gives a bad effect and the dotting of statues about both the public gardens of Paris and London is destructive of all repose.[23]

In the end, as Miss Jekyll wrote

It is upon the right relation of the garden to the house that its value and the enjoyment that is to be derived from it will largely depend. The connection must be intimate, and the access not only convenient but inviting.[24]

It sounds obvious but it was not always so. Miss Jekyll, with Lutyens as collaborator and teacher, knew all about this and the value of what we now call 'hard landscape', that is, walls, paving and ponds in the garden. She also compiled a whole book of photographs with comments on anything from entrance gateways to stone vases and sculptures. There is not space to go into the subject in any depth, but it is worth quoting her attitude to gardening with the house or hard features in mind.

The whole question of the relation of vegetation to architecture is a very large one, and to know what to place where, and when to stop, and when to abstain altogether, requires much knowledge on both sides. The horticulturist generally errs in putting his plants and shrubs and climbers everywhere, and in not even discriminating between the relative fitness of any two plants whose respective right use may be quite different and perhaps even antagonistic. The architect, on the other hand, is often wanting in sympathy with beautiful vegetation. The truth appears to be that for the best building and planting, where both these crafts must meet and overlap and work together, the architect and the gardener must have *some* knowledge of each other's business and each must regard with feelings of kindly reverence the unknown domains of the other's knowledge.[25]

When writing this she must have been thinking of her own relationship with Lutyens, and perhaps also casting her mind back to a dispute which affected Robinson and, indirectly, the rest of the horticultural world.

In 1892, an architect called Reginald Blomfield published a book that was to incense Robinson to such an extent that he dashed off one the same year in reply. Blomfield's book, *The Formal Garden in England*, was notable for its containing, for the first time, the word 'formal', used in the context of garden design. Blomfield, being an architect and also somewhat opinionated and even, at times, ill-informed, took

exception to the 'natural' ways of gardening then gaining ground, and desired to relegate the garden designer to a subordinate position *vis-a-vis* the architect. He was also a proponent of topiary. The enraged Robinson published, as a counterblast, *Garden Design and Architects' Gardens* in 1892, and returned to the subject in the first two chapters of *The Garden Beautiful* in 1906. At the same time he took issue with John Sedding, whose *Garden-Craft, Old and New*, had been published posthumously in 1891.

The Blomfield–Robinson controversy was stupid and bitterly intemperate on both sides. If the protagonists had bothered to study properly what each other was saying, they would have found much to agree upon. The truth was that, though Blomfield did see the architect as the principal designer of gardens, he did not utterly reject the importance of the flowers and their arrangement, and Robinson, as can be seen at Gravetye, was fully aware of the importance of a formal structure in garden design.

On the subject of topiary, it seems to me that Robinson was on safer ground. *Garden Design and Architects' Gardens* is subtitled 'Two reviews, illustrated, to show, by actual examples from British gardens, that clipping and aligning trees to make them "harmonise" with architecture is barbarous, needless and inartistic'. For Blomfield however, 'it is no more unnatural to clip a Yew tree than to cut Grass'.[26]

Robinson replied:

I do not clip my Yews, because clipping destroys the shape of one of the most delightful in form of all trees, beautiful, too, in its plumy branching. It is not my own idea only that I urge here, but that of all who have ever thought of form, foremost among whom we must place artists who have the happiness of always drawing natural forms. Let Mr. Blomfield stand near one of the Cedar-like Yews by the Pilgrim's Way on the North Downs, and, comparing it with trees cut in the shape of an extinguisher, consider what the difference means to the artist who seeks beauty in form.[27]

Elsewhere Robinson implied that it was morally wrong.

... What right have we to deform things given us so perfect and lovely in form? No cramming of Chinese feet into impossible shoes is half so wicked as the wilful and brutal distortion of the beautiful forms of trees[28]

He concluded his argument:

Thus while it may be right to clip a tree to form a wall, dividing-line, or hedge, it is never so to clip trees grown as single specimens or groups, as by clipping such we only get ugly forms—unnatural too.[29]

Miss Jekyll obviously found the argument intriguing. In 1896 she published an article in the *Edinburgh Review* called 'the Idea of a Garden' in which were reviewed historical developments in garden design, and she commented on the row between Blomfield and Robinson.

Within the last few years ... another war of controversy has raged between the exponents of formal and the free styles of gardening, and against it is to be regretted that it has taken a somewhat bitter and almost personal tone. The formal army has hurled javelins poisoned with the damning epithet 'vulgar'; the free has responded with assegais imbued with an equally irritating 'ignorant'. Both are right and both are wrong. The formal army are architects to a man; they are undoubtedly right in upholding the simple dignity and sweetness and quiet beauty of the old formal garden, but they parade its limitations as if they were the end of all art; they ignore the immense resources that are the precious possession of modern gardeners, and therefore offer no sort of encouragement to their utilisation. If for a moment they leave the safe harbourage of encircling Yew hedge, or let go the handrail of the balustrade, and venture for an excursion into the unknown country of horticulture, they exhibit the weakness of any army that is campaigning at too great a distance from its 'base', and certainly do expose themselves to the shaft of the enemy. [She went on to say that they treated gardeners as if they were just brickmakers or modern builders.] ... Moreover, they do not suggest who is to play the very needful part of artist-gardener—who is to say what is to be planted where, and why, and how.[30]

She leaves us in little doubt which view she favoured.

Harold Falkner, who had been apprenticed in Blomfield's architect's office, and who was won over from the formalists' camp by the charm of the Munstead garden, recorded that: 'She used to relate with great glee the fact that Robinson designed himself a garden all squares, and Reggy a garden on a cliff with not a straight line in it.'[31]

Miss Jekyll did not underestimate the difficulties of free gardening, knowing that it required constant restraint and even sacrifice as well as knowledge and discrimination. It was her view that it was not so easy to go wrong in the formal garden because of its limitations.

Despite the difficulties inherent in free gardening, it became very popular with gardeners. However, the disciples of 'the prophet' as Farrer called Robinson, inevitably went too far. Farrer commented in a passage, written in 1907, that has at least a kernel of fairness in it, on what happened.

It is the grief of humanity that from one extreme of error it must always sway back into another ... In gardening we are now enduring the backwash of just such a terrific wave, whose recession down the naked shingles of the world leaves our horticultural future rather doubtful ...[32]

After describing the excesses of the Victorian era, he went on to say,

But suddenly there comes a Moses to our need. Out of the dense darkness arises the immortal Mr. Robinson, pointing the way to escape. He reminds us of beauties which we had almost forgotten and leads us on to a land flowing with sweetness and delight. Yet all these emancipations have excesses ... and, in their contempt for the abuses of the formal system, Mr. Robinson's successors and disciples have been driven into the foolish extreme of denying all value to form, of insisting on anarchy in the garden, of declaring that every restraint is hateful. Now we have nothing but weak lines in our gardens, vague, wibble-wobble areas that have no meaning nor explanation; our borders meander up and down and here and there like sheep that have no shepherd; our silly lawns erupt into silly little beds like pimples. All is uncertainty, formlessness—a vain impotent striving after the so-called natural. Mr. Robinson, the great and good, with all the incalculable benefits that he has given, has given also, against his will, incalculable harm. For the prophet's words are always exaggerated and abused; and, in reacting violently against the heartless formalism of the eighteenth century, Mr. Robinson's creed has been used also against the large, orderly splendour of the sixteenth ...

Truth, that unseizable thing, lies ever between two extremes; and, while the garden of multi-coloured gravel is an offence to the blessed sun, hardly less so is the amorphous foolishness that now makes our borders undulate and flounder so feebly. The garden proper, as seen from the house, is a part of the house, neither more nor less than the frame is part of the picture. From which it follows that the garden must be built on calm, trim lines— either straight or intelligibly strongly curved. It must have a definite scheme, coherence, unity—not to be a mere reckless jumble of features. It must also make one individuality with the house it belongs to, harmonise with it, continue its plan, and carry out its intention.[33]

Whether Farrer exaggerated preposterously or not it is now, at this distance in time, hard to say. His criticism presumably had some foundation. However, in the process Robinson's image was damaged, and he surely was not responsible for his readers' actions. Likewise, he could not be blamed for putting emphasis, as he did in *Hardy Flowers* published in 1871, on placing groups of plants in turf near shrubberies. He was thinking of 'architectural' plants such as Kniphofia and Acanthus, but in the wrong hands, it would not have had a happy outcome and probably gave point to Farrer's comment about 'silly little beds like pimples'.

The argument smoulders on about who it was exactly devised the idea of the herbaceous border. It was for a long time ascribed to Robinson and Miss Jekyll, but it is obvious they were adapting and popularising an existing concept. The Arley Hall borders have been mentioned before and, in the following extract, Robinson specifically referred to the mixed border as a historical fact; he was, however, obviously anxious that it should be improved. It is also apparent that he was not wholehearted about it, preferring the wild garden as a suitable place for many hardy plants.

We must again have our mixed borders, not the old mixed borders, but better than we have ever seen.

There are several other ways of arranging hardy plants in a more beautiful, natural, and pleasing manner, but the mixed border forms a sort of reception room for all comers and at all times. On its front margin you may place your newest Sedum or silvery Saxifrage; at the back or in the centre your latest Delphinium, Phlox or Gladiolus; and therefore it is, on the whole, the most useful arrangement, though it should as a rule be placed in a rather isolated part of the garden, where the extent of the place permits of that. Not that a mixed border is not sufficiently presentable for any position; but, having many more suitable things to offer for the more open and important surfaces of the garden, this had better be kept in a quiet, retired place, where indeed its interest may be best enjoyed. [He suggested the kitchen-garden.] ... In old times the borders on each side of the main walk of the kitchen garden were mostly appropriated to herbaceous plants; and, if well done, this is a good practice, especially if the place be small ...

The mixed border is capable of infinite variation as to plan as well as to variety of subjects. The most interesting variety is that composed of choice herbaceous plants, bulbs, and alpine plants.[34]

He also suggested as an alternative a border consisting of only bedding plants, i.e. dahlias and gladioli, which shows that he was not against the plants themselves but only against the poor arrangement of them. Whatever the plants used, he was adamant that they should not be planted symmetrically or at regular intervals.

The herbaceous border has acquired a bad reputation, because of its propensity for 'going off' in the late summer and also because of the degree of staking and tying required but, as Miss Jekyll pointed out, three months was the maximum span for a border to look very well, and even then the gardener must resort to ways of filling the gaps that would inevitably appear.

There is frequent complaint among horticultural amateurs to the effect that they cannot keep borders of hardy flowers well furnished with bloom throughout the summer. But in an ordinary garden it is quite unreasonable to expect that this can be done. It can only be done where there are the means of having large reserves of material that can be planted or plunged in the borders to take the place of plants gone out of bloom. Owners of gardens should clearly understand that this is so—acceptance of the fact would save them from much fruitless effort and inevitable disappointment. If a really good display is desired, it can only be conveniently done by restricting the season to a certain number of weeks—by devoting separate borders or other garden spaces to a definite time of year . . .

The earliest of the season gardens will be for April and early May: the one next to follow for May and June. Then will come the main display for July, August and September. If there may be besides a special border or double border for August and another for September, and even one for October, there will be a succession of seasonable displays, each one of which may be made perfect of its kind . . .

Interestingly, she went on to say:

Although the main occupants of the border are hardy plants, there is no reason why the best of the so-called bedding plants should not also have a place, especially as their blooming time is that of the late summer and early autumn. Therefore we shall look to Geraniums, Calceolarias, Salvias, Gazanias, and Heliotrope to take their places, according to their colourings, in and near the front of the border . . .

There is one matter that is commonly overlooked . . . This is the provision of what may be called 'between' plants. For masses of colour, even if arranged in quite a good sequence, are only truly pictorial if between and among the colour groups there are other masses or accompaniments of neutral colouring.

For these she advised, especially, grey foliage plants.

Even with the permanent perennials, the bedding plants and the annuals, a border is apt, here and there, to show a place that might be better furnished. To remedy this it is well to have some plants in pots in reserve [and she suggested lilies and hydrangeas and the Pyramid Campanula] ready to drop in where

they will make the best effect. No means [she said sternly] should be neglected or despised that will make the border handsome and effective, and all such ways of doing it are so many spurs to further beneficent inventiveness.[35]

It is small wonder that the herbaceous border has gone out of fashion and has been replaced in many, often unsuitable, places by conifer and heather gardens or yards of dreary groundcover. Miss Jekyll does not address herself to the problem of bare soil in winter, as far as I know, but her view was that you did not go near a border that was out of flower. After all, she had seasonal borders, and even, in the case of the Michaelmas daisy borders, ones given over entirely to one genus.

Robinson veered more towards the modern concept of what we now call the mixed border, i.e. one with shrubs as well as hardy perennials; this is now the most popular idea. It was practised by Miss Sackville-West at Sissinghurst, for she was no advocate of the purely herbaceous border, and also by Major Lawrence Johnston at Hidcote. When referring to the formal beds near the house and with what they could be planted when bedding was abolished, Robinson suggested beds of shrubs, arranged in an open uncrowded way, and placing

... the *finest hardy flowers in groups between the free untortured shrubs* [his italics]. The advantage of the shrubs is that they would 'adorn' the earth all the winter as well as all the summer, and give us a broken surface as well as a beautiful one . . . The beds, filled with shrubs and garlanded with evergreens and creepers, would everywhere afford nooks and spaces among the shrubs where we could grow some of the many fine hardy Lilies with the Gladioli, Phlox, Iris, tall Anemone, Peony and Delphinium. The choice shrubs suited for such beds are not gross feeders, like trees, but on the other hand encourage the finer hardy bulbs and flowers. They also relieve the plants by their bloom or foliage, and when a Lily or Cardinal Flower fades after blooming it is not noticed as it might be in a stiff border. In this way we should not need the wretched and costly plan of growing a number of low evergreens in pots, to 'decorate' the flower garden in winter.[36]

To graduate the vegetation from the taller

subjects behind to the very margin of the grass is of much importance, and this can only be done thoroughly by the greater use of permanent evergreen and very dwarf subjects. Happily there are quite enough of these to be had suitable for every soil ... Look, for example, at what we could do with the dwarf green Iberises, Helianthemums, Aubrietias, Arabises, Alyssums, dwarf shrubs and little conifers ... All these are green, and would spread out into dense wide cushions, covering the margin, rising little above the grass, and helping to cut off the formal line which usually divides margin and border.[37]

His idea was to 'steal in' herbaceous plants where it would not show when they died down, but to fill the front of the border with evergreen plants and, especially, alpines.

It is well known that Miss Jekyll's attitude towards garden planning was influenced by the cottage garden which she had known from her childhood rambles in rural Surrey, and from which she continued to derive much inspiration in later life. She was unwittingly responsible for a good deal of gush and unrealistic idealism about the cottage garden, perpetrated by later writers who never knew what she knew. The fault is partly hers; she did not point out sufficiently, it seems to me, that some cottage gardens were, and are, unsatisfactory muddles. In the 1870s, however, those which had escaped the bedding-out craze that spread like wildfire through the estates of the rich, must have seemed to exhale a breath of sweetly scented fresh air. Nowadays a cottage garden is as likely to be filled with garish, glaring, dissonant colours, and the old cottage garden plants to be found in the borders of the Old Rectories and Manor Houses. Robinson was also instrumental in enhancing the reputation of the cottage garden, for he remembered what first-class hardy plants he had seen on his walks in southern England in the 1860s, when they had been largely banished from the gardens of the well-to-do; the propaganda campaign was triumphantly concluded by Miss Sackville-West. This is Miss Jekyll:

I have learnt much from the little cottage gardens that help to make our English waysides the prettiest in the temperate world. One can hardly go into the smallest cottage garden without learning or observing something new. It may be some two plants growing beautifully together by some happy chance, or a pretty mixed tangle of creepers, or something that one always thought must have a south wall doing better on an east one.[38]

This is Robinson, published a year earlier in 1898.

English cottage gardens are never bare and seldom ugly. Those who look at sea or sky or wood see beauty that no art can show; but among the things made by man nothing is prettier than an English cottage garden, and they often teach lessons that 'great' gardeners should learn, and are pretty from Snowdrop time till the Fuchsia bushes bloom nearly into winter. We do not see the same thing in other lands ... I often pass a small cottage garden in the Weald of Sussex never without a flower for nine months of the year. It is only a square patch, but the beauty of it is far more delightful than that of the large gardens near, and it is often pretty when they are bare.

What is the secret of the cottage garden's charms? Cottage gardeners are good to their plots, and in the course of years they make them fertile, and the shelter of the little house and hedge favours the flowers. But there is something more and it is the absence of any pretentious 'plan' which lets the flowers tell their story to the heart. The walks are only what are needed, and so we see only the earth and its blossoms.[39]

I do not myself see entirely what is wrong with a plan. There is an element of sentimentality expressed here, although they would no doubt strongly have denied it. Bowles was not immune either:

Pyrethrum uliginosum ... seems to have fallen into disfavour in many gardens of late, but has established itself very successfully in cottage gardens. We owe a vast debt of gratitude to the conservative instincts of our peasantry. Just think, for instance, how often it has happened that the weathercock of fashion has turned out the Chippendale chairs from the dining-room of the Hall first to some stable loft and then to the cottages on the estate to be discovered and brought back half a century later. The same change of taste, or lapse and abeyance of good taste we might say, turned out the old Roses and herbaceous plants to make way for showier bedding sorts. Again, Cottage Tulips, rescued from cottage gardens, are clearly the throw-outs of various Tulip fanciers who discarded breeders that broke not, [bulbs which did not exhibit contrasting splashes of colour on the petals, an attribute prized by Tulip hybridists in earlier times] and even those that would not behave just as they wished, and their self-imposed rules decreed ... I have got many a hardy, sturdy treasure from cottage gardens, besides *Pyrethrum uliginosum*, and the pink Chrysanthemum, and anyone with a keen eye for a good plant might do good work by keeping that eye open on cottage plots. A really hardy, reliable plant of good habit is what the cottage gardener wants and it is after all not a bad standard to set up for the larger garden, and a plant that has thriven and been found worth growing for fifty years in a cottage garden is certain to have many good qualities in it.[40]

Miss Sackville-West called the cottage garden

all a flurry of flowers and a paved perplexity of paths, probably the loveliest type of small garden this country has ever evolved.[41]

Her love of profusion was fuelled by her admiration for cottage gardens. Elsewhere she wrote about planting a small garden:

For my own part, if I were suddenly required to leave my own garden and to move into a bungalow on a housing estate, or into a council house, [that was slightly disingenuous, for she knew that such an occurrence would *never* have happened] I should have no hesitation at all about ruffling the front garden into a wildly unsymmetrical mess and making it as near as possible into a cottage garden ... I should plant only the best things in it, and only the best forms of the best things, by which I mean that everything should be choice and chosen.[42]

If she had done that she would *not* have made it a cottage garden.

Both Miss Sackville-West and Miss Jekyll had areas of their gardens specifically set aside for cottage garden plants, laid out in the way they thought appropriate. They were careful, however, only to use those plants that were proven worthies of respectable and unadventurous habit, much like the owners of the gardens they so admired. They gave more care to the colour schemes of their 'cottage' gardens than was perhaps common amongst those owners. The making of garden pictures, where plants were grouped in interesting ways, was, after all, axiomatic to them.

If [wrote Miss Jekyll] ... I have laid special stress upon gardening for beautiful effect, it is because it is the way of gardening that I love best, and understand most of, and that seems to me capable of giving the greatest amount of pleasure. I am strongly for treating garden and wooded ground in a pictorial way, mainly with large effects, and in the second place with lesser beautiful incidents, and for so arranging plants and trees and grassy spaces that they look happy and at home, and make no parade of conscious effort.[43]

Whether the picture be large as of a whole landscape, or of lesser extent as in some fine single group or effect, or within the space of only a few inches as may be seen in some happily-disposed planting of Alpines, the intention is always the same ... And so it comes about that those of us who feel and understand in this way do not exactly attempt to imitate Nature in our gardens, but try to become well acquainted with her moods and ways, and then discriminate in our borrowing, and so interpret her methods as best we may to the making of our garden-pictures.[44]

For Miss Jekyll, the way to achieve good garden pictures was to concentrate on planting several of a few sorts, rather than to seek restlessly after variety.

There are many people who almost unthinkingly will say, 'But I like a variety'. Do they really think and feel that variety is actually desirable as an end in itself, and is of more value than a series of thoughtfully composed garden pictures? There are no doubt many to whom, from want of a certain class of refinement of education or natural gift of teachable aptitude, are unable to understand or appreciate, at anything like its full value, a good garden picture, and to these no doubt a quantity of individual plants give a greater degree of pleasure than such as they could derive from the contemplation of any beautiful arrangement of a lesser number.[45]

That should put most of us in our place.

The opposite of garden picture composition is the dotting of large numbers of different plants in an incoherent assortment. This is especially likely in gardens where there are collections of plants. Farrer described a tour of Cornish gardens which he had made. As is well known, these are blessed by a mild, wet climate so that an immense range of normally tender plants may be grown there.

> What did I see in Cornwall? Well, I saw ... the perils in to which too soft circumstances, and specialism, can lead a gardener ... I ... saw ... many a spectacle of bewildering gorgeousness and splendour ... But, will my Cornish friends allow me to say it, I saw no gardens ... I saw collections beyond price, and culture high beyond imagining. But of a garden I saw never a trace. Everything was aimless, formless, haphazard. Precious Rhododendrons dumped in a straight line through a wood, tree-ferns in a sort of square paddock-like clearing, Bamboos in a jostle down a glade, with no attempt to show up

their individual graces or masses—nowhere, in fact, the least or most elementary notion of design, neither for garden-proper nor for garden-wild.[46]

Robinson must have had a similar experience, for before praising a garden called Offington which obviously had not fallen into the trap of specialism, he wrote:

> Large collections are rarely in the hands of those who have any thought for general effect, and no garden is more likely to be inartistic than the one rich in plants ...[47]

Farrer described, in the Preface to *My Garden in Spring*, what a really good garden looked like, i.e. one that had steered a path away from a mere collection towards a unified garden picture, but where every plant was jealously guarded and cared for. He was referring, of course, to the Myddelton House rock-garden.

> The highest art is to conceal art; and accordingly the first and last essential of the good rock garden is that it should not look like a garden at all, but like the unharvested flower-fields of the hills—effortless, serene, and apparently neglected. And to achieve this

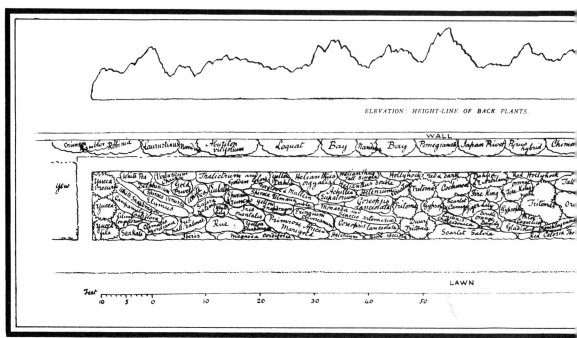

Figure 7.2 Plan of the Main Flower Border at Munstead Wood. (From Colour Schemes for the Flower Garden, *by Gertrude Jekyll)*

effect, as all who have tried it well know, is the final ambition of the real gardener, and the very last to be attained. For nothing is harder, in any walk of art, than to strike the perfect note of calm assurance ... without falling into the death in life of spick and spanness on the one hand, or the more ferocious life in death of slovenliness and anarchy on the other. But at first sight, like all great works, from the Monna Lisa [sic] downwards, the really good garden looks so simple and unaffected and easy that those who base their admiration on a sense of money spent and obvious artificial difficulties surmounted, will be inclined to conclude at a glance that such a mass of inter-mingled happy plants is a simple matter of luck and neglect that any one could achieve. And this verdict is the crowning prize of the good gardener, more worth than many Stan-dard cups. For let these complacent people only try, that's all; let them learn by experi-ence what it is to cope with things that want to be weeds, in such a way that they do not succeed, and yet retain their own spontaneous happiness; then they will ere long begin to learn that right letting alone and right meddl-ing are the beginning and the ending of good gardening, and that the simplest effects are just precisely those which defy money and

ambition and effort, and everything but tire-less patience, attention and knowledge bought at first hand with pain.[48]

In famous passages repeated in so many words in many books and articles, including a piece attributed to her in *The English Flower Garden*, Miss Jekyll wrote of her colour schemes for her large summer border. This extract is from *Col-our Schemes for the Flower Garden*.

The planting of the border is designed to show a distinct scheme of colour arrange-ment. At the two ends there is a groundwork of grey and glaucous foliage—Stachys, San-tolina, *Cineraria maritima*, Sea-Kale and Lyme-Grass, with darker foliage, also of grey quality, of Yucca, *Clematis Recta* and Rue. With this, at the near or western end, there are flowers of pure blue, grey-blue, white, palest yellow and palest pink; each colour partly in distinct masses and partly intergrouped. The colouring then passes through stronger yel-low to orange and red. By the time the middle space of the border is reached the colour is strong and gorgeous, but, as it is in good harmonies, it is never garish. Then the colour strength recedes in an inverse sequence through orange and deep yellow to pale yel-

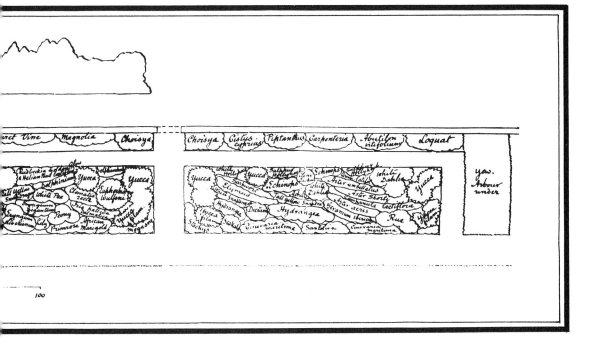

low, white and palest pink; again with blue-grey foliage. But at this, the eastern end, instead of the pure blues we have purples and lilacs.

Looked at from a little way forward, for a wide space of grass allows this point of view, the whole border can be seen as one picture, the cool colouring at the ends enhancing the brilliant warmth of the middle. Then, passing along the wide path next to the border, the value of the colour arrangement is still more strongly felt. Each portion now becomes a picture in itself, and every one is of such a colouring that it best prepares the eye, in accordance with natural law, for what is to follow. Standing for a few moments before the endmost region of grey and blue, and saturating the eye to its utmost capacity with these colours, it passes with extraordinary avidity to the succeeding yellows. These intermingle in a pleasant harmony with the reds and scarlets, blood-reds and clarets, and then lead again to yellows. Now the eye has again become saturated, this time with the rich colouring, and has therefore, by the law of complementary colour, acquired a strong appetite for the greys and purples. These therefore assume an appearance of brilliancy that they would not have had without the preparation provided by their recently received complementary colour.[49]

Miss Jekyll's scheme was a stable and unchanging one, which she used also in her Spring Garden.

A word of dissent, or at least caution, is voiced by Bowles, and I have sympathy with his view. Miss Jekyll was far too clever to make the mistake, but presumably her disciples were not.

I fear I am a little impatient of the school of gardening that encourages the selection of plants merely as artistic furniture, chosen for colour only, like ribbons or embroidery silks. I feel sorry for plants that are obliged to make a struggle for life in uncongenial situations because their owner wishes all things of those shades of pink, blue or orange to fit in next to the grey or crimson planting, and I long to shift the unhappy *Lilium pardalinum* away from its sun-loving Alstroemeria partners and plant it across the path among the shade-loving [and presumably clashing] Phloxes.[50]

Miss Sackville-West solved the problem of designing in an existing garden.

I have a gardening dodge which I find very useful. It concerns colour-schemes and plant-groupings. You know how quickly one forgets what one's garden has looked like during different weeks progressively throughout the year? One makes a mental note, or even a written note, and then the season changes and one forgets what one meant at the time. One has written 'Plant something yellow near the yellow tulips', or 'Plant something tall behind the lupins', and then the autumn comes and plants have died down, and one scratches one's head trying to remember what on earth one meant by that.

My system is more practical. I observe, for instance, a great pink, lacy crinoline of the May-flowering tamarisk, of which I put in two snippets years ago, and which now spreads the exuberance of its petticoats twenty feet wide over a neglected corner of the garden. What could I plant near it to enhance its colour? It must, of course be something which will flower at the same time. So I try effects, picking flowers elsewhere, rather in the way that one makes a flower arrangement in the house, sticking them into the ground and then standing back to observe the harmony. The dusky, rosy *Iris Senlac* is just the right colour: I must split up my clumps as soon as they have finished flowering and make a group of those near the tamarisk for next May. The common pink columbine, almost a weed, would do well for underplanting, or some pink pansies, *Crimson Queen*, or the wine-red shades, as a carpet; and, for something really noble, the giant fox-tail lily, *Eremurus robustus*, eight to ten feet high. I cut, with reluctance, one precious spike from a distant group, and stick it in; it looks fine, like a cathedral spire flushed warm in the sunset. Undoubtedly I should have some *eremuri* next year with the plumy curtains of the tamarisk behind them, but the *eremuri* are too expensive and one cannot afford many of them.

This is just one example. One has the illusion of being an artist painting a picture—putting in a dash of colour here, taking out a dash of colour there, until the whole composition is to one's liking, and at least one knows exactly what effect will be produced twelve months hence.[51]

She professed to love best of all the colour white, hence the deep satisfaction she derived from the success of the White Garden. Apropos of *Spiraea thunbergii*, she wrote:

There comes a moment at twilight when white plants gleam with a peculiar pallor or ghostliness. I dare to say of white, that neutral tint usually regarded as an *absence* of colour, that it is every bit as receptive of changing light as the blues and reds and purples. It may perhaps demand a patiently observing eye, attuned to a subtlety less crude than the strong range of reds and purples that we get in, say, the herbaceous phloxes which miraculously alter their hue as the evening light sinks across them. I love colour, and rejoice in it, but white is lovely to me forever. The ice-green shades that it can take on in certain lights, by twilight or moonlight, perhaps by moonlight especially, make a dream of the garden, an unreal vision, yet one knows that it isn't unreal at all because one has planted it all for effect.[52]

It is a cause for marvelling how sophisticated she was in her understanding of colour. But then she had the professional, Miss Jekyll, as her example and literary mentor.

In the Austrian Copper, the vivid scarlet of the inside of the petal is laid on in a thin film over a ground of yellow. To get the same powerful quality of red colouring a painter has to use exactly the same artifice. I notice that Nasturtiums are painted in the same manner, but here the film of colour is laid on still more delicately, for whereas in the Brier petal one can peel off the red surface and show the yellow ground, one cannot do it in the Nasturtium. Here the texture of the petal is not so tough, and the most delicate touch with a fine needle breaks up the fragile skin, leaving a wet discoloured wound. The surface colour seems to be lightly dusted on, and by taking a flower of a middle orange colour, not too deep, one may see on the lower petals, where the colour lightens towards the little fringe of pointed slashings, how the brilliant powdering gradually ceases, and here and there how the yellow ground is laid bare, where the surface of the flower has received some gentle abrasion, more delicate than can be done by hand, as of wind-rubbing of one petal upon another.[53]

Miss Jekyll is usually credited with the idea of particular colour gardens, even though she considered she only had room for one, a grey garden, at Munstead Wood. The following extract seems to suggest that the idea was not entirely new.

It is extremely interesting to work out gardens in which some special colouring predominates ... occasionally I hear of a garden for blue plants, or a white garden, but I think such ideas are but rarely worked out with the best aims. I have in mind a whole series of gardens of restricted colouring, though I have not, alas, either room or means enough to work them out for myself, and have to be satisfied with an all-too-short length of double border for a grey scheme. But besides my small grey garden I badly want others, and especially a gold garden, a blue and a green garden; though the number of these desires might easily be multiplied.

It is a curious thing that people will sometimes spoil some garden project for the sake of a word. For instance, a blue garden, for beauty's sake, may be hungering for a group of white Lilies, or for something of palest lemon-yellow, but it is not allowed to have it because it is called the blue garden, and there must be no flowers in it but blue flowers. I can see no sense in this; it seems to me like fetters foolishly self-imposed. Surely the business of the blue garden is to be beautiful as well as blue. My own idea is that it should be beautiful first, and then just as blue as may be consistent with its best possible beauty ...[54]

It seems to me a certainty that Miss Sackville-West did not pluck the idea of one-colour gardens out of the air. It is futile, however, to conjecture whether, if she had never read Miss Jekyll, she would nevertheless have conceived such a plan herself. The White Garden at Sissinghurst would certainly have pleased Miss Jekyll for its imaginative design and the skill and conviction in its execution.

My grey, green and white garden will have the advantage of a high yew hedge behind it, a wall along one side, a strip of box edging along another side, and a path of old brick along the fourth side ... I visualize the white trumpets of dozens of Regale lilies ... coming up through the grey of southernwood and artemisia and cotton-lavender, with grey-and-white edging plants such as *Dianthus Mrs. Sinkins* and the silvery mats of *Stachys Lanata* ... There will be white pansies, and white paeonies and white irises with their grey leaves at least, I hope there will be all these things.[55]

She did not, however, assume that colour was everything.

... I believe that one ought always to regard a garden in terms of architecture as well as of colour. One has huge lumps of, let us say, the shrub roses making large voluminous bushes like a Victorian crinoline, or flinging themselves about in wild sprays; or, putting it another way, some plants make round fat bushes, and seem to demand a contrast in a tall sharp plant, say delphiniums, sticking up in a cathedral spire of bright blue amongst the roses instead of in the orthodox way at the back of the herbaceous border. It is all a question of shape. Architectural shape, demanding the pointed thin ones amongst the fat rounds, as a minaret rises above the dome of a mosque. ... [She advised *Yucca gloriosa*, a plant incidentally much used and admired by Miss Jekyll, as it] will come as a fine surprise on the grand scale in July, and will carry out my contention that you want variety of shape and height to make an aesthetic composition instead of just an amorphous muddle.[56]

The more I see of other people's gardens the more convinced do I become of the value of good grouping and shapely training. These remarks must necessarily apply most forcibly to gardens of a certain size, where sufficient space is available for large clumps or for large specimens of individual plants, but even in a small garden the spotty effect can be avoided by massing instead of dotting plants here and there.

It is a truly satisfactory thing to see a garden well schemed and wisely planted. Well schemed are the operative words. Every garden, large or small, ought to be planned from the outset, getting its bones, its skeleton, into the shape that it will preserve all through the year even after the flowers have faded and died away. Then, when all colour has gone, is the moment to revise, to make notes for addi-

tions, and even to take the mattock for removals. This is gardening on the large scale, not in details. There can be no rules, in so fluid and personal a pursuit, but it is safe to say that a sense of substance and solidity can be achieved only by the presence of an occasional mass breaking the more airy companies of the little flowers.

What this mass shall consist of must depend upon many things: upon the soil, the aspect, the colour of neighbouring plants, and above all upon the taste of the owner. I can imagine, for example, a border arranged entirely in purple and mauve—phlox, stocks, pansies, *Clematis Jackmanii* trained over low hoops— all planted in bays between great promontories of the plum-coloured sumach, *Rhus cotinus foliis purpureis*, but many people, thinking this too mournful, might prefer a scheme in red and gold. It would be equally easy of accomplishment, with a planting of the feathery *Thalictrum glaucum*, gaillardia, *Achillea eupatorium* (the flat-headed yellow yarrow), *helenium*, *Lychnis chalcedonica*, and a host of other ordinary, willing, herbaceous things. In this case, I suppose, the mass would have to be provided by bushes of something like the golden privet or the golden yew, both of which I detest when planted as 'specimens' on a lawn, but which in so aureate a border would come into their own.

The possibilities of variation are manifold, but on the main point one must remain adamant; the alternation between colour and solidity, decoration and architecture, frivolity and seriousness. Every good garden, large or small, must have some architectural quality about it; and, apart from the all-important question of the general lay-out, including hedges, the best way to achieve this imperative effect is by massive lumps of planting such as I have suggested.[57]

We are so thoroughly imbued with the Robinson and Jekyll view of how a garden should be laid out, and with what we should plant it, that much of what has been said in this chapter seems self-evident and obvious. It is extremely difficult to put ourselves in the shoes of our great-grandparents. Most gardeners who consider themselves sophisticated, and many who do not, take care over colour-schemes, plant associations, foliage effects and planting patterns. Although it would be a mistake to see the pre-

11. *Narcissus* 'Weardale Perfection', painted by
     E.A. Bowles (see Ch. 12)

12. *Galanthus nivalis var. scharlokii*, painted by
     E.A. Bowles

13. *Gentiana farreri*, painted by Reginald Farrer (see Ch. 6)

14. *Eritrichium nanum*, photographed in the Pordoi Pass in the Dolomites where Farrer found it (see Chs. 6 and 10)

15. A group of Oncocyclus irises (see Ch. 12)

Robinsonian era as a Dark Age of error and slavish acceptance of silly fashion, as Robinson would have liked us to, it is nevertheless true, that if the shades of these two walk in gardens today, they must see their work as a lasting success.

Notes

1. W. Robinson, *The Wild Garden*, 1st edn (John Murray, 1870), pp. 1–2.

2. W. Robinson, *Alpine Flowers for English Gardens*, 1st edn (John Murray, 1870), pp. 38–41.

3. W. Robinson, *The English Flower Garden*, 6th edn (John Murray, 1898), pp. 5–6.

4. Ibid, pp. 51–2.

5. Robinson, *Alpine Flowers for English Gardens*, pp. xiii–xiv.

6. Robinson, *The English Flower Garden*, p. 78.

7. G. Jekyll, *Wood and Garden*, facsimile of 1st edn (Antique Collectors' Club, 1981), p. 349.

8. G. Jekyll, *A Gardener's Testament*, Francis Jekyll and G.C. Taylor (eds.) facsimile of 1937 edn (Antique Collectors' Club, 1982), p. 154.

9. E.A. Bowles, *My Garden in Summer*, 1st edn (T.C. and E.C. Jack, 1914), pp. 252–3.

10. Jekyll, *Wood and Garden*, pp. 349–50.

11. Ibid., pp. 353–4.

12. E.A. Bowles, *My Garden in Spring*, 1st edn (T.C. and E.C. Jack, 1914), p. 95.

13. Bowles, *My Garden in Summer*, p. 256.

14. Robinson, *The English Flower Garden*, p. viii.

15. W. Robinson, *The Wild Garden*, 4th edn (John Murray, 1894), pp. xxviii–xxix.

16. Ibid., pp. 7–8.

17. Ibid., p. 9.

18. Robinson, *The English Flower Garden*, p. 160.

19. G. Jekyll, *Colour Schemes for the Flower Garden*, facsimile of 1936 edition (Antique Collectors' Club, 1982), p. 44.

20. Jekyll, *Wood and Garden*, pp. 358–9.

21. Robinson, *The English Flower Garden*, p. 16.

22. Ibid., p. 12.

23. Ibid., p. 24.

24. G. Jekyll and L. Weaver, *Gardens for Small Country Houses*, facsimile of 1912 edition (Antique Collectors' Club, 1981), p. i.

25. G. Jekyll, *Wall and Water Gardens*, 5th edn (Country Life, 1913), pp. 54–5.

26. W. Robinson, *Garden Design and Architects' Gardens*, 1st edn (John Murray, 1892), p. 53.

27. Ibid., p. 55.

28. Robinson, *The English Flower Garden*, p. 299.

29. Robinson, *Garden Design*, p. 58.

30. Jekyll, *A Gardener's Testament*, p. 47.

31. Harold Falkner, quoted in Betty Massingham, *Miss Jekyll*, 1st edn (Country Life, 1966), p. 83.

32. R.J. Farrer, *My Rock Garden*, facsimile of fourth impression (Theophrastus, 1971), pp. 3–4.

33. Ibid., pp. 5–6.

34. Robinson, *Alpine Flowers*, pp. 44–5.

35. Jekyll, *A Gardener's Testament*, pp. 114–17.

36. Robinson, *The English Flower Garden*, p. 39.

37. Robinson, *Alpine Flowers*, pp. 48–9.

38. Jekyll, *Wood and Garden*, p. 18.

39. Robinson, *The English Flower Garden*, p. 30.

40. E.A. Bowles, *My Garden in Autumn and Winter*, 1st edn (T.C. and E.C. Jack, 1915), p. 98.

41. V. Sackville-West, *Even More for Your Garden*, 1st edn (Michael Joseph, 1958), p. 81.

42. V. Sackville-West, *More for Your Garden*, 1st edn (Michael Joseph, 1955), pp. 26–8.

43. Jekyll, *Wood and Garden*, p. 16.

44. Ibid., p. 266.

45. G. Jekyll, *Home and Garden*, facsimile of 1900 edition (Antique Collectors' Club, 1982), pp. 346–8.

46. R. J. Farrer, *In a Yorkshire Garden*, 1st edn (Edward Arnold, 1909), pp. 25–6.

47. Robinson, *The English Flower Garden*, pp. 55–6.

48. E.A. Bowles, *My Garden in Spring*, 1st edn (T.C. and E.C. Jack, 1914), pp. xi–xii.

49. Jekyll, *Colour Schemes*, pp. 128–30.

50. Bowles, *My Garden in Spring*, pp. 18–19.

51. V. Sackville-West, *In Your Garden*, 1st edn (Michael Joseph, 1951), pp. 76–8.

52. Sackville-West, *More for Your Garden*, pp. 69–70.

53. Jekyll, *Home and Garden*, pp. 97–8.

54. Jekyll, *Colour Schemes*, p. 218.

55. Sackville-West, *In Your Garden*, p. 20.

56. V. Sackville-West, *In Your Garden Again*, 1st edn (Michael Joseph, 1953), pp. 100–1.

57. Ibid., pp. 124–6.

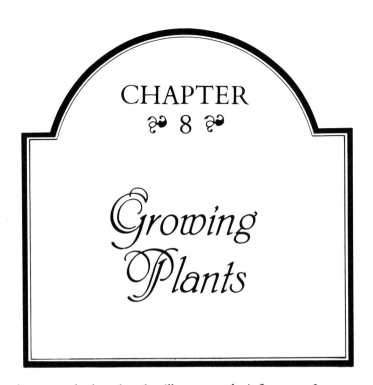

CHAPTER
❧ 8 ❧

Growing Plants

Reared, as I have been, on the bread-and-milk diet of modern garden writing, I know how dull much of it, especially that dealing with practical matters, can be. It is wholesome and nutritious but unexciting. The prime aim appears to be the imparting of accurate and unambiguous advice, but that should properly be the first and not the only consideration. It may be that the laborious spadework required to make certain the information is correct quite exhausts the garden writer, and leaves him with no energy to turn his phrases neatly. The writers represented in this collection suffered from no such weakness.

They were all enthusiastic practical gardeners who took great pride in work well done, and often had strong views on how particular operations should be carried out. Robinson was the only one with a formal training, the others picking up the business as they went along by observing others at work and by methodical practice, but they all knew the satisfaction of getting their hands dirty. Their delight in, and their recognition of, the importance of practical gardening is as evident as the pains they took.

It used to irritate Miss Jekyll so much if visitors did not properly appreciate the care and trouble she had taken.

[Many people] will ascribe it [any success] to chance, to the goodness of my soil, and even more commonly to some supposed occult influence of my own—to anything rather than to the plain fact that I love it [her garden] well enough to give it plenty of care and labour. [She went on to give an example of one such ungenerous visitor.] I had been saying how necessary good and deep cultivation was, especially in so very poor and shallow a soil as mine. Passing up through the copse where there were some tall stems of *Lilium giganteum* [see Chapter 9 for description] bearing the great upturned pods of seed, my visitor stopped and said, 'I don't believe a word about your poor soil—look at the growth of that Lily. Nothing could make that great stem ten feet high in a poor soil, and there it is, just stuck into the wood!' I said nothing, knowing that presently I could show a better answer than I could frame in words. A little farther up in the copse we came upon an excavation about twelve feet across and four deep, and by its side a formidable mound of sand, when my friend said, 'Why are you making all this mess in your pretty woods? . . . and what on earth are you going to do with that great heap of sand? Why, there must be a dozen loads of it.' That was my moment of secret triumph, but I hope I bore it meekly as I answered, 'I only wanted to plant a few more of those big Lilies, and you see in my soil they would not have a chance unless the ground was thoroughly prepared; look at the edge of the scarp and see how the solid yellow sand comes to within four inches of the top; so I have a big wide hole dug; and look, there is the donkey-cart coming with the first load of Dahlia-tops and soft plants that have been for the summer in the south border'.[1]

She continued with a litany of compost ingredients with which the holes were to be filled.

Care very often goes hand-in-hand with a methodical approach. Farrer maintained he did not have such a thing, and in doing so, I feel sure, gained the warm approval of his readers.

I do wish I had more method. Generally in the garden, how do I envy the neat methodicalness of people who never stir out without their knives, and their magnifying-glasses, and their stud-book, and their note-book, and their pencil and their basket, and stakes and labels and scissors and balls of string and balls of wool ...

One ought, I say, always, incessantly, unremittingly, to cultivate hardness of heart, decision, and, above all, method, in the garden. Enter your crossings at once in the stud-book, with full notes, and not an illegible hieroglyph that means a great deal to you as you scrawl it, but absolutely nothing by the day after to-morrow. Never pass a superior or an inferior plant without signalising it firmly, for further commendation, or for rejection. Never fail, as you go by, to record what bush is to be moved, and which retained, and which is pretty, and which, on consideration, is held unworthy of too prominent a place. Oh dear, oh dear, I give you this advice, weightily as the bottom secret of success. And now hastily slide from this painful subject.[2]

Once these first principles have been established, what advice was given that might prove helpful to the modern gardener? These days it is common practice to cut all the stems of dying herbaceous plants in the autumn, in order, we are told, to prevent them harbouring pests and diseases during the winter and for aesthetic reasons, too, it being thought that bare expanses of chocolate-brown earth punctuated by slightly raised mounds of dormant crowns are preferable to the subtle colours of sere stalks and stems. The gardener who is not incurably tidy-minded, or insensitive to changing, if muted, colour, might like to consider this.

The stems of all herbaceous plants, reeds and tall grasses in winter are very good in colour, and should always be allowed to stand through the winter and not be cut down in the fidgety tidy way that is so common, sweeping away the stems in autumn and leaving the surface as bare and ugly as that round a besieged city. The same applies to the stems of all waterside and herbaceous plants, stems of plants in groups often giving beautiful brown colours in many fine shades. Those who know the plants can in this way identify them in winter as well as in summer—a great gain in changing one's plantings and in increasing or giving away plants.[3]

Robinson also advocated something else which would be anathema to those of a neat mentality, namely not raking the leaves from borders in the autumn. It is commonly assumed that if they are left to rot, they will provide a safe haven for the slug, one of God's creatures that no gardener has any compunction about trampling under his foot. However, there is some evidence that slugs feed most happily on dead matter and that, if leaves are left, they will more contentedly live on them than the fresh and succulent new shoots in springtime. Robinson asked, rhetorically:

How do the swarming plants of the woods and copses of the world exist in spite of the slugs? In the garden we may please ourselves as to leaves, and beside all gardens are frequently enriched by soil and other things, but not one leaf would I ever allow to be removed from a clump of shrubs or trees on lawn or pleasure ground, and I should prefer the leaves all over the place to dug borders. [But what about the leaves blowing about in the wind?] In a plantation of choice trees, their branches resting on the ground, with low shrubs and hardy plants like, say, Starworts [his word for Michaelmas daisies] between, there are impediments to the leaves rushing about in the way mentioned. Our annual digging, mutilation, raking away of leaves, and exposing on bare earthy borders plants that in Nature shelter each other, and are shielded from hard frost and heat by layers of fallen leaves, which gradually sink into light soil for the young roots, are practices that must be given up by all who look into the needs of our hardy garden flora. In my plantation 10,000 stems of Starworts and other plants all the winter standing brown in their place, keep hold of all the leaves that may get among them![4]

It was the practice in the nineteenth century, especially in the public parks, to dig up shrubbery borders each year.

When winter is once come, almost every gardener, with the best intentions, prepares to make war upon the roots of everything in his shrubbery. The practice is to trim and mutilate the shrubs and to dig all over the ground that is full of feeding roots. Choice shrubs are disturbed, herbaceous plants are disrooted, bulbs are injured, the roots as well as the tops of shrubs are mutilated, and a miserable aspect is given to the borders; while the only 'improvement' that comes of the process is the darkening of the surface of the upturned earth!

Illustrations of these bad practices are seen by the mile in our London parks in winter. Walk through any of them at that season and observe the borders around masses of shrubs. Instead of finding the earth covered with vegetation close to the margin and each shrub grown into a fair example of its kind, we find a wide expanse of dug ground, and the shrubs upon it with an air of having recently suffered from a whirlwind, that led to the removal of mutilated branches. Rough pruners go before the diggers and trim in the shrubs for them, so that nothing may be in the way: and then come the diggers, plunging their spades deeply about plants, shrubs or trees. The first shower that occurs after this digging exposes a whole network of torn-up roots.[5]

Wiser counsels fortunately have prevailed; no one now would dream of doing such a thing.

One of Robinson's most novel ideas was the conserving of moisture by what he called 'mulching with Life'. This had the virtue of being both utilitarian and highly ornamental, and I cannot imagine why such an idea has never been more widely accepted.

... I am very fond of covering the surface with dwarf living plants of fragile nature, which do not much exhaust the soil, and which in very hot weather may help to keep it moist. This is done in the case of Roses and other plants which, being rather small and bare at first, want some help to cover the ground, and a number of very pretty plants may be used for this purpose which will give us bloom in spring and good colour on the ground. This, of course, prevents the use of manure, hitherto common on the surface of the flower beds, Roses especially. It is much better that the aid of manure should be given at the root instead of the surface, and if we have plenty of manure and rich soil, there is no need for surface mulching it. Covering the surface with living plants is worth doing, for the sake of effect alone, even if we have to pay for it in other ways. The result of it is that we may have a beautiful spring garden in addition to the summer garden—that is to say, if our garden is planted for summer and autumn with Roses and the like, by the use of Tufted Pansies and other dwarf plants in the beds we get pretty effects early in the year, and through this living carpet may come up many pretty plants.[6]

Miss Sackville-West, who followed his lead at Sissinghurst, recalled in an article in the *Observer* asking Robinson whether not being able to feed the rose-beds mattered, and his snorting in reply and saying it was quite unnecessary.

She, being a more-or-less self-taught amateur, had a respect, verging on the reverential, for the truly experienced gardener. She referred quite often to such a paragon when relating some piece of advice to her largely amateur readership, as, for instance, when talking about moving plants.

Experienced gardeners have a theory that it doesn't matter so much *when* you move a plant as *how* you move it. Up to a point, I agree. I am no great believer in the green fingers mystique; I think every finger, all eight of them, ten if you include the thumbs, must be attached by some string to the information office in the brain. In other words, you can't rely on a cheerfully optimistic instinct unsupported by no knowledge at all. Thus the experienced gardener knows that he must instantly cover up the freshly exposed roots, even with a sheet from today's newspaper, to the annoyance of anyone who hasn't yet read the paper, anything rather than let fibrous roots dry out in the air. He wraps them at once, within one minute; he would use his handkerchief, or tear a bit off the tail of his shirt, if nothing else were available. I have even seen a handful of damp grass or leaves wrapped round and secured with twine. Then he will rush his treasure home, and plant it, possibly puddling it in if he thinks it needs a drink, and in all cases will shade it from the sun for the first few days until it has re-established itself after its upheaval.[7]

All that is required in fact is common sense, coupled with attention to detail, and the ability, or at least the predisposition, to observe. This was shown by Miss Jekyll when she discussed division of herbaceous plants. It is a job she must have done a great deal, for not only did she have herbaceous borders of considerable breadth and length, but she also recommended that a great many herbaceous perennials be divided, to retain their vigour, every year. We now realise that this is much too often; only the most strong-growing such as heleniums and rudbeckias need that treatment to flourish.

A plasterer's hammer is a tool that is very handy for dividing plants. It has a hammer on one side of the head, and a cutting blade like a small chopper on the other. With this and a cold chisel and a strong knife one can divide any roots in comfort. I never divide things by brutally chopping them across with a spade. Plants that have soft fleshy tubers like Dahlias and Paeonies want the cold chisel; it can be cleverly inserted among the crowns so that injury to the tubers is avoided, and it is equally useful in the case of some plants whose points of attachment are almost as hard as wire, like *Orobus vernus* or as tough as a door-mat, like *Iris graminea*. The Michaelmas Daisies of the *Novae Angliae* section make root tufts too close and hard to be cut with a knife, and here the chopper of the plasterer's hammer comes in ... The Christmas Rose is one of the most awkward plants to divide successfully. It cannot be done in a hurry. The only safe way is to wash the clumps well out and look carefully for the points of attachment, and cut them either with knife or chisel, according to their position. In this case the chisel should be narrower and sharper. Three-year-old tufts of St. Bruno's Lily [*Paradisea liliastrum*] puzzled me at first. The rather fleshy roots are so tightly interlaced that cutting is out of the question; but I found out that if the tuft is held tight in the two hands, and the hands are worked opposite ways with a rotary motion of about a quarter of a circle, they soon come apart without being hurt in the least.[8]

It is one thing to desire to propagate your plants, quite another to wish to raise new hybrids. Most of us can go through our gardening lives without falling prey to this sort of obsessive interest, such a mixture of the scientific and egotistic. It appealed to the botanist in both Farrer and Bowles. Farrer recognised perfectly well the dangers of becoming an hybridist.

For in the arrogating of a Creator's function, it appears inevitable that the human being must develop the creator's callousness and high indifference. [He referred, with characteristic understatement to 'putting his soul in grievous perils'. But there is a serious point here.] For I seem to notice that the true gardener does tend to become crusted and groovy till, in the end, he will pass unseeing through a wood of blue-bells, to rhapsodise over the last new Daffodil of his raising ... To create life for the mere fun of taking it away again afterwards, or with the thought that you will do so if it doesn't please you, must always be an evil thing in the eyes of any Buddhist, whether the life be that of bird or plant.[9]

Whether Bowles was afflicted with such moral doubts, we do not know. In his writings we derive only the impression that he thoroughly enjoyed himself.

Raising crocus seedlings has proved such a source of interest and pleasure to me, and such a means of enrichment to my collection, that I wish I could persuade more garden lovers to carry it on. It has certainly the great disadvantage of a wait of at least three years for the first flowering, but years pass only too swiftly in a garden and once that period is over every succeeding season brings fresh babes to flowering strength, and I know no garden joy equal to a visit on a sunny morning to the crocus beds when seedlings are in full flowering. To see a dozen, or score, or better still a century, of some old favourite reproduced in a new generation is good, but still better is the thrill of spotting a pure white bloom in a row of orthodox lilac ones. Forms with larger flowers, deeper or lighter colour, or extra markings as compared with the normal type, fill the heart with joy and pride when found in one's own seedbeds, and it is a happy being who carefully lifts them out from among the common herd ...[10]

And what success he had, especially with seedlings of *Crocus chrysanthus*, of which there are several colour types to be found in the wild. The first, which he raised that had stripes on the back of the petals, he called 'Yellowhammer'; he continued to name this 'series' after birds that he thought they resembled. 'Bullfinch' was 'so round and chubby', and there was 'Snowbunting', often the first to open in gardens. One of the very best is a *Crocus chrysanthus pallidus* seedling named 'E.A. Bowles' by its raiser Thomas Hoog of the Haarlem firm, van Tubergen. Such reliable, easy and pretty flowers are, not surprisingly, still in commerce today.

No gardener has the slightest doubt of the importance of good tools in order to do his work well and with pleasure. Miss Jekyll, who had an extraordinary affinity with the tools she used, being above all a craftswoman, demonstrated how attached she could become to particular familiar tools.

One feels so kindly to the thing that enables the hand to obey the brain. Moreover, one feels a good deal of respect for it; without it brain and hand would be helpless. When the knife that has been in one's hand or one's pocket for years has its blade so much worn by constant sharpening that it can no longer be used, with what true regret does one put it aside, and how long it is before one can really make friends with the new one! I do not think any workman really likes a new tool. There is always some feeling about it as if something strange and unfamiliar and uncongenial, somewhat of the feeling that David had about Saul's armour. What an awkward thing a new spade is, how long and heavy and rough of handle! And then how amiable it becomes when it is half worn, where the square corners that made the thrust so hard are ground away, when the whole blade has grown shorter, when the handle has gained that polish, the

Figure 8.1 Miss Jekyll's Boots by Sir William Nicholson

best polish of all, that comes of long hand-friction. No carpenter likes a new plane; no house-painter likes a new brush. [She felt the same way about clothes.] I suppose no horse likes a new collar; I am quite sure I do not like new boots![11]

Judging by Sir William Nicholson's painting she was writing no more than the truth.

Bowles was most attached to cook's forks which he obtained regularly from the Army and Navy Stores. I wish I knew what such a thing looked like for he found it invaluable for selecting crocus seedlings in his frames. Nor was that the only unusual tool he used. When digging for the bulb of a Chionoscilla, he found that:

This burrowing is difficult when one has to go some eight or more inches among the plants, and I use another special tool of my own compose for it. An ordinary 'lady's fork' of four tines furnishes the raw material for my inventive genius to work upon, a coarse file my coadjutor: mind and muscle and metal then get to work, and off come the two outer tines, and I have a lovely giant's toothpick that almost always accompanies me when in the garden. Hark to a list of its virtuous uses. It goes to the root of the evil in cases of Dandelions and Docks unlike any other weapon: a plunge, a twist, and the tap-rooted fiend lies vanquished at my feet. More gently and lovingly inserted, it fetches up a choice bulb, a rogue among the tulips, or a new seedling of great price and depth. Again, when the gardening visitor comes with a basket and wants a bit of something good, nothing removes a side crown so neatly without disturbing the main plant, or so unerringly extracts the very piece your critical eye selects as best spared, and your affection for your guest settles the extent of, as this two-pronged walking stick.[12]

It is now in a glass case near the 'Bowles' Corner' garden created by the Royal Horticultural Society at Wisley.

Farrer's favourite tool, which he was for ever losing, was even more extraordinary.

That tie-pin of mine is to me what Napoleon's star is said to have been to him. On any horticultural expedition it is my unvarying companion ... It has pollinated plants uncounted, Orchids, Saxifrages, Primulas; it has helped to pot Odontoglossums [a kind of Orchid] and often in the potting, slipped away into heaps of soil and been awfully lost; it has been the sword of Gideon against slugs in the Orchid-house ... it has carved out Androsaces from the living granite of the cliffs above Arolla; it has pecked seeds of them, most daintily, out of the gaping, ripened capsules ... In fact there has been no end to its functions, its escapades, its elopements and recoveries.[13]

Incomprehension sets in between gardeners and non-gardeners as to why the gardener feels the urge always to know what his plants are and to give them a name. This is as much because the seeking out of knowledge is a habit which dies very hard, as because we do not want to order from nurseries an excess of what we already have. There is, of course, an element of egotism involved. Much more approbation accrues to the man who remarks that the Fremontodendron is flowering well than merely exclaiming about the pretty yellow wall-shrub; but then it is that egotism that spurs respectable ambition. To retain that knowledge, however, the gardener needs labels, and there is no such thing as an attractive label. When considering the rockery, Miss Jekyll wrote:

... even if ... one succeeds in cheating oneself into thinking that it [the rockery] is something like a bit of rocky nature, there is pretty sure to be the zinc label with its stark figure and ghostly colouring looking as if it were put there of cruel purpose for a more effectual shattering of the vain illusion. I suppose that of all metallic surfaces there is none so unlovely as that of zinc, and yet we stick upright strips of it among, and even in front of, some of the daintiest of our tiny plants. We spend thought and money, and still more money's worth in time and labour, on making our little rocky terraces, and perhaps succeed in getting them into nice lines and planted with the choicest things, and then we peg it all over with zinc labels! I am quite in sympathy with those who do not know their plants well enough to do without the labels; I have passed through that stage myself and there are many cases where the label must be there. But I considered that in dressed ground or pure pleasure ground, where the object is some scheme of garden beauty, the label, even if it must be there, should never be seen ... And then one finds how seldom one really wants the label. In my own later practice, where the number of different plants has been reduced to just those I like best and think most worthy of a place, they are so well known to me that their names are as familiar as those of my best friends; and when I admit a new plant, if I cannot at once learn its name, it is purposely given a big ugly label, as a self-inflicted penance that shall continue until such time as I can expiate by remembrance.[14]

Failing to learn a plant's name is a species of laziness, an unworthy indolence that comes over every gardener at one time or another. The most common form of sloth afflicted Farrer, a man of considerable energy and drive; that of avoiding the myriad of small tasks which should not take a moment and so never get done. This is what he had to say about trying to remember to segregate a particular form of the primrose called 'Miss Massey'.

This year ... I must really buckle to and rise to the enormous effort of poking in a piece of stick to Miss Massey.

I wish it were not so awfully difficult to do these tiny little simple things; the fact is that being so very small, one has a contempt for them, and thinks that any moment will serve for their doing, so that, in the end they never get done at all. I imagine that St. George, despite his success as a killer of dragons, was probably badly pestered with black beetles— boring little things which he would always mean to go for with his shield and spear—and always put off the job till tomorrow, because in such a simple piece of work tomorrow would obviously be just as convenient as today ... we are so vulgar at heart that we can do things which require efforts and splashing fusses, but instinctively despise all plans that are easy of fulfilment. Well anyhow, we dally with them and do not take them seriously, just because they would be so very easy to deal with if we did. And therefore there is nothing about them to challenge our pride or put us on our mettle.[15]

I have said that Miss Sackville-West had great respect for the experienced gardener, and of course at Long Barn and Sissinghurst she had plenty of professional help. She was lucky, but from the following extract it would appear that her gardeners did not always please, and it demonstrates quite well the gulf between those who garden in spare and snatched moments for pure pleasure, and those for whom there is always tomorrow, and for whom the rewards, however hard the work, are always the same. She may have been unfortunate, or she may have been unfair, but in this respect, times have improved for, with the dearth of openings available in what used to be called 'private service', no one now becomes a gardener who has not an aptitude for the work. I can imagine how infuriated she must sometimes have become over the cutting of the yew hedges.

The amateur gardener finds an endless fascination in watching the procedure of the professional. The employer of labour, if he be garden-minded, will stop to pull up a seeding groundsel. Not so his employee. Any timid suggestion that a certain corner is getting into rather a mess and hadn't something better be done about it is instantly countered by the reply 'I haven't got round this way yet!' Murmurs about one year's seeds meaning seven years' weeds are of no avail. He hasn't got round that way yet, and nothing will get him round before he means to.

The same observation applies to the annual clipping of hedges. By the end of the summer, when clipping time arrives, hedges of yew and box have become so fluffy as to add to the slatternly appearance of the September garden. One longs to see them resume their sharp outlines, and the snip-snap of the shears one morning is the most welcome sound we can hear. But where has the man started on his job? Not at the front of the hedge, where it shows, oh no. One discovers him somewhere at the invisible back, where it least matters, and one knows that it will be days or even weeks before he reappears to human view. One tries to explain this curious habit by thinking that he wants to get the dullest part over first, saving up the more amusing and repaying part for, so to speak, a treat. One could not be more mistaken. The professional's attitude towards his work is not fun, but plod. Impatience is unknown to him as it is, alas, known only too well to you and me.

There must be a reason. I shall be told that the answer is Method. You waste more time 'dodging about' than by going to work methodically. This contention has probably been evolved by the experience of generations, and I have too much respect to dispute it. At the same time, might one not plead for a little more elasticity? [But, lest she should nettle those on whom she undoubtedly depended for the upkeep of the garden at Sissinghurst, she finished with the following soothing words] There can be fewer happier collaborations, properly managed, than between an employer and his gardener; a pity if they should ever be allowed to degenerate into a source of mutual exasperation.[16]

Notes

1. G. Jekyll, *Wood and Garden*, facsimile of 1st edn (Antique Collectors' Club, 1981), pp. 198–9.

2. R. J. Farrer, *In a Yorkshire Garden*, 1st edn (Edward Arnold, 1909), pp. 22–3.

3. W. Robinson, *The English Flower Garden*, 6th edn (John Murray, 1898), pp. 248–9.

4. W. Robinson, *The Wild Garden*, 1st edn (John Murray, 1870), pp. 81–2.

5. Ibid., pp. 75–6.

6. Robinson, *The English Flower Garden*, pp. 351–2.

7. V. Sackville-West, *Even More for Your Garden*, 1st edn (Michael Joseph, 1958), p. 156.

8. Jekyll, *Wood and Garden*, pp. 192–3.

9. Farrer, *In a Yorkshire Garden*, pp. 13–14.

10. E.A. Bowles, *My Garden in Spring*, 1st edn (T.C. and E.C. Jack, 1914), p. 64.

11. G. Jekyll, *Home and Garden*, facsimile of 1900 edn (Antique Collectors' Club, 1982), p. 142.

12. Bowles, *My Garden in Spring*, pp. 97–8.

13. Farrer, *In a Yorkshire Garden*, pp. 82–3.

14. Jekyll, *Home and Garden*, p. 142.

15. Farrer, *In a Yorkshire Garden*, pp. 144–5.

16. Sackville-West, *Even More for Your Garden*, pp. 162–3.

CHAPTER
❧ 9 ❧

Herbaceous Plants

As a counterbalance to the eye-jarring unsubtleties of most bedding plants, increasing efforts were made by garden writers, from the late nineteenth century onwards, to publicise the advantages of the herbaceous perennials, plants which die down to ground level in winter, but which come to life once more when the soil warms up in the spring. They were cheaper because they were permanent and, once established, required no great annual effort of planning and placing. The range of form and colour also far exceeded that of tender annuals. At the same time the growing of hardy annuals and biennials was also encouraged.

Amongst the herbaceous plants recommended, were some whose charm was not immediately or obviously striking. The euphorbias and hellebores, plants with greenish flowers that had little place in the High-Victorian garden, experienced a rapid improvement in their fortunes. This was partly, especially in the case of hellebores, because they could be found in quantity in the wild.

> In ample room and in deep rich soil at the foot of the rock garden, [wrote Farrer] or in broad sunny (or cool) slopes together with Colchicums, all the Christmas Roses and Lent Roses are in place, ample in their splendid foliage, and in their blossom either weird and sumptuous or pure with a dazzling chastity

that seems inappropriate and hypocritical in plants so poisonous and sophisticated. Yet *Helleborus niger* is one of the candours of the world, in all its forms of a white and unchallengeable flawlessness. Many forms it has indeed, and one day in winter or earliest spring in the sub-alpine woods of Garda or Como—even within a quarter of an hour of Menaggio and all its hotels and old maids—will yield you half a dozen extra-special Christmas Roses pre-eminent in size or precocity, or lateness, or whiteness, or breadth of petal—all being true prizes each in its own way, advancing the hour of the bloom or protracting it. So now we have a period from October to the end of April that is never without *H. niger*, so called because its heart, or root, is black, while its face shines with a blazing white innocence unknown among the truly pure of heart.[1]

Miss Jekyll grew the Lenten hellebores, *Helleborus orientalis*, of which there are a myriad of differing colour forms, in borders in her Nut Walk.

> It is interesting to observe the large variety of colouring and marking, for even among the purples alone there is considerable difference, though what is most usual is a finely splashed spotting of a darker colour. In general the

purple flowers have a lustreless surface, in many cases with a faint film of plum-like bloom. Their spotting is only on the front or inner side, for turning the flower over, the back shows only a straight veining.

The pure whites are charming flowers. A mature plant carrying a quantity of blooms is a striking object in the still misty woodland or in some sheltered garden corner; an occasional tinge of green only seems to make the white purer. Sometimes there comes a remarkable break—pure white flower heavily spotted inside with dark crimson. When this occurs the spots show faintly through to the outside. There are a number of plants showing intermediate colouring. Some have a rather coarse habit of growth, but one well suited for woodland planting; they have large leaves and light-coloured bloom. Some gardeners or growers might think them worthless because of the undecided colouring, but to anyone with a trained colour eye they are charming and full of interest, with their tender flushes of pink, suffused with a still tenderer hint of green and sometimes a thread-like picotee edge of rosy red.[2]

Much as she did to enhance the reputation of hellebores, she did even more with the standing of primroses, developing her own 'Munstead' variety of *Primula acaulis (vulgaris) elatior*.

It must be some five-and-twenty years ago, [she wrote in 1899] that I began to work at what I may now call my own strain of Primroses, improving it a little every year by careful selection of the best for seed. The parents of the strain were a named kind, called Golden Plover, and a white one, without name, that I found in a cottage garden ...

They are, broadly speaking, white and yellow varieties of the strong bunch-flowered or Polyanthus kind, but they vary in detail so much, in form, colour, habit, arrangement, and size of eye and shape of edge, that one year thinking it might be useful to classify them I tried to do so, but gave it up after writing out the characters of sixty classes! Their possible variation seems endless. Every year among the seedlings there appears a number of charming flowers with some new development of size or colour of flower, or beauty of foliage, and yet all within the narrow bounds of—white and yellow Primroses.[3]

There is one great favourite that I call Lemon Rose; it is of a pure primrose colour, with six wide petals that have handsomely waved edges and a pale lemon blotch; a flower of refined and yet rich effect ... Then there is a whole range of purest canary, many of them as nearly as possible self-coloured, the blotch either disappearing entirely or remaining only in the softest suffusion of slightly deeper colouring. It seems curious that, as they must all have been originally derived from the common Primrose, the pale greenish yellow of the type flower should be the rarest colour among them, but so it is ...[4]

Miss Sackville-West, no doubt, modelled her Cob-Nut Walk, underplanted with polyanthus and coloured primroses, on the Munstead garden. Bowles rather enjoyed the story of the occasion when his imperious friend, Mrs Robb, who gave her name to that dull but useful shade-loving plant, *Euphorbia robbiae*, found a good purple form of the primrose, *Primula acaulis* var. *rubra*, in Greece.

She saw it on Mount Olympus, and much to the annoyance of her magnificent dragoman, who was dressed in a uniform richer in gold lace than that of the most distinguished general, she insisted on his dismounting from his horse and digging up some roots with a broken potsherd, the only weapon that offered itself. She told me its purple glory always reminded her of the rueful face of that glittering dragoman.[5]

A little later than the primroses, comes the first of the rhizomatous bearded irises. Bowles grew them, in colour-graded groups, in long beds close to the New River. For once, the water-tightness of the banks was an advantage for these irises hate moisture, and they must have thrived in his light and gravelly soil. A particular pet of his, and one that Miss Jekyll also loved massed in a border, was the Dalmatian form of *Iris pallida*.

I[ris] *pallida dalmatica* is the most glorious of them; in fact I rather think it is the most glorious of all Irises when it does well. It has grown here for a long time, and was one of the very few really good plants I found a large stock of in the garden when I began to sit up and take notice of garden affairs. It has the widest blue leaf of all my Flags, and is wonderfully distinct and effective even when out of bloom; but how can I fitly describe its blossoms? It is too well known to need describing, except in as much as I must try to make good my assertion as to its exceeding glory ... Dalmatica's shade is a mingling of Rose-madder and Ultramarine blue, as I have learnt from painting it, and one must keep on squeezing one's tube of Rose-madder at a ruinous rate to give the warmth of the shades in hollows and on the sides of the falls. It is that soft rosy lilac to be found in certain Crocuses ... but much purer and cooler than the rosy-mauve I associate with Cattleyas [tropical orchids] and their musky heavy balsamic scent and vulgarly rich, purple and gold blotchings ... [He then digressed on plants that he disliked]

Now scurry we back to *Iris pallida dalmatica*'s charms, another of which is the way the ample standards open out and show the remarkably wide style branches, as if the flower knew how beautiful they are. I think pellucid must be the right adjective for them, only one must free one's mind of visions of the pale pellucid periwinkle soup of the Nonsense Book and think of an opal without any fire. They are a pale bluish lilac, as pale as a basin of starch, and just transparent enough to show a trace of the orange lower portion of the beard. Aha! now I've got it—they are like a delicious plover's egg just shelled and ready to eat ...[6]

Flowering at the same time, but grown principally for its autumn berries, is the British native, *Iris foetidissima*.

A spike of the brightest orange caught my eye, [wrote Miss Sackville-West] half hidden by a clump of *Berberis Thunbergii* which had turned very much the same colour. They were both of an extraordinary brilliance in the low afternoon sunshine. I could not remember if I had planted them deliberately in juxtaposition, or if they had come together by a fortunate chance. Investigation revealed further spikes: three-sided seed-pods cracked wide open to expose the violent clusters of the berries within.

This was our native *Iris foetidissima* in its autumn dress ... No one would plant *I. foetidissima* for the sake of its name, which in English is rendered the Stinking iris and derives from the unpleasant smell of the leaves

if you bruise them. There is, however, no need to bruise leaves, a wanton pastime, and you can call it the Gladdon or Gladwyn iris if you prefer, or even the Roast-beef Plant. Some etymologists think that Gladdon or Gladwyn are corruptions of Gladiolus, owing to a similarity between the sword-like leaves; but I wish someone would tell me how it got its roast-beef name.

Its flowers, small, and of a dingy mauve, are of no value or charm, nor should we be wise to pick them, because it is for the seed pods that we cherish it. Not that it needs much cherishing, and is even one of those amiable plants that will tolerate shade ... The seed pods are for late autumn and winter decoration indoors, for the seeds have the unusual property of not dropping out when the pods burst open, and will last for a long time in a vase; they look fine, and warm, under a table lamp on a bleak evening. Miss Gertrude Jekyll used to advise hanging the bunch upside down for a bit, to stiffen the stalks; I dare say she was right; she was usually right and had an experimental mind.

Let me not claim for the Gladdon iris that its crop of orange berries makes a subtle bunch or one which would appeal to flower-lovers of very delicate taste; it is frankly as coarse as it is showy, and has all the appearance of having been brought in by a pleased child after an afternoon's ramble through the copse. Nevertheless, its brightness is welcome, and its coarseness can be lightened by a few sprigs of its companion the berberis.[7]

Amongst the thousands of hardy perennials in the summer border few add such an air of upright, sombre distinction, like a general invited to a tea-party of chattering, brightly dressed women, as the acanthus. According to Miss Sackville-West,

The expression *foliage plants* carries something of a Victorian sound for us, like the echoing of a gong through a linoleumed, encrusted boarding-house, but in spite of this grim association some of the foliage plants hold a high decorative value in the garden. They fill up gaps in the border, and richly deserve to be called handsome.

I am thinking in particular of the acanthus. This is a plant with a classical tradition, for it provided Greek architects with the design for

the Corinthian capital to their columns. The
form of acanthus they used must have been
Acanthus spinosus or *spinosissimus*, which has
dark green leaves and a most prickly spike of
purple bracts, at least 18 in. in length, very
showy in July. For some odd reason it is popu-
larly known as Bear's Breeches, though I
should be sorry for any bear that had to wear
them ...[8]

Bowles liked them too.

A(canthus) mollis with its huge shining
leaves and tall spikes of prickly blossoms, is
handsome all the year except when snow or
very severe frost destroys its great leaves ...
A. longifolius has leaves longer than broad and
something like those of *mollis* but more deeply
cut. It disappears altogether below ground in
Autumn, but arises in a wondrous hurry as
soon as Spring calls it, and flowers more freely
than any kind I know ... *A. Caroli-Alexandri*
ought to be something of unusual
magnificence to carry off such a double-
barrelled name but up to the present has
looked like a sick and sulky *spinosus*. That is
one drawback of the Acanthus family, its
members will sometimes sulk for years after a
removal; but once they forgive you they
ramp, and if you try to curb this form of
letting off steam peculiar to vigorous plants
and heraldic animals by removing large portions to other sites, it is quite possible that
large plants removed will begin the hunger-
strike method once again and dwindle for a
season or two; while every atom of broken
rootlet you have left in the bottom of the
two-feet deep hole you took them out of will
sprout up into stronger plants than those
removed.[9]

For the autumn border Michaelmas daisies, in
their many different varieties, receive more than
ample coverage, despite their proneness to mil-
dew and their need for careful and deep cultivation. Miss Jekyll gave them a garden to themselves, in order to show them to their best
advantage.

The early days of October bring with them
the best bloom of the Michaelmas Daisies, the
many beautiful kinds of the perennial Asters.
They have, as they well deserve to have, a
garden to themselves. Passing along the wide

path in front of the big flower border, and
through the pergola that forms its continuation, with eye and brain full of rich, warm
colouring of flower and leaf, it is a delightful
surprise ... to come suddenly upon the
Michaelmas Daisy garden in full beauty. Its
clean fresh, pure colouring of pale and dark
lilac, strong purple, and pure white, among
masses of pale green foliage, forms a contrast
almost startling after the warm colouring of
nearly everything else; and the sight of a region where the flowers are fresh and newly
opened, and in glad spring-like profusion,
when all else is on the verge of death and
decay, gives an impression of satisfying
refreshment that is hardly to be equalled
throughout the year.[10]

How much she would have enjoyed the modern varieties with their improved disease-
resistance, even if she might have dubbed some
of the colours 'aniline'.
Robinson was equally enthusiastic.

There is a quiet beauty about the more
select Starworts, which is charming in the
autumn days, and their variety of colour, of
form, and of bud and blossom are delightful ...
As yet gardeners seldom look at general
effects—at the whole of things. The flowers
are so dear to them that the garden, as a picture, is left to chance, and hence there is so
much ugliness and formality in gardens, to
those at least who regard the robe as more
than the buttons. Some years ago Starworts
were rarely seen except in bundles in botanic
gardens. Since the hardy flower revival, they
have become more frequent in collections but
as yet they have no important place in gardens
generally ... The bad effect of staking and
bundling may be wholly got rid of, if the
plants were supported and relieved by the
bushes, and their flowers massed above them
here and there. Asters, dwarfer than the
shrubs among which we place them, are not
less valuable, as they help to give light and
shade, and to avoid the common way of setting plants to a face as if they were so many
bricks. This is not the only way of growing
these hardiest of northern flowers, but it is a
charming one, and it lights up the garden with
a new loveliness of refined colour.[11]

It would be misleading to give the impression that just because the system of bedding-out was thoroughly discredited it necessarily meant that the individual plants used in such displays were equally disliked. In fact, the opposite was true. All the authors prided themselves on their appreciation of plants as individuals, but they did rebel against their use *en masse* without any thought given to placing or colour blending. In the same way a crowd of people in a room may irritate by their noise and press although we know them all to be attractive individuals. I would not like to suggest either that they considered all half-hardy annuals lovable, seeing beauty even in the most garish products of an hybridist's warped imagination, but they tempered their distaste by concentrating on those plants that did appeal. After two pages of condemning bedding-out in an unhysterical way (see Chapter 7), Bowles admitted:

> ... I confess to adoring Scarlet Pelargoniums, rejoicing in Blue Lobelia and revelling in Yellow Calceolaria. But they must be certain varieties, well grown and well placed. An aged Pelargonium, King of Denmark, with a tree-like trunk, numerous branches, and in a pot three sizes too small for it, can be a glorious cloud of warm salmon blossoms; and Paul Crampel is worth similar ill-treatment. Of course fat sappy cuttings stuck out in rich soil, and that grow leaves fit for cooking and serving with white sauce are not what we want. I love to seize a few pot-plants in the conservatory or greenhouse, and to take them out for a Summer airing in the garden, sinking their pots among other plants, where they fit in and look as if they have been there all their lives. There is a raised bed near the house bordering the carriage drive that is getting filled up by degrees with permanent tenants, but among them at present are still a few lodgings to let, and here all sorts of tender plants pass their Summer.[12]

Miss Sackville-West took an intelligent and unprejudiced look at lobelia.

> Today I should like to put in a good word for the lobelia, dear to the heart of some suburban and most municipal gardeners, but despised by those who pride themselves on a more advanced taste. The poor lobelia has suffered terribly and most unjustly from its traditional use and from association. Association has been the worst enemy of many plants. I suppose that the first time anybody saw pink tulips coming up through forget-me-nots they may have exclaimed in delight. Similarly, the Victorian-Edwardian combination of lobelia and sweet alyssum may once have given pleasure. No longer now.
>
> But can you discard all your preconceived ideas and think of the lobelia as though you had never seen it before? What a fine blue, as good as a gentian, is it not? And so dense, so compact, such a rug, such a closely woven carpet, you could put a pin though not a finger into the mat of flower. Think of it in this way, and you will instantly begin to see it in a different light and full of different possibilities.
>
> Think of it as a great blue pool. Think of it in terms of waves and washes; think of it in terms of the Mediterranean at its best; think of it in spreads and sweeps and wapentakes and sokes and bailiwicks and tithings. Or, if you have not quite so much space at your disposal, do at least plant it in really generous patches, not just as an edging, and remember the variety called Cambridge Blue, which lives up to its name.
>
> If you must have it as an edging, and if you must combine it with alyssum, try it with the alyssums called Lilac Queen, Violet Queen, and Royal Carpet, instead of the traditional white. The blue of the lobelia mixes into something very sumptuous with their mauves and purples. And I did observe an amusing and original use of lobelia last summer. The dark blue and the bright blue were planted in neat squares up either side of a narrow path leading from the garden gate to the front door. It was like a slice of chessboard; an Oxford and Cambridge chess-board.[13]

The influence of Robinson and Miss Jekyll was such that the growing of half-hardy annuals in many gardens suffered a steep decline. Bedding-out has never entirely disappeared, however, which demonstrates the tenacity and steadfastness of popular taste in the face, since the war, of vastly increased fuel prices and a chronic shortage of labour. It would be a shame, in any event, if bedding were to vanish altogether, for, in public parks especially, large beds of considerable visual impact, placed at some distance from the spectator, are striking and even cheering. Many public authorities, notably the Royal Botanic Gardens at Kew, have shown that bedding can be impressive if only care is taken to blend the colours of the constituent plants and match their shapes and foliage.

Nevertheless there has been a decline, and with it a corresponding rise in the fortunes of the hardy annual, sown where it is to flower, requiring nothing like as much upkeep and labour, and often achieving more harmonious effects. Miss Sackville-West was fond of hardy annuals and experimented with many kinds in her garden, sometimes with disastrous results which she disarmingly admitted, as when she decided one year to mix all her annual seed in an old tobacco tin, sow them and let them take their chance. The outcome was a predictable failure.

The charm of annuals is their light gaiety, as though they must make the most of their brief visit to be frivolous and pleasure-giving ... They must always be youthful, because they have no time to grow old. And so their colours are bright, and their foliage airy, and their only morality is to be as cheerful as possible, and to leave as much seed as they can behind them for their progeny to continue in the same tradition. This, of course, is the one thing you must not let them do: all seeding heads must ruthlessly be snipped off if you want to prolong the exuberance of flowers.[14]

The question of not allowing annuals to seed is a vexed one, very easy to say, very difficult to do. Often there seems to be no need to halt the prodigality anyway, as in the case of *Viola* 'Bowles' Black'. In Bowles' rock-garden there was

a queer little black *Viola tricolor* that starting from this point has gone about the world a good deal under the name of Bowles' Black ... I got it from Dr. Lowe [a kindly and immensely knowledgeable mentor of Bowles' in his early days of enthusiasm] who told me it always bred true, and so it does if kept to itself ... but I know that it readily influences other Violas, and its dusky charms appear in Mulattoes, Quadroons, and Octaroons all over the place ... Canon Ellacombe saw it here, and having lost it at Bitton, carried it back again, where it was seen, admired and coveted by the stream of

visitors that ever flows to view the perennial display of good plants in that garden. They were told that Bowles was throwing it away, and many a begging letter came here asking for *my* black Pansy and most of those to whom I sent it labelled it Bowles' Black, and soon after sent it on to other gardens under that hideous name. Not so bad, though, as one I saw at the last Chelsea Show, for there it was labelled Viola Black Bowles! I am not as black as I was painted on that label, so I altered it. It is a very charming little weed, sowing itself freely and when in full bloom it has a wonderfully friendly and cheerful look in the yellow Cyclopian eye in the middle of its almost black face.[15]

While on the subject of Bowles' plants I feel sure *Cheiranthus* 'Bowles' Mauve' would have found favour with Miss Jekyll, who had a special garden devoted solely to wallflowers. The usual way of growing these is by sowing seed in June outside, planting out the seedlings into a nursery row, and transplanting them again in the autumn to the place where they are to flower. Miss Jekyll preferred self-sown seedlings.

Like the inhabitants of some half-barren place who have never been in touch with abundance or ease of life or any sort of luxury, they are all the more sturdy and thrifty and self-reliant, and I would venture to affirm that their lives will be as long again as those of any sister plants from the same seedpod that have enjoyed more careful nurture and a more abundant dietary. No planted-out Wallflower can ever compare, in my light soil, with one sown where it is to remain; it always retains the planted-out look to the end of its days and never has the tree-like sturdiness about the lower portions of its half-woody stem that one notices about the one sown and grown in its place. Moreover, from many years' observation, I notice that such plants only, show the many variations in habit that one comes to recognise as a kind of individual or personal characteristic, so that the plant acquires a much greater and almost human kind of interest. I have one such seedling that gives me great pleasure. The flower is of a full, clear, orange colour, more deeply tinged to the outer margins of the petals with faint thin lines of rich mahogany, that increase in width of line and depth of colour as they reach the petal's outer edge, till, joining together, the whole edge is of this strong, rich colour. The back of the petal is entirely of this deep tint, and though the flower is of some substance, I always think the richness of colouring of the back has something to do with the strong quality of the deep yellow of the face. The calyx, which forms the covering of the unopened bud, is of a full purple-brown. The leaves are of a dark dull green, tinged with brown-bronze, much like the colour of the brown water-cress.[16]

She tantalisingly refrained from naming this desirable seedling, if indeed it ever had a name.

It might be amusing to end this chapter with a miscellany of curiosities: what Miss Sackville-West referred to as 'joke plants'.

Amongst other seeds for spring sowing I ordered a sixpenny packet of *Mimosa pudica*, the Humble Plant. Most people, including some nurserymen, call it the Sensitive Plant, a name that should be reserved for *Mimosa sensitiva* which contradictorily, is less sensitive than *M. pudica*. So humble is the Humble Plant, so bashful, that a mere touch of the finger or a puff of breath blown across it will cause it to collapse instantly into a woebegone heap, like the once popular Ally Sloper. One grows it purely for the purpose of amusing the children. The normal child, if not an insufferable prig, thoroughly enjoys being unkind to something; so here is a harmless outlet for this instinct in the human young. Shrieks of delight are evoked, enhanced by the sadistic pleasure of doing it over and over again. 'Let's go back and see if it has sat up yet.' It probably has, for it seems to be endowed with endless patience under such mischievous persecution.

I must admit that I would like to see it in its native home in tropical America, where, I have been told, acres of pigmy forest swoon under the touch of a ruffling breeze. Nominally a perennial there, it is best treated as a half-hardy annual here ... By late summer it will have grown up into quite a tall plant about a foot high; and then you may observe that, like most sensitive people, it is not only sensitive but prickly. It develops large spiky thorns, but still retains its shivering fright. It then becomes not only an amusement for

children but a symbol for many of our friends. [She also referred to] the Burning Bush, *Dictamnus fraxinella* or Dittany, which you can set alight into a blue flame, especially on a warm summer day, without any harm to the plant. The explanation of this apparent miracle is the presence of a volatile oil; but why seek for explanations when you can so easily entertain your young guests?[17]

She wrote too about

the Marvel of Peru, *Mirabilis Jalapa*, familiarly called Four o'clock, because it opens only at tea time and shuts itself up again before breakfast. It is an old-fashioned herbaceous plant, seldom seen now, but quite decorative with its mixed colouring of yellow, white, red, or lilac, sometimes striped and flaked like some carnations ...

Then there is the Obedient Plant, *Physostegia virginiana*. The form of amusement provided by this object is the readiness of its flowers to remain in any position you choose to push them round the stem. I never could get it to work, until a Scottish friend told me that I did not poosh it hard enough. If you look carefully, you will see that they have a sort of little hinge ...

Perhaps the oddest plant of all is The Monarch of the East, *Sauromatum guttatum*. The name comes from saurus, a lizard, and guttatum means dotted or spotted. The flower, which resembles an arum lily in shape, is indeed dotted and spotted like some oriental lizards, only in different colours. The Monarch rejoices in the decadent livery of green and purple, with purple bruises on the pale green. Its colouring, however, is not the chief queer thing about it. The chief queer thing is the way it will agree to grow. You set the tuber down on a saucer, just like that, plonk! with no soil and no water, and quite soon it will begin to sprout, and within a few weeks will begin to show signs of flowering.

When it has flowered, you should plant the tuber out in a rather damp corner of the garden to let it develop its leaves during the summer. Then in August or September you lift the tuber, dry it off, and eventually put it back into its saucer, when it will perform again, year after year.[18]

Notes

1. R. J. Farrer, *The English Rock Garden*, fourth impression (2 vols., T.C. and E.C. Jack, 1928), vol. 1, pp. 411–12.

2. G. Jekyll, *A Gardener's Testament*, Francis Jekyll and G.C. Taylor (eds.) facsimile of 1937 edn (Antique Collectors' Club, 1982), p. 235.

3. G. Jekyll, *Wood and Garden*, facsimile of 1st edn (Antique Collectors' Club, 1981), p. 295.

4. Jekyll, *A Gardener's Testament*, p. 249.

5. E.A. Bowles, *My Garden in Spring*, 1st edn (T.C. and E.C. Jack, 1914), p. 144.

6. E.A. Bowles, *My Garden in Summer*, 1st edn (T.C. and E.C. Jack, 1914), pp. 21–3.

7. V. Sackville-West, *In Your Garden Again*, 1st edn (Michael Joseph, 1953), pp. 142–4.

8. V. Sackville-West, *More for Your Garden*, 1st edn (Michael Joseph, 1955), p. 104.

9. Bowles, *My Garden in Summer*, pp. 117–18.

10. Jekyll, *Wood and Garden*, pp. 180–1.

11. W. Robinson, *The English Flower Garden*, 6th edn (John Murray, 1898), pp. 410–11.

12. Bowles, *My Garden in Summer*, pp. 253–4.

13. Sackville-West, *More for Your Garden*, pp. 20–1.

14. V. Sackville-West, *In Your Garden*, 1st edn (Michael Joseph, 1951), p. 54.

15. Bowles, *My Garden in Spring*, pp. 271–2.

16. G. Jekyll, *Home and Garden*, facsimile of 1900 edn (Antique Collectors' Club, 1982), pp. 52–4.

17. Sackville-West, *In Your Garden Again*, pp. 32–3.

18. Ibid., pp. 33–4.

CHAPTER
❧ 10 ❧

Rock-gardens
&
Alpines

It is hard now to appreciate what furious and not always good-natured arguments raged eighty or a hundred years ago about the best ways of building a rock-garden and what to plant in it. Those arguments have lost their force over the years because there are fewer rock-gardens built; they have been replaced to a great extent by the dry wall and raised bed. The knowledge of the debates is nevertheless interesting and instructive because, in the process of them, the best ways of cultivating rock plants in this country were firmly established.

In the eighteenth century, grottoes had enjoyed a vogue in the landscapes of the well-to-do, but they were not places for growing plants; far from it. William Beckford, the rich eccentric, had an alpine garden in a quarry at Fonthill at the end of the eighteenth century and there were a few rock-gardens that dated from the 1830s, notably Lady Broughton's mini Chamonix valley at Hoole House, Chester; a fairly naturalistic one at Redleaf near Penshurst, and the still extant one at Lamport Hall, Northamptonshire. In 1831 there was actually a discussion in a gardening magazine about the importance of studying nature when placing rocks in a rockery, and it is evident that the author of the article was trying to show those with rock-mounds of brick and flint the error of their ways. The most famous rock-garden before the Robinsonian era, though, was surely the one built by James Backhouse at his nursery at York. He was a friend of Robinson, and built his rock-garden in the late 1850s. Backhouse must receive the credit for being the first man to attempt to grow alpines on a large scale in conditions that were both naturalistic and suitable for their well-being. Mrs Lawrence, at her villa at Drayton, was more representative in having a garden full of rustic stone arches, and extravagant but ultimately barren rockwork. Robinson satirised her efforts in *Alpine Flowers for English Gardens*. It is perhaps salutary to comment, however, that all the argument that we shall read of the artificial versus natural rock-garden was in itself artificial for, in lowland Britain where most readers lived, the concept of any rockwork was an odd one. The rock-gardens of Kew and Wisley, built in 1882 and 1911 respectively, are models of naturalness where much care was taken with the rock strata, but that does not alter the fact that they were set down in gardens situated not far above sea level.

The impact that Robinson, and Farrer after him, made, was as much in teaching people what to grow in rock-gardens as in how to set stones 'naturally'. Thanks in part to pioneering work by these men so much became known about the habits and habitats of rock plants that any amateur can now grow all but the very fussiest high alpines with a reasonable chance of success, using well-draining gritty composts.

Figure 10.1 'Frontispiece of a book on alpine plants'. (From First Edition of Alpine Flowers for English Gardens, *by William Robinson)*

The composition of such composts has been tested and details can be found in any book on the subject.

Much of what Farrer and Robinson said was polemic. They wished to convert readers to their view of what a rock-garden should look like and also that alpines were not impossible plants which needed the utmost care to survive at all. In the process they very often overstated their case and, because we have absorbed most of their precepts so completely, it is hard for us to understand why much of what they said was not taken for granted in the half-century before the First World War.

By 1870 the fashion for growing the flowers of the European Alps, and also those sent from mountainous regions of North America, had increased, promoted by the botanists, travellers and plain tourists who were making mountain walking in the Alps such a popular pastime and bringing back collected species in quantity. Gardeners were, however, encountering considerable difficulties in growing them successfully, and Robinson saw the need to enlighten the public, for he believed it was faulty rockwork construction that was doing the harm.

He had a section on 'What to Avoid' in *Alpine Flowers for English Gardens* and illustrated it.

In the selection of a few illustrations showing on what a mistaken principle and with what deplorable taste, rockwork is generally made, my first intention was to have had them engraved from drawings taken in various gardens, public and private; but as this course might have proved an invidious one, I have preferred to take them from our best books on Horticulture ... From these the reader may glean some idea of popular notions on this subject, and it is scarcely needful to add that, if such ridiculous objects occur in our most trustworthy books yet more must they be in many gardens.

The first simple beauty is copied from the frontispiece of a small book on alpine plants, published not many years ago. Growing naturally on the high mountains, unveiled from the sun by wood or copse, alpine plants are grouped here beneath what appears to be a weeping willow—a position in which they could not possibly attain anything like their native vigour and beauty, or do otherwise than lead a sickly existence. The degree of contentment and delight felt by the artist for his subject is shown by his planting the ponderous vase in the centre of the group, and the introduction of the railing is beyond all praise.

In the same passage he ridiculed the picture of a rustic arch at Mrs Lawrence's garden at Drayton, Middlesex, portrayed in John Loudon's *The Villa Gardener* of 1838.

Frequently they are formed out of burrs, and occasionally of clinkers, but even if composed of the finest stone obtainable, they are utterly useless for the growth of alpine vegetation. How many Saxifrages, or Pinks, or Primroses, could find a home on such a structure planted in a part of the Alps highly favourable to vegetation? Probably not one, and should a few succulents establish themselves on its lower flanks, they would in all probability perish from heat and drought if their roots had not a free course to the earth beneath. Even persons with some experience of plant life may be seen sticking plants over such objects as these, as if their tender roots were capable of bearing as many vicissitudes of heat and cold as a piece of copper wire. The fact that plants push their roots far into masses of old brickwork is no justification for the rustic arch as a home for alpine flowers ...

Our next figure shows a truly laudable attack upon monotony. The tall stones are to the smaller ones as the Lombardy Poplar is to his round-headed brothers of the grove. The front margin of this graceful scene consists of two rows of prostrate and one row of erect clinkers, and is much less irregular and more hideous than the engraver has had the heart to make it. The back wall is of a very common type, and precisely of that texture on which alpine plants will *not* exist. This cut is not extracted from the great books of Loudon or of Macintosh: it is a comparatively recent improvement, and was sketched during the past summer in a botanic garden not one hundred miles from London.[1]

It is small wonder he made enemies.

Mainly as a result of Robinson's publicity, matters did change initially for the better. However, by the time Bowles' *My Garden in Spring* came out in 1914, the old wicked money-spending show-off days of bedding-out were back again with a vengeance; according to Farrer that is, who wrote the Preface. This passage

Figure 10.2 'After Loudon'. (From First Edition of Alpine Flowers for English Gardens, *by William Robinson)*

Figure 10.3 'A truly laudable attack on monotony' from 'a botanic garden not one hundred miles from London.'

landed him and the poor unfortunate Bowles into hot water because of the argument that resulted, which has come to be known as the Crispian Row.

> Everyone must have their 'rockwork', and the very rich are out to purchase the glories of the Alps at so much a yard—with all the more contentment if the price be heavy, so that their munificence may be the more admired. Passion for display appears the ruling note in English horticulture of every kind and in every period: we want a show.

He continued,—and this was a tilt at Robinson—with the observation that when carpet-bedding had gone out of fashion, for a short time there was a movement to return to 'Nature', but which he said was 'merely wobbly anarchy reduced to a high art' (see Chapter 7), but that rock-gardens at least were then places for trying to grow particular plants well.

> But now the accursed thing is once more rearing its head, and carpet-bedding is bursting up to life again in the midst of the very rock garden itself, of all places impermissible and improbable. For the rich must have their money's worth in show; culture will not give it them, nor rarity, nor interest of the plants themselves: better a hundred yards of Arabis than half a dozen vernal Gentians. So now their vast rockworks are arranged like the pattern of a pavement: here is a large triangle filled neatly with a thousand plants of *Alyssum saxatile* neatly spaced like bedded Stocks, and with the ground between them as smooth and tidy as a Guardsman's head; then, fitting into this, but separated by stone or rock, more irregular great triangles of the same order—one containing a thousand Aubrietia 'Lavender', and the next a thousand *Lithospermum prostratum*. But nothing else; neither blending nor variety—nothing but a neat unalloyed exhibit like those on 'rock-works' at the Chelsea Show. [The first show held in the grounds of the Royal Hospital was in 1912. Before that it was held in the Temple Gardens.] But what a display is here! You could do no better with coloured gravels. Neat, unbroken blanks of first one colour and then another, until the effect indeed is sumptuous and worthy of the taste that has combined such a garden. But 'garden' why call it? There

are no plants here; there is nothing but colour, laid on as callously in slabs as if from the paintbox of a child. This is a mosaic, this is a gambol in purple and gold; but it is not a rock garden, though tin chamois peer never so frequent from its cliffs upon the passer-by, bewildered with such a glare of expensive magnificence.[2]

The tin chamois referred to were a feature of Sir Frank Crisp's rock-garden, at Friar Park near Henley, which covered an area of four acres with large blocks of millstone grit and was designed to resemble closely the Matterhorn. The 'summit' was topped with alabaster to look like snow. Crisp was a rich, and it must be said vain, man, with wide and scholarly interests, who was by profession a solicitor. He was much absorbed in his hobby; he even went to the lengths of sending his head gardener to Switzerland to study the mountain he was copying in miniature.

He was enraged when *My Garden in Spring* was published in the spring of 1914. He reacted swiftly and intemperately, and in so doing put himself firmly in the wrong. At the Chelsea

Figure 10.4 Sir Frank Crisp of Friar Park, Henley-on-Thames

Figure 10.5 Miss Ellen Willmott of Warley Place, Essex

Show in May, Miss Ellen Willmott (she of the 104 gardeners), distributed to all and sundry from a large leather bookmaker's bag leaflets entitled, 'MR E.A. BOWLES AND HIS GARDEN', 'A New Parable of the Pharisee and the Publican'. In this Bowles was attacked for puffing up his own achievements in the Preface. The elementary mistake of confusing the author of the Preface with that of the book is astonishing, but so it was that Bowles' name was dragged through the dirt. It seems to me that the Crispians thoroughly overreacted, especially as Farrer was well known to exaggerate preposterously at times. It was particularly unfair that their wrath should descend on Bowles who was an innocent spectator. Farrer, in his Preface was comparing these large extravagant rock-gardens with Bowles' 'plantsman's' approach, but it seems extremely doubtful that Bowles had a say in what Farrer wrote. Being the mildest-mannered of men he was, I suspect, thoroughly upset by the furore, but restricted his contribution to a gently reproachful letter to Robinson after Crisp's pamphlet had been reproduced in *Gardening Illustrated*. For a long time it was

assumed that Robinson had behaved badly in reproducing such scurrility, but it is apparent from a letter from Farrer in Lanchow to Robinson that he knew Robinson, confined to Gravetye through ill-health, was not responsible, and that it was the fault of his sub-editor. There was little love lost between Robinson and Farrer, however, so it may be that Robinson had some idea of what was afoot.

Robinson commended Friar Park in the 1910 edition of *Alpine Flowers for Gardens*, as well as Warley Place where Miss Willmott lived. There

... we may see not only the rarest Alpine plants admirably grown, but efforts and colour not unworthy of the Alpine fields.[3]

Miss Jekyll, usually so keen on restraint and proportion, also praised Friar Park in 1913. She called it one of the most remarkable of private gardens, and mentioned that over ten thousand tons of rock had been used in its making. She continued by quoting approving remarks made by Professor Henri Correvon. It cannot have pleased Farrer that his arch-rival should admire Crisp's rock-garden. Although he must have had a sneaking admiration for Correvon, a very fine botanist and plant-hunter who worked in Geneva and cultivated successfully many alpines that even Farrer had difficulty with, he made Correvon the butt of many side-swipes in *My Rock Garden* and *The English Rock Garden*. Everything points to Farrer having been in a silly and unbridled mood, but it was a shame that Bowles' good name should have been muddied in the process, and also that he overstated what, generally speaking, was a good case. He had picked the wrong target.

What were Farrer's legitimate targets? Having expatiated on the folly of Robinson's extreme disciples (see Chapter 7) he went on to survey current practices in rock-garden building.

The ideal rock garden must have a plan. But there are three prevailing plans, none of which are good. The first is what I may call the Almond-pudding scheme, and obtains generally, especially in the north of England. You take a round bed; you pile it up with soil; you then choose out the spikiest pinnacles of limestone you can find, and you insert them thickly with their points in the air, until the general effect is that of a tipsy-cake stuck with almonds. In this vast petrified porcupine nothing will grow except Welsh Poppy, Ferns, and some of the uglier Sedums. The second style is that of the Dog's Grave. It marks a higher stage of horticulture, and is affected by many good growers of alpines. The pudding-shape is more or less the same in both, but the stones are laid flat in the Dog's Grave ideal. Plants will grow on this, but its scheme is so stodgy and so abhorrent to Nature that it should be discarded. The third style is that of the Devil's Lapful, and prevailed very largely when Alpines first began to be used out of doors. [Here he singled out the botanic gardens in Dublin and Edinburgh] The plan is simplicity itself. You take a hundred or a thousand cartloads of bald square-faced boulders. You next drop them all about absolutely anyhow; and you then plant things amongst them. The chaotic hideousness of the result is something to be remembered with shudders ever after.[4]

He went on to praise the Glen at Kew, still in being, and the Gorge at Warley Place, which is not. Warley Place was Miss Willmott's garden, and it is hardly surprising that the preceding passage was published in 1908, some years before the Crispian Row.

In a passage which owes much to Robinson, he wrote of the stone to be used:

... all artificial 'stone', by whatever name described, is invariably and absolutely to be refused. Far better a rock-garden without a single rock than ill-furnished acres of Portland cement blocks or sham stalactites.

All derelict artificial rubbish, burrs, clinkers, odds and ends of Norman arches, conglomerated bricks, and such like, must be refused with equal sternness.

All granite, flint, slate, porphyry, syenite or calliard is only to be used as a resource of despair. These rocks are lifeless, arid, and unprofitable, innutritious in substance, hard and hostile of texture and outline, unfriendly to beauty, whether of conformation or plant life. They are only capable of producing chaotic gaunt piles from which a few species peer fitfully.[5]

So now we know what they were making so much fuss about.

It is easy enough to say, however, how it should not be done, but what was, and is, the best way of making a rock-garden for the health of the plants and the best display of their charms?

Bowles' rock-garden, was for him, along with his frames of 'croci', the horticultural love of his life, and though little remains of it now, and it will probably never be possible to recreate it in any major way, his description of what it was like is still worth quoting.

My rock garden is a home-made affair, that is to say I planned, built, and planted it, and have had the chief hand in caring for it for twenty years. When I say built I mean I chose out the stone for each position, helped to move it and generally gave it the final lift or shove, or jumped up and down on the top of it, to fix it in place just as I wanted it, but, of course, several heads and hands helped me, especially with the large blocks and the excavating and shovelling up of soil ... It is a rock garden but by no means an alpine garden, for though alpine plants have a first choice of places I have always been ready to plant any bush or even tree in it, that I think will grow better for the advantages of drainage and protection the chosen site will afford it. I often say that I must reserve a new wing for choice alpines only or clear out an older range for them, then I come along with a choice young Eucalyptus in a pot ... or some other son of Anak; a suitable cosy nook is given to the poor homeless waif, and so long as plants flourish I cannot bring myself to destroy their happiness. So do not expect the orthodox grouping of dwarf alpines, or even carefully-stratified stones, for I have never hesitated to stand a large, flat block up on end to form a miniature south wall for tender sun-lovers, but I have always had the sense to fill in the back of such an one with soil and continue the rise above the stone, and so treated the bank looks natural enough. I have used Kentish rag throughout, and until my ship comes home with a cargo of more guineas than I know what to do with I shall not change it for mountain limestone.[6]

Grappling with the problem of how to make a rock-garden, so artificial a conception, look natural, Robinson wrote:

It is a trite observation to say that what pleases us in Nature is the perfect fitness of things which pervades all her belongings. The most rugged, abrupt and even grotesque rock masses, when untouched by man, never repel us by a sense of incongruity; they may be pleasing or awful, as the case may be, but they do not strike us as being out of place. Who on the other hand, has not seen a lovely view marred by some unintelligent human hand, whether its work took the form of a quarry, a statue, or a vase?[7]

Farrer was positively dismissive of the whole idea of the 'natural'. In this passage he appears deliberately to wish to contradict Robinson.

... to talk of imitating nature, as so many vainly do, is to encourage a rank and empty delusion. To make a thing look 'natural' is by no means to imitate nature. Nature often looks more artificial than the worst forms of artificial art; nature in the mountains is often chaotic, bald, dreary, and hideous in the highest degree. By making a rock-garden look natural, then, we merely mean that it must have a firm and effortless harmony of hill or vale, cliff or slope. Conventionally 'natural' effects are best unaimed at—rock-gardening, like all great arts, is not imitative, but selective and adaptive. Vast congeries of rounded boulders are 'natural', but neither beautiful nor helpful in the rock-garden; lowering kopjes of up-ended spikes and obelisks, ragged, vast, and gaunt, are frequent in the granitic ranges, but in the rock-garden are presumptuous, violent, and disproportionate in effect; unless the composition be on the very vastest scale, and then pyramids of chaos can close some deep and huge ravine.[8]

His rule for the ideal rockery was just one:

Have an idea, and stick to it. Let your rock-garden set out to be something definite, not a mere agglomeration of stones. Let it be a mountain gorge, if you like, or the stony slope of a hill, or a rocky crest, or a peak. But, whatever it be, it must have definiteness of scheme. It is, in effect, an imitation of Nature, and, to be successful, must aim at reproducing with fidelity some particular feature of Nature—whatever you may choose.[9]

He cannot, therefore, have objected to the layout of the Friar Park garden, but only to the planting.

Great care had to be taken in the siting of the rock-garden, the materials used for its construction and the building of it. This is Robinson on the subject.

No very formal walk—that is to say, no walk with regularly trimmed edges—should come near the rock-garden. This need not prevent the presence of good walks through or near it, as by allowing the edges of the walk to be broken and stony, and by encouraging Stonecrops, Rockfoils, and other little plants to crawl into the walk at will, a pretty margin will result. There is no surface of this kind that many not be thus adorned. Violets, Ferns, Forget-me-nots, will do in the shadier parts, and the Stonecrops and many others will thrive in the full sun. The whole of the surface of the alpine garden should be covered with plants as far as possible, except a few projecting points.[10]

Farrer, following in Robinson's footsteps, stated, for no very good reason that I can see, that the rock-garden should not be placed near a wall (what about his New Rock Garden at Ingleborough?), or a formal path, border or house; nor in sight of any regular and artificial construction. The view was that rock-gardens were best placed near the Wild Garden. This is certainly what happened at Wisley but, as have I said before, the use of the words 'natural' and 'artificial' in this context are arbitrary anyway. Farrer did also point out, sensibly, that the rock-garden should be sited in an open place, not overhung by trees which spread shade and dripped. And, with the full weight of magisterial authority gained from extensive experience, he declared his view on the proper rock-garden foundations.

Having chosen an open aspect and conceived your plan, you must invariably excavate the soil to a foot or fifteen inches below ground level. You must then fill up this excavation with rough coarse curs, clinkers, and coke-blocks for drainage. This is the alpha and omega of success; it was never understood in the past, when we compiled our heaps of any impervious old rubbish, and then were surprised because our choice Alpines, in prepared 'pockets' pecked in the mass, proved miserable and sullen. From that day dates the bad reputation of many a beautiful plant, which has now become happy and free and easy, since we have discovered that the vital secret of success in rock-gardening is to build the whole fabric soundly, on proper principles, with good soil and perfect drainage, from the very base.[11]

As for the stone that was the most suitable, he did not entirely rule out the usefulness of sandstone, for which builders of rock-gardens such as the one at Wisley must have been grateful to him, but, cheerfully partisan to the last, he recommended limestone, and especially that from the Craven Highlands. I suppose one should have guessed. I can just imagine what he said to Bowles about his Kentish rag. For him, weather-worn limestone

> forms naturally into flutings and ribbings, bays and inlets, 'moutonnements' and ripples of primeval effect, enhancing with lights and shadows the tender grey-whiteness of the stone itself, in texture soft and tender to the plants it nourishes so well, yet leonine and stark in its moulded forms, which have the rare gift of so obvious a solidarity, that block fits to block like the sections of a jigsaw puzzle, so that the merest child at work with these could hardly help compiling, without thought or effort, a rock-work that shall really look all of a piece, the creation not of man, but of the untrammelled forces of the world at work since the hills first were.[12]

Even in those days, rock-gardens did not constitute the only milieux in which rock plants were grown. Miss Jekyll and Robinson favoured the dry wall; that is, the wall held together by gravity rather than by cement. Robinson opined that:

> It is not without considerable observation of the capabilities of walls, even walls in good repair, to grow numerous rare and pretty plants, and, moreover, keep them in perpetual health without trouble, that I recommend everybody who takes an interest in the matter to have the fullest confidence in growing them easily in this way. Most of those who are blessed with gardens have usually a little wall surface at their disposal; and to all such I can name some plants that will grow thereon better than in the best soil. A mossy old wall, or an old ruin, would afford a position for many

dwarf rock-plants which no specially prepared situation could rival; but even on straight and well-preserved walls we can establish some little beauties, which year after year will abundantly repay the tasteful cultivator for the slight trouble of planting or sowing them. Those who have observed the way dwarf plants grow on the tops of mountains, or on elevated stony ground, must have seen in what arid positions many grow in perfect health—tufts springing from an almost imperceptible chink on an arid rock or boulder. They are often stunted and diminutive in such places, but always more floriferous and long-lived than when grown fat and large upon the ground; in fact, their beauty is often intensified by starvation and aridity.[13]

Elsewhere Robinson wrote:

> In garden formation, especially in sloping or diversified ground, what is called a dry wall is often useful, and may answer the purpose of supporting a bank or dividing a garden quite as well as masonry. Where the stones can be got easily, men used to the work will often make gently 'battered' walls, which, while fulfilling their object in supporting banks, will make homes for many plants which would not live one winter on a level surface in the same place.[14]

This remark called down Farrer's scorn on his head, although the latter was, in my opinion, being unnecessarily captious. He maintained that because the wall garden is both wall and garden it is never wholly satisfactory as either.

> The real, dignified wall-garden is that which set out originally to be a wall, and a wall only, with no *arrière-pensée*, or ambition after frills of any kind. Such are the great walls of St. John's College at Oxford. The only gardener that they know is Time, who sows them cunningly, with the result that they end by being doubly beautiful—a magnificent wall in the first place, and essentially; and then, accidentally, a garden of pleasant flowers. But the wall that is built for wall-gardening has always to be built at a slant, instead of with a stern straightness of the real thing. Thus it gives away its duplicity of purpose at a glance, and as you look at it leaning back against a bank, conveys an inevitable

feeling of weakness. The poor creature looks as if it had unfortunately got drunk, and could not stand without support. It is of no use to try combining the artificial with the natural, or the imitation of the natural. [In that access of honesty he gives the lie to his whole point of view.] A wall is, *ex hypothesi*, an artificial product, flop it about as drunkenly as you will; while the rock-garden is, *ex hypothesi*, an attempt to give the impression of Nature. There the wall-garden is discord, naturally and invariably; nor do I see, in spite of all that is said and written, that it grows the plants any better than a well-set rockwork.[15]

All that would have made Miss Jekyll, who wrote half a book on wall gardens, snort. She was a zealous advocate of the dry terrace wall and the planting thereof, and the results of her work can still plainly be seen at Hestercombe, for example. She described what could be planted where a stairway cut through the bank between two dry walls.

Little Ferns are planted in the joints on the shadier side as the wall goes up, and numbers of small Saxifrages and Stonecrops, Pennywort and *Erinus, Corydalis* and Sandwort. Then there will be hanging sheets of *Aubrietia* and Rock Pinks, *Iberis* and *Cerastium*, and many another pretty plant that will find a happy home in the cool shelter of the rocky joint. In some regions of the walling Wallflowers and Snapdragons and plants of Thrift can be established; as they ripen their seed it drifts into the openings of other joints, and the seedlings send their roots deep into the bank and along the cool backs of the stones, and make plants of surprising health and vigour that are longer lived than the softer-grown plants in rich flower-borders.

I doubt if there is any way in which a good quantity of plants, and of bushes of moderate size, can be so well seen and enjoyed as in one of these roughly terraced gardens, for one sees them up and down and in all sorts of ways, and one has a chance of seeing many lovely flowers clear against the sky, and of perhaps catching some sweetly-scented tiny thing like *Dianthus fragrans* at exactly nose-height and eye-level, and so of enjoying its tender beauty and powerful fragrance in a way that had never before been found possible.

Then the beautiful detail of structure and

marking in such plants as the silvery Saxifrages can never be so well seen as in a wall at the level of the eye or just above or below it; and plain to see are all the pretty ways these small plants have of seating themselves on projections or nestling into hollows, or creeping over stony surface as does the Balearic Sandwort [*Arenaria balearica*] or standing like *Erinus* with its back pressed to the wall in an attitude of soldier-like bolt-uprightness.[16]

As for the arrangement of plants in the wall, Miss Jekyll argued that:

Often walls are planted with too large a variety of plants that are in sight at the same time, with no particular thought as to their suitability as companions; a case of want of judgement that spoils many a garden. For whether it concerns flower borders or rockwork or watery places, the same main rule is one that is safe to follow—that is, to have only a few kinds of flowering plants at a time in view together, and that those few should be chosen for their pleasant interharmony, to be quietly enjoyed before passing on to another satisfying association. In rock-work or planted dry-walling some such vigilance is specially desirable, for the vertical presentment arrests the eye more readily than the horizontal, and therefore demands the more careful consideration.[17]

Farrer is often credited with inventing the 'Moraine'. This is highly unlikely, however for the Reverend Charles Wolley-Dod made what he called 'potato ridges' at Edge Hall in Cheshire and he died when Farrer was only 24. However, the latter did popularise the idea through his writings to such an extent that he was known, by Bowles at least, as the 'Moraine Magician'. Needless to say, an idea that he took to himself was bound to become shrouded in hyperbole. In *In a Yorkshire Garden* he referred to it as quite the most important discovery ever made in the culture of alpine plants in England.

One vast and invaluable advantage that the moraine possesses is that even the smallest gardens can have one; and that it costs literally nothing. No rocks, no heavy carting, no big purchase of soil or stone, not any handsome lie of the land required—four small rocks, perhaps, to hold up the bed, and even this is an artistic finick, and quite unnecessary; as, for utilitarian purposes, you can make your moraine just anywhere you like, by merely taking out so much soil from a bed or border, and then filling up the whole with fine road-metal and a little dust or soil. My first moraine, as a matter of fact, *is* an artistic finick; and I contemplate it with eternal pleasure. I made it all with my own two hands, and I do sincerely contemplate the result and find it good.[18]

He arranged four large blocks of limestone in a hollow square, which he filled full of sharp drainage material covered by blue limestone chips and a very little soil. In this he grew mossy and silver saxifrages, *Eritrichium* and *Edraianthus pumilio*. The word 'moraine' is of course a misnomer; the modern one 'scree' is more descriptive and less misleading. As Farrer admitted:

This is no more than an extreme extension of the chip principle, and though it bears the name, has no relation to the barren moraines of the glaciers, but rather to the upmost shingle-slopes in the highest folds of the mountains, where the loveliest and choicest of all their flowers are gathered in the fine loose slides of stone, moistened beneath by the rivers of the melting snow.[19] [As I said—'scree'.]

This moistening beneath is important and led Farrer and others to water their moraines from below with pipes which even had taps that could be turned on and off. He advised sinking a perforated pipe attached to a water-cock, twelve inches below the ground.

For, and this is a point I want to rub into the hard of heart and unbelieving, the essential quality of a moraine, which looks so utterly arid and dry on a sunny day, is that it is never, never, never, too dry or too wet ... In the wettest and most torrential downpours of autumn, the moraine sends the surplus moisture running quickly down among the stones, till there is no excess of it left to corrode the dormant roots; and in summer again, when the whole garden is cracked and panting with thirst, that moraine is always cool and moist a couple of inches under the surface ... The fact is, that while rain or watering-pot showers run quickly away down through the chips, the resultant dampness can never run away, nor

evaporate, through all the layers of stone that fill the depths, and lie on the surface, for ever checking any transpiration of moisture from the ground beneath.

And therefore I say it again, with all the weight of a Pope pronouncing *ex cathedra*, no summer drought that ever parched need make you unhappy about your moraine ... for, while all the rest of the garden is agonising and gaping for water, that most thirsty-looking place of all, mere wilderness of dry stone-flakes that it is, will be showing its plants as green and healthful as you please; and, if you poke your finger below the arid, hot surface, you will come at once into a region of uniform and most pleasant cool humidity.[20]

He advised that the tap be on from April till the end of September. The moraine was a most ingenious idea, especially because he proposed that it be raised, rendering major excavation unnecessary and making the tiny plants more easy to see.

Bowles mentioned in *My Garden in Spring* the raised mounds at Wolley-Dod's Edge Hall, but:

Then arose the prophet. The abundant rainfall of Ingleborough and the local limestone ... aided and abetted by river silt from the lake's mouth and chips of all sizes from the mountain side, were only waiting for Mr. Farrer's master mind to plan their combination and lo! a new era dawned. The most discontented of his alpine treasures flourished, the great news went forth to the world, a series of books in slate-coloured covers became the foundation of conversation, even at dinner, to the great annoyance of those who wait and therefore should expect all things to come to them. This is a fact: a head gardener, in speaking of the extraordinary wave of the fashion of gardening, told me that the men in the house complained bitterly that, whereas once upon a time they picked up innumerable sporting tips and had much interesting gossip to listen to, nowadays the talk at dinner was all Latin names and about soils and gardening books. Now the moraine holds the field.[21]

In Farrer's moraine, he even had some success with that most difficult of high alpine rarities, *Eritrichium nanum*, and also *Androsace glacialis*, its 'peer in glory, and in general mimpish miffiness'.[22]

Farrer will be remembered also, at least by me, for his Cliff, but then I have scrambled along the track, more fitting for goats than humans, that leads to this sheer and magnificent limestone face beside the Ingleborough Lake. Sadly, all that it yields up after 50 years is a few ferns and one or two plants of ramonda, probably because, in the intervening time, trees have grown above and dripped remorselessly on the moisture-haters below. It was however, an inspired idea.

There is a story that Farrer rowed out on the Lake in a boat, and shot seed from an air-rifle towards the Cliff, hoping it would stick and germinate. He certainly admitted that:

... choice treasures were sown by me in detail, last year, [1907] when I spent many a long afternoon of the most finicking needlework, pricking a pattern of rare plants into every line of crevice, no matter how minute,

inserting each pricked seed on the point of the tie-pin, previously licked to make the seed adhere. Sometimes the seed, despite the precaution, fell off and was lost; sometimes, by a too-firm pressure into its cranny, it was burst and spoiled. On the whole, though, that was a successful work, and little plants are now bushing where you would not have thought it possible that even a lichen could find lodgement.[23]

He wrote of its 'Great Crevice', where he planted his saxifrages, the plants that he most wished to succeed there,

... this has all been planted thoroughly, and sown as well, ... On rope ladders up and down went the nimble toilers; my [Nursery] Manager has no less a zeal for this magnificent place than I myself, and takes vast pride in it; and accordingly, if you look up from the path,

Figure 10.6 The Limestone Cliff Beside Ingleborough Lake

and crick your neck, you will see all the little crevices and couloirs, up and up and up, planted with lines of Silver Saxifrages . . . until you lose all notion of any artifice, but imagine that you are, indeed, looking up to some unattainable Saxifrage-cliff in Dolomites or Pyrenees.

As for me, the sight makes me say *Nunc Dimittis*: so far and away more satisfactory is it than any other thing I have yet seen achieved upon this sinful and ineffectual earth.[24]

In the light of later circumstances I find this passage almost unbearably affecting. It is no one's fault that his saxifrages no longer glisten amongst the limestone gullies; perhaps we should simply marvel that they ever did.

. . . I don't think I have ever written about an Alpine lawn. [wrote Miss Sackville-West, in 1954] Those fortunate people who have walked over the high alpine pastures of Switzerland or French Savoy or the Austrian Dolomites will know what I mean. In that clean, pure air, fresh as iced water and fluty as a glass of hock, the bright flowers bejewel the turf and cluster up against the natural outcrops of grey rock, edging the quick, narrow rills, silvery as minnows as they trickle from their source: blowing in the mountain breeze and crouching inch-low to the ground in an instinct of self-protection against the mountain gales.

We cannot aspire to so majestic a setting, but in a humble way we can reproduce a patch of Alpine meadow in an English garden. It makes the ideal approach to the little foothills of a rock-garden. The essential thing is to make it as dense as possible; it must be woven, tight as a carpet or a tapestry. Clearly we cannot use grass as a foundation, unless we are prepared to clip it with nail-scissors, so I suggest some of the close-carpeting plants: the creeping thymes, the little mints, the common yellow stone-crop, the camomile, the blue speedwell, anything which crawls and creeps and mats itself into a green drugget mosaiced in its season by its small gay flowers. If the spring-flowering gentian *acaulis* will grow for you, so much the better; it usually grows all right, forming a thick green mat, even if it does not flower, and a thick green mat is all-important. Again, patches of the silvery *Raoulia australis* are densely matted,

but a little apt to take on a moth-eaten appearance. I should not mind some aubretia, discreetly used and not allowed to encroach, nor should I mind some wild violets, reminiscent of the Alpine viola or of our own harebell on the Downs.[25]

So much for the situations in which alpines could thrive, but what constituted an alpine anyway? On the face of it, Farrer's definition was nonsensical but it had an inner logic.

. . . my own definition includes everything that will look well in a rock-garden. The definition, therefore, is the loosest possible, for all depends on the size of your ground. On a big bold bank bamboos and *Lilium auratum* and Japanese Cherries have their place, and look superb. In a small garden their very notion is disproportionate . . . I myself would only plead for the absolute exclusion of all double flowers, except the Double Orange Welsh Poppy [I disagree; I think it looks like a garish and indifferently-made tissue paper flower] from the rock-garden, and of all Annuals, only admitting a few of tiny nature and special beauty. It is possible to cram a bare rock-garden with Godetias and annual Linums and *Eschscholtzia*—you may even get a pretty, dazzling effect. But this effect is bastard art, illegitimate, ungenuine. It is no more right or appropriate than to put the prettiest of French picture-hats on the Venus of Milo. The rock-garden is a place sacred to the brave perennials of the mountains; therefore to contrast their antlike perseverance with the grasshopper frivolity of an annual is to perpetrate a crying discord . . .

But even when you have excluded Annuals, and reckoned with your available space, the question of what constitutes fitness for the rock-garden still remains. All plants of the rock-garden are by no means mountain or rock-species—who would do without *Anemone robinsoniana* or *Iris gracilipes*? Nor are all rock-plants by any means eligible for cultivation—who wants to be bothered with the ugly little glacial Camomiles or Plantains?[26]

He was not saying that the mass of the plants grown on the rock-garden would exist as well elsewhere; only that some plants would look well there even though not strictly alpine plants.

Figure 10.7 Anemone robinsoniana. *(From Fourth Edition of* The Wild Garden, *by William Robinson)*

What is so terrible and, I suppose, fascinating about rock-gardening, is that you can take all the advice on offer as Gospel, and go to great lengths to cultivate alpines well, but, because so many of the plants that you wish to share your climate are alien, failure is assured. That may be partly the reason why Farrer liked British alpine natives so much for many of them grew on Ingleborough mountain and would condescend to move down the hill a little way and settle in his garden. There is always a special pleasure in seeing a plant you have met in the wild, flourishing in your garden; certainly that was half the fun of plant-hunting for Farrer. But some plants he did have difficulty with, and these he divided into two categories, the 'miff' and the 'mimp'.

16. The old Alpine House at Wisley in early spring (see Ch. 13)

17. The White Garden – Sissinghurst (see Ch. 5)

18. The Rose Garden – Sissinghurst (see Ch. 5)

A miff [in this case *Myosotis rupicola*] is a plant which, in the midst of seeming life, is in death and expires abruptly; a mimp [for example, *Gentiana verna*] is one that for ever hangs on the edge of death, trailing a sickly existence towards inevitable extinction.[27]

For many people, the mere mention of the word rock-garden banishes all notion of arrangement and colour combinations; these are suffocated under the weight of the anxiety to give plants the conditions they require. The growing of alpines and their natural arrangement are not mutually exclusive considerations, however, nor should they be.

Robinson believed in

the great superiority of natural grouping over the botanical or labelled style of little single specimens of a great number of plants. [This is a sin that particularly besets rock-gardeners, probably because they feel they will never learn the names of alpines otherwise.] In a few yards of border, in the ordinary way, there would be fifty or more kinds, but nothing pretty for those who have ever seen the beautiful mountain gardens ... Through bold and natural grouping we may get fine colour without a trace of formality. But most gardeners find it difficult to group in this natural way, because so used to setting things out in formal lines. But a little attention to natural objects will help us to get away from set patterns, and let things intermingle here and there and run into each other to form groups such as we may see among the rocks by alpine paths.[28]

I mentioned in the Introduction what a painful task of selection this was, and nowhere do I feel the burden more heavy than when choosing pieces on alpine plants. Farrer's two volumes of *The English Rock Garden* alone make this difficult. The lion's share must go, of course, to him because the study and appreciation of alpines was his life's work.

Take it all in all, perhaps Gentiana offers the rock-garden more glory than any other race, and more persistently denies it. To please Primula is possible, to cope with Campanula is even comfortable; but there is no jesting with a Gentian, except, indeed, when the Gentian does the jesting—grows ample and splendid and hearty, only to gratify you at the end with dingy little flowers amid a mass of foliage so ill-pleasing that you feel indeed more mocked by such a success than if the plant has followed the example of its beautiful cousins and wholly refused to grow. All the more noble Gentians, indeed, may be said to be a kittle cattle, and hard to please; but when pleased, with what pleasure do they not repay the pleaser! Those all are children of pure mountain air and moisture, Oreads beyond all others impatient of the plain-lands; they have no down like Androsace to threaten danger and show dislike of wet; they are not living limpets of the rock, like the saxatile Campanulas and Primulas. But their hunger is always for the air of the hills, and, even more, for that persistent aura of moisture in the clear atmosphere which the sunlight draws from the steaming flanks of the mountains when the high snows are gone or going, throughout the growing period of the Gentians on their slopes. Therefore ... the alpine section, where all the Queens of the family are gathered together, require undoubtedly the most especial conditions. But these granted, the difficulties fade as the silver clouds of morning fade from the Tombea in sunrise, leaving the blue and violet masses of *Gentiana verna* jewelled with fine dew-drops in the early freshness of day.[29]

Dear also to Farrer's heart were the saxifrages; of these he had at one time a greater number than anyone else, in Britain at least. For him the most valuable of them, as a rock-garden plant, was *Saxifraga aeizoon*, a plant that Robinson described rather unkindly in *Alpine Flowers for English Gardens* as 'not a pretty-flowering kind' of saxifrage. Farrer, however, had found a particularly good form of it in the Bernese Oberland, which has remained firmly in cultivation.

My dearest pride ... is a certain very wonderful *aeizoon* that I found myself last year— on a precipitous unprolific shale-slope below the Tossenhorn ... there, in that unprofitable place, did I run plump on *Saxifraga aeizoon Rex* ... and there was only one solitary clump of him! The *King-aeizoon*, in the first place, is an *aeizoon* pur-sang, with no drop of blood inherited from any other Saxifrage: in the second place, he is by far the tallest, stoutest, solidest *aeizoon* I have ever seen: in the third place, even in that vigorous clan he seems the most vigorous; in the fourth place, his tall and stalwart stems are an ardent carmine; in the fifth place, his gracefully-carried abundant flowers are larger than any of his kindred's, and of an infinitely brighter and cleaner unflecked whiteness, most effulgent to behold.[30]

But he warned of the perils he had found in specialising in saxifrages.

For years I have gone on acquiring saxifrages, until I have now got together a collection which is said to be about the largest known. And this I say not in pride, but for an excuse: for such is the welter of spurious forms in which I lie entangled that I envy from afar the neat simplicity of those gardens that rest content with two or three unquestioned and distinct species ... But if once one sets out to specialise, as I have done, one has to accumulate every form, spurious or not, in order to collate false and true, and get some idea of the entire race; and then, when you have got to know the impostors, you never dare resist one of the great names if you see it in a catalogue, on the chance that it may really cover the plant it belongs to. And so the tale grows, and when you have all the innocent impostors filling frames and beds they are most of them so pretty and all of them so innocent of intentional fraud, that no heart could find itself capable of ejecting them into the outer darkness of the rubbish-heap. I hate destroying, or throwing away—I can only do it with coarse uglies and herbaceous stuff; and even they have to be planted out in the wild garden at a vast cost of time and trouble. But it does seem to me such black ingratitude to kill a plant that has been at all the trouble of growing and flowering ... It is true I have neither mourned nor replaced [*Saxifraga*] *androsacea* and *varians* but to be calm about a guest's departure is quite a different thing from hoofing him violently out.[31]

I have written of Farrer's joy and triumph at finding *Eritrichium nanum* in the high Alps (see Chapter 6). Here is a description of the difficulties of cultivating it in the moist atmosphere of the Yorkshire Moors.

But the King of the Alps, when all is said and done, should be adored not touched. He is so impossible of cultivation that to take him from his native crevices seems murder as clear as to bruise a butterfly in our hands—an act more certain to put the blue heavens (whence the plant has surely descended straight and undefiled upon our dusty earth) in a rage, than any number of robin redbreasts in cages. Impossible? Yes not impossible, with great pains and fusses, to keep alive, alone and palely loitering, in his pot or prepared nook; but impossible, indeed, to make anything but a homesick exile, impossible to inspire with the air of his lost hills amid our pallid temperatures, or fill his veins with the blood of blueness that he draws from the blasts of the wind-swept arêtes where he has his home. And yet, and yet—what gardener worth his salt will ever give up hope of a happy and hearty Eritrichium? Somewhere, somewhere in the world, on some strange mountain or penguin-haunted Arctic isle, there must surely be an Eritrichium, form or species, that shall prove of happier temper, and gratify the lucky gardener with the garter of his highest ambition. Indeed Eritrichium is more to blame than the collector, for it looks so happy, so indestructible and cosy in its crevice or sandy slope, that it does not seem possible for a mass so compact of blossom, so tidily rooted in a ball of fibre, to prove anything but as robust as it looks. The plant provokes the trowel. In cultivation then, let us do the best we can, seeing that no amount of wise words will ever induce us to come empty-handed off a mile-long ridge, turquoised with round slabs of blue; let Eritrichium be *bone-dry* in light sandy gritty mould all the winter through, from September to March, and from that time onward let it be in a sunny moraine, or very morainy chipful mixture, with water flowing underneath. For it is not perhaps always realised how much water the root will not only take but actually demand throughout its growing period—so long as that water is not administered over the soft and silver-silky coat. Another point that is not realised is one that too much escapes the notice of those who cope not only with this but with other presumably difficult alpine species. Our natural first inclination is to put something rare and difficult into a rare choice place all by itself, where it cannot be invaded and worried by rivals. But this is precisely what the poor thing does not want; it misses in its loneliness the cheery society of the little grasses and weeds of the hills, that made company for it at home, gave its roots something to fight, something to carry off superfluous moisture and fatness, kept it going, in fact, with the interest and keenness of life which is always sure to flag, alike in plants and humans, under the system of too elaborate shelter and seclusion. So Eritrichium rarely if ever grows alone, and is always happiest and at his widest tuffets and broadest expanses of blue smile, if he is wrestling it out with the smallest and finest of herbage, Arenarias, Sedums, minute high-alpine Gentians, and all the little lovely fry that fill the upmost gaunt ridges with life.[32]

Equal to his knowledge of the forms of Saxifrages was that of the genus Primula which he sought both in Europe and in the Far East. *Primula marginata* especially took his heart; and Bowles' too. One of the easiest of the European primulas, he wrote, it needed to be set into vertical rock-work because that is what happened in Nature. In a border it grew out of the ground and looked leggy.

In time it will form a sheet; the trunks are fibrous and woody, haunted by golden meal among the fibrosities of their coat; the rosettes are built of handsome leathern foliage, thick and grey, picturesquely toothed, and with the ample toothing outlined, especially when the leaves are young, with the same golden meal in a conspicuous hem. Early spring calls forth the flowers ... of a beauty unbelievable: wide-open saucers of the loveliest lavender-blue, pure and clear, with infinitesimal atoms of white powder hovering densely on their eye, like globules in a shower on the surface of a pool.[33]

Hybrids in the wild had long been sought in vain, but in 1913, in the Cottian hills, Farrer and Bowles found a crossing between *marginata* and *viscosa*, which was named *Primula × Crucis* Bowles. And they found other crossings between the same parents.

There was one form among them of a beauty so overwhelming that it can only be realised when I say that it was three times offered by its finder to the eponymous disco-

verer, and no less than three times refused, thus postulating a heart-breaking degree of virtue on the part of the refuser, no less than on that of the offerer, such as could be called out by no less momentous occasion than a matter of horticultural life and death.[34]

This he named *Primula × Crucis*, Blue Bowl, which was a pun on his friend's name, and the sort of joke Farrer enjoyed. I can just picture the scene on the mountainside, Bowles chivalrously offering Farrer the honour of having the plant named after him, and Farrer histrionically but resolutely refusing.

And so on to Edelweiss, probably the most overrated of all alpines; overrated in its charms and overrated in the supposed difficulties of its cultivation. I have seen it growing perfectly content in a gritty soil a few feet above sea level in Lincolnshire.

And now we come to the arch-imposter of the garden—the Flannel-flower of the Alps, so ridiculously sought after and marvelled at. The man who first called it 'Edelweiss' was a master of humour; the plant is neither noble or white. I am far from denying the strange, wonderful beauty of the thing—the hoary leaves and hoary star-flowers are marvellously fascinating. It is the monstrous claims of the plant that I protest against. Many people regard it as a typical alpine plant—as *the* typical plant of high, perilous peaks; many people yearly topple off precipices in their attempts to find it; and the first question that all strangers put on entering a rock-garden is the reverent whisper, 'Do you grow the Edelweiss?' Now, so far from being *the* typical plant, the Edelweiss is not even an alpine plant at all. It is a desert plant (from the great Siberian wastes), whose fluffy seeds allow it to spread far and wide ...

He denied any merit in being able to grow the Edelweiss.

A more robust weed doesn't exist ... Plant it high, give it poor soil, and a dressing of lime to whiten it; then there isn't anything of stouter health in the garden ... If only Edelweiss would stand on his own merits, and be content with recognition as a very beautiful, interesting Siberian, that would be all right; it is when this alien immigrant presumes to pose as the type-plant of the mountains, that we are forced to unveil his imposture, and declare him the easiest of border-species; when he falsely absorbs the homage that is really due to *Eritrichium* and *Androsace*, that we find ourselves bound to denounce him as a flannelette fraud, composed entirely of deception, without and within, a bunch of whitened leaves masquerading as a blossom, and an easygoing, sand-loving parvenu from the deserts masquerading as a peer to the real, proud-tempered aristocracy of the mountains.[35]

Notes

1. W. Robinson, *Alpine Flowers for English Gardens*, 1st edn (John Murray, 1870), pp. 72–7.

2. E.A. Bowles, *My Garden in Spring*, 1st edn (T.C. and E.C. Jack, 1914), pp. vii–viii.

3. W. Robinson, *Alpine Flowers for Gardens*, 4th edn (John Murray, 1910), p. xviii.

4. R. J. Farrer, *My Rock Garden*, facsimile of 4th impression (Theophrastus, 1971), pp. 7–8.

5. R. J. Farrer, *The English Rock Garden*, 4th impression (2 vols., T.C. and E.C. Jack, 1928), vol. 1, pp. xxix–xxx.

6. Bowles, *My Garden in Spring*, pp. 252–3.

7. Robinson, *Alpine Flowers for Gardens*, p. 99.

8. Farrer, *The English Rock Garden*, vol. 1, pp. xxxii–xxxiii.

9. Farrer, *My Rock Garden*, p. 8.

10. W. Robinson, *The English Flower Garden*, 6th edn (John Murray, 1898), pp. 143–5.

11. Farrer, *The English Rock Garden*, vol. 1, p. xxvii.

12. Ibid., p. xxx.

13. Robinson, *Alpine Flowers for English Gardens*, pp. 33–4.

14. Robinson, *The English Flower Garden*, p. 152.

15. Farrer, *My Rock Garden*, p. 75.

16. G. Jekyll, *Wall and Water Gardens*, 5th edn (Country Life, 1913), pp. 2–3.

17. G. Jekyll, *A Gardener's Testament*, Francis Jekyll and G.C. Taylor (eds.) facsimile of 1937 edn (Antique Collectors Club, 1982), pp. 239–40.

18. R. J. Farrer, *In a Yorkshire Garden*, 1st edn (Edward Arnold, 1909), pp. 167–8.

19. Farrer, *The English Rock Garden*, vol. 1, xxxv.

20. Farrer, *Yorkshire Garden*, pp. 172–3.

21. Bowles, *My Garden in Spring*, pp. 104–5.

22. Farrer, *Yorkshire Garden*, p. 231.

23. Ibid., p. 276.

24. Ibid., pp. 286–7.

25. V. Sackville-West, *More for Your Garden*, 1st edn (Michael Joseph, 1955), pp. 63–5.

26. Farrer, *My Rock Garden*, pp. 20–1.

27. R. J. Farrer, *Alpines and Bog Plants*, 1st edn (Edward Arnold, 1908), p. 136.

28. Robinson, *The English Flower Garden*, p. 151.

29. Farrer, *The English Rock Garden*, vol. 1, pp. 359–60.

30. Farrer, *Yorkshire Garden*, pp. 54–5.

31. Farrer, *My Rock Garden*, pp. 90–1.

32. Farrer, *The English Rock Garden*, vol. 1, pp. 337–9.

33. Ibid., vol. 2, p. 153.

34. Ibid., p. 155.

35. Farrer, *My Rock Garden*, pp. 142–3.

CHAPTER
❧ 11 ❧

Trees & Shrubs, including Roses

The current intense interest in the growing of trees and shrubs, especially shrubs, is due in large part to the inspirational writings of Robinson, Miss Jekyll and Miss Sackville-West, absorbed by the last few generations and handed on, like a baton in a relay race, to later writers. Even now, when few gardens are more than a half-acre in size, we still consider planting at least one or two trees and succeed in making, in many instances, little exotic forests. The impulse is good, even if the result sometimes lacks restraint. Our response to the dwarfing of our gardens is often to use smaller trees, which on the whole works well in the case of Malus, Pyrus, Sorbus and Acer, although it is even possible to overplant these. After all, trees of moderate height may have considerable girth or spread. Where the gardener may truly make a mistake, and the fault often lies with misinformation from the nurseryman, is in the setting down of, say, a blue Atlas cedar, a tree that in Britain has been known to reach thirty metres, no more than two metres from the sitting-room picture window. In 30 years time, if an infuriated future owner does not cut it down before that, nothing will be discernible of the view except the cedar's graceful glaucous branches. The anxiety I feel about overplanted gardens is nothing new. In 1924, Miss Jekyll wrote,

There are some places, unfortunately only too many, where there were once wide clean sweeps of ancient lawn beautiful and restful in themselves, that have been sadly spoilt by the intrusion of specimen conifers. It was tempting to plant them when about fifty years ago they were first brought to England, especially as a young conifer has a certain attractive trimness that commends it to favour. But it is sad to see in what one remembers as a beautiful widespread lawn, already sufficiently furnished with noble cedars and other large surrounding trees, a miscellaneous collection of these conifers, one each of perhaps a dozen kinds, now of forty years' growth and almost meeting and obstructing the garden prospect in every direction. If only they had been given some near spaces of parkland, with time to see how they would develop, they would by now have been well-grown trees of value as specimens for botanical observation.[1]

The Victorian era was the great time for the introduction of trees, especially evergreens. David Douglas (1799–1834), for example, introduced in his short life the Douglas fir (*Pseudotsuga menziesii*), the sitka spruce (*Picea sitchensis*), *Abies grandis, Abies nobilis, Thuja plicata* and the Monterey pine (*Pinus radiata*). It is hard for us now to realise to what extent the landscape was changed by the arrival of these exotics. It is, however, still possible to see plantations of conifers close to Victorian houses, consisting of a miscellany of cypresses and firs, often very large and very close together. Naturally, the introduction of all these hardy trees gave the impetus to nurserymen to develop new forms from them. They were helped by the conifer's amenable habit of 'sporting', that is, throwing out shoots of a different colour or size, which could be propagated by cuttings and the desirable characteristic perpetuated. These forms of conifer put Robinson in fighting mood.

One of the most baneful things in our gardens has been the introduction of distorted and ugly conifers which often disfigure the fore-grounds of beautiful houses. These are often sports and variations raised in modern days as is the case with the too common Irish Yew. It is not only that we have to deplore the tender trees of California, which in their own country are beautiful, though, unhappily, not so in ours, [here he was too harsh; it has only been through trial and error that beautiful conifers like *Cupressus macrocarpa*, a most useful species that will withstand salt winds, have been found to be hardy in many parts of the British Isles] but it is the mass of distorted, unnatural and ugly forms—the names of which disfigure even the best catalogues—that is most confusing and dangerous. In one foreign catalogue there are no less than twenty-eight varieties of the Norway Spruce, in all sorts of dwarf and monstrous shapes—some of them, indeed, dignified with the name monstrosa—not one of which should ever be seen in a garden. The true beauty of the pine comes from its form and dignity, as we see it in old Firs that clothe the hills of Scotland, California or Switzerland. It is not in distortion or in little green pincushions we must look for the charm of the Pine, but rather in storm-tossed head and often naked stems; and hence all these ridiculous forms should be excluded from gardens of any pretence to beauty![2]

He had another dislike, about which he was inordinately unfair.

Of all ugly things, nothing is worse than the variegated conifer, which usually perishes as soon as its variegated parts die, the half dead tree often becoming a bush full of wisps of hay.[3]

Care and understanding are obviously necessary when deciding where and how to place trees so foreign in appearance as most conifers are. The task is easier with the native ones. Despite being umbrageous and poisonous, no one has a bad word to say for the English yew. Bowles was fond of the ancient ones in his garden which lined the bank of the New River. That may, however, have been more for the warming work they gave him in winter than anything else.

The fine old Yews along the river have been there some three centuries, and never look better than during the winter months. When the weather is too abominable for any other garden work I put on an old coat and take a scrubbing-brush and work away under the shelter of their umbrella-like heads, and get warm and pleasantly tired by the good exercise derived from scrubbing their stems. I learnt this form of winter sport from Glasnevin ... I do not believe anyone can know what an absorbing and fascinating job is the peeling of an old Yew tree. The scaling off of the loose flakes first, then peeling off large flat pieces and leaving the smooth surface below, and the pleasure grows as one gradually reveals the real outline of the trunk. But the best bit of all is the final brushing over, when the colour turns from that of the lean of a rather dry ham to a rich warm crimson under the scrubbing-brush.[4]

Miss Jekyll liked the native conifers in her wood, especially a fine, double-stemmed Scots pine, and the native juniper, *Juniperus communis*, which she considered thoroughly underrated, uncommon in the wild and hard to procure from nurseries. In one of her best descriptive passages, she depicted it in minutest detail.

Among the many merits of the Juniper, its tenderly mysterious beauty of colouring is by no means the least; a colouring as delicately subtle in its own way as that of cloud or mist, or haze in warm, hot woodland. It has very little of positive green; a suspicion of warm colour in the shadowy hollows and a blue-grey bloom of the tenderest quality imaginable on the outer masses of foliage. Each tiny, blade-like leaf has a band of dead, palest bluish-green colour on the upper surface, edged with a narrow line of dark green slightly polished; the back of the leaf is of the same full, rather dark green, with slight polish, it looks as if the green back had been brought up over the edge of the leaf to make the dark edging on the upper surface. The stems of the twigs are of a warm, almost foxy colour, becoming darker and redder in the branches. The tips of the twigs curl over or hang out on all sides towards the light and the 'set' of the individual twigs is full of variety. This arrangement of mixed colouring and texture, and infinitely various position of the spiny little leaves, allows the eye to penetrate unconsciously a little way into the mass, so that one sees as much tender shadow as actual leaf surface, and this is probably the cause of the wonderfully delicate and, so to speak, intangible quality of colouring.[5]

The serious drawback of conifers, especially in restricted surroundings, is the amount of shade they cast, especially in winter-time; they are therefore passive agents of overcrowding, something which Robinson could not tolerate.

After all is said about shade, the most essential thing about it in British gardens is not to have too much of it. Most of us plant too thickly to begin with. The trees get too close and we neglect to thin them, the result being mouldy, close avenues, dripping, sunless groves, and dismal shrubberies, more depressing than usual in a wet season. It is only when we get the change from sun to shade with plenty of movement for air that we enjoy shade. We cannot feel the air move in an over-planted place, and there are in such no broad breadths of sunlight to give the airy look that is so welcome ...

Very harmful in its effect on the home landscape is the common objection to cutting down of ill-placed trees crowded to the detriment of the landscape and often to the air and light about a house. The majority of the trees that are planted in and near gardens are planted in ignorance of their mature effects, the landscape beauty of half the country seats in England being marred by unmeaning trees and trees out of place. I have known people who wanted to remove a solid Georgian house rather than take down a tree of moderate dimensions which made the house dark and mouldy and obscured the view of far finer trees beyond it, and it is not long since a man

wrote to the *Times* after a storm to say that one of his elm trees had fallen through the dining-room ceiling when he was at luncheon and that elms were not good trees to put over the house![6]

These words of advice should weigh even more heavily on modern readers.

Another disadvantage of conifers is that, though by no means the same in all seasons, often taking on enriched colouring in the winter-time and splendid in their new growth and male and female 'flowers' in the spring, they do not afford us the satisfaction of seeing the shape of their naked branches in winter.

On the other hand, wrote Miss Jekyll,

In summer-time one never really knows how beautiful are the forms of the deciduous trees. It is only in winter, when they are bare of leaves, that one can fully enjoy their splendid structure and design, their admirable qualities of duly appointed strength and grace of poise, and the way the spread of the many-branched head has its equivalent in the wide-reaching ground grasp of the root. And it is interesting to see how, in the many different kinds of tree, the same laws are always in force, and the same results occur, and yet by the employment of what varied means. For nothing in the growth of trees can be much more unlike than the habit of the oak and that of the weeping willow, though the unlikeness only comes from the different adjustment of the same sources of power and the same weights, just as in the movement of wind-blown leaves some flutter and some undulate, while others turn over and back again. Old apple-trees are specially noticeable for their beauty in winter, when their extremely graceful shape, less visible when in loveliness of spring bloom or in rich bounty of autumn fruit, is seen to fullest advantage.[7]

Also more obvious in winter are the barks of trees, many of which are very beautiful. Miss Jekyll planted rhododendrons amongst the birches in her wood because she liked the contrast of the white bark with the green leaves.

How the silver stems, blotched and banded with raised browns and greys so deep in tone that they show like a luminous black, tell among the glossy Rhododendron green; and how strangely different is the way of growth of the two kinds of tree; the tall white trunks spearing up through the dense, dark, leathery leaf-masses of solid, roundish outline, with their delicate network of reddish branch and spray gently swaying far overhead![8]

Miss Sackville-West liked

the tattery trees, whose bark curls off in strips like shavings. There is one called *Arbutus Menziesii*, with cinnamon-red bark which starts to peel of its own accord, and which you can then smooth away with your hand into something like the touch of sand-papered wood of a curious olive-green colour. It likes a sheltered corner, for it is not absolutely hardy. Then there is *Acer griseum*, the Paper-bark maple, with mahogany coloured-bark replaced by a brighter orange underneath and brilliantly red leaves in autumn. It is, in fact, one of the best for October–November colour. *Betula albo-sinensis var. septentrionalis* is a birch with a beautiful white and grey trunk ... It is, I think, one of the loveliest, though *Betula japonica* drips with most attractive little catkins in spring ...
Prunus serrula, sometimes sold as *serrula tibetica*, is a very striking tree with a shining mahogany bark. This does not take on so shaggy an appearance as some, but sheds its outer covering in circular strips, leaving the trunk with annular ridges that make it look as though it were wearing bracelets. Reddish and glossy, the freshly-revealed surface suggests the French polish sometimes used on fine old tables. It should be grown in very rich soil and planted where it can be seen, with the sun shining on it.[9]

The single most compelling reason, I would suggest, why trees are planted in gardens, is because of the colour of their leaves in autumn. Bowles wrote at length about it in *My Garden in Autumn and Winter*.

... an Autumn of brilliant tints, and a peaceful fall of leaves following the earlier frosts, should be looked upon as good and true signs of ripened wood and promise for the future, and if only it were not so fleeting, here to-day and gone in the night, the glory of autumnal tints would be as joyous as that afforded by any of the seasons. But only too frequently

when it is approaching its best and fullest pageantry a squall of heavy rain, lasting perhaps less than half an hour, a frost of anything over six degrees, [Fahrenheit] or a sudden change of wind may turn a scarlet pyramid of fire into bare black bones. One November day I received a telegram in fulfilment of a kind promise, bidding me hasten next day to Westonbirt [in Gloucestershire, now managed by the Forestry Commission] to see the autumnal tints, as they were at their best and might go at any minute. I rushed off and was in time, and that afternoon and next morning enjoyed a feast of beauty that far surpasses anything I had ever imagined possible in old England ... I carried away a wonderful vision of beauty to live in my memory, which I think, is all the more precious because, when next we met, Sir George [Holford] told me it was but a few hours after I left him in that fairyland of colour, that a storm of rain and wind swept over the hills and robbed him of all the best of the display.[10]

I can imagine Bowles deriving a certain unmalicious pleasure from that.
Miss Sackville-West suggested the placing of plants that coloured well in one portion of the garden to make the most effect.

In spring and summer one tends to forget the autumn days, but, when they arrive, with their melancholy and the spiders' webs so delicately and geometrically looped from the hedges, how grateful we are for the torch of a little tree or the low smoulder of leaves on azaleas and peonies. I feel sure that these effects should be concentrated into one area of the garden, preferably at a distance if space allows so that they may be seen from the windows in a rabble incarnadine.[11]

How typical of her that when searching for a simile for blood-red she should have used a Shakespearian word, with all the romance of old association.
Bowles believed that the Swamp Cypress, *Taxodium distichum*,

colours as finely as anything in the garden, first getting touched with yellow that deepens to orange, but ending off with a wonderful shade of deep red brown, the like of which I can only recall in a fox or a Hereford ox. Perhaps Indian red is the nearest thing in paints to its fullest and deepest colouring. It generally keeps its leaves on for a long period after they have turned colour, and is often the latest of the brightly coloured trees to lose them. And what a mess it does make if a high wind blows its feathery leaves all over the lawn and flower beds, giving these last the appearance of having been mulched with cocoanut fibre.[12]

One garden feature that has passed out of sight, as a result of the onslaught delivered by, amongst others, Robinson and Miss Jekyll, is the evergreen shrubbery, such a common feature of Victorian gardens. It is still to be found occasionally, composed of Phillyrea, spotty aucubas, laurels, box and privet in ill-favoured corners of Old Rectory gardens, remembered by generations of children as a dusty, evil-smelling refuge in games of 'Hide and Seek'. Robinson's view was that *flowering* shrubs were infinitely preferable to glossy, dripping evergreens in what he referred to as the 'choke-muddle shrubbery'. The publication of his views coincided with considerable activity on the part of plant-hunters like George Forrest and E.H. Wilson who were opening up the floral treasure chest of China.

The idea of the murderous common shrubbery is so rooted in the popular mind that it is almost hopeless to expect much change for the better. The true way is to depart wholly from it as a mass of *mixed* shrubs and beautiful families should be grouped apart. Each family or plant should have a separate place free from the all-devouring privet and laurel, and each part of the shrubbery should have its own character, which may easily be given to it by grouping instead of mixing, which ends in the starvation of the choice kinds. We do not allow stove and green-house plants to be choked in this way, yet no plants are more worthy of a distinct place and of care than hardy shrubs. Low flowering trees, like Hawthorns, group admirably on the turf, but the finer kinds of flowering shrubs should be planted in beds. The shrubbery itself need no longer be a dark dreary mass, but light and shade may play in it, its varied life be well shown and the habits and forms of each thing may be seen.[13]

Bowles grubbed out the old shrubbery in the garden at Myddelton House, in order to plant up his 'Lunatic Asylum'.

In the days of my early youth a vast clump ... of evergreens occupied the space which now forms my home for demented plants ... Portugal Laurels there were, and the still more objectionable Common Laurel; Laurustinus bushes, which in showery weather exhale an odour of dirty dog-kennel and an even dirtier dog; leprously spotted Aucubas and Privet jostled one another round the feet of two Weymouth Pines [*Pinus strobus*] and a dead Yew covered with Ivy, the whole dismal crew being rendered more awful and uninteresting by having all their attempts to show any beauty that might be inherent in their natural manner of growth nipped in the bud by the garden shears. This agglomeration consequently bore the semblance of a magnified dish of Spinach with a few trees emerging from the top, where a giant poached Roc's egg or two might have lain.[14]

The twisted Hazel was the first crazy occupant, and is perhaps the maddest of all even now. [It had been first found by Lord Ducie in a hedgerow, and he had given rooted layers to friends like Canon Ellacombe, who in turn gave a sucker to Bowles.] It is a most remarkable form, for it never produces a bit of straight wood, the stem between each leaf is curved as though one side had grown much faster than the other, and alternating lengths are generally curved in opposite directions; frequently they are twisted spirally as well, so that the whole bush is a collection of various curves and spirals, a tangle of crooks and cork screws from root to tip. They do not straighten out with age and thickening, and in winter, when leafless, the interlacing twigs are beautiful as well as curious, but when covered with the large crumpled leaves it has a heavy and somewhat diseased look, for each leaf is twisted or a little rolled, and they look as though attacked by leaf-rolling caterpillars. I have not seen catkins or nuts on it, and wonder whether the former would be curly lambs' tails, and the latter coiled like rams' horns.[15]

Most climbing plants are, of course, flowering shrubs, and Robinson in particular did much to popularise the idea of clothing house and gar-

Figure 11.1 White Climbing Rose Scrambling over Old Catalpa Tree

den walls with them, as well as tree stumps and even living trees. In a memorable passage (in Chapter 7) he bewailed the fact that when he was called in to redesign the garden at Shrubland Park in Suffolk, that had been laid out in the old way by Barry, the house was completely bare of softening climbing plants. He was obviously scandalised at such a missed opportunity for beauty.

To what extent it is desirable [wrote Miss Jekyll towards the end of her long life in 1924] to have climbing plants on house walls is a question that often arises. In the case of many houses, either of mean or of over-pretentious architecture, the more they are covered up the better; for if their designer has left a building that can only be considered to be in bad taste, it behoves the gardener to do what he can to give it decent clothing, if only of Ivy or a rampant growing Ampelopsis, either of which will save him the trouble of training. But in the case of a good building, though a carefully and duly restrained planting of its walls may give it an added grace, great care should be taken that nothing essential be hidden. Many a noble building has been shamefully buried under Ivy; moulded doors and windows have been reduced to dark holes, beautifully wrought pinnacles look like nothing but May-Day Jacks-in-the-green; buttresses have become shapeless green lumps; the whole wall face has lost every feature of plinth, string course and detail of good masonry. Better taste and knowledge are now remedying this desecration of worthy architecture and some of the grandest monuments of the past centuries have lately been relieved of their encumbrances of rampant vegetation.[16]

Robinson recognised that the training of climbers on houses often meant wiring and nailing, and so he advocated, as an alternative, growing vigorous climbers up trees, and fragile climbers, such as Clematis, through evergreen shrubs. This is, of course, what happens in nature.

Often stiff, unbroken masses of Rhododendrons and Evergreen flowering shrubs will be more varied if delicate flakes of Clematis (white, lavender, or claret-red) or the bright arrows of the Flame Nasturtium come among them here and there in autumn. The great showy hybrid Clematises of our gardens are not so good for this use as the more elegant wild Clematises of N. America, Europe and N. Africa such as the Hairbell and others of the less vigorous Clematis. These are so fragile in growth that many of them may be trusted among groups of choice shrubs like Azaleas, training themselves and throwing veils over the bushes here and there.[17]

Snobbishness [wrote Miss Sackville-West] exists among gardeners, even as it exists among other sections of the community. The gardener's special brand consists in a refusal to grow plants which, of startling beauty in themselves, have become too trite to seem worthy of a place in any self-respecting gardener's garden ... I must agree that we all get tired of seeing certain plants all over the place [like aubrieta and] the Virginia creeper, *Ampelopsis Veitchii*, glued to red-brick houses, where its colour swears horribly with the brick when it turns to flame in autumn. Yet, could we but behold either of these for the first time, we should shout in amazement.

It is too late to hope for such an experience, but I do suggest that much can be achieved by using these poor vulgarized plants in a different way and in the right place. There is, for instance, a big silver birch of my acquaintance into which a Virginia creeper has loosely clambered. When I first saw it, I couldn't think what it was. Great swags and festoons of scarlet hung in the sunlight amongst the black and silver branches of the tree, gracefully and gloriously looping from bough to bough, like something (I imagine, perhaps incorrectly) in a tropical forest, or at any rate like a stained glass window or like glasses of wine held up to the light. It convinced me once and for all that *Ampelopsis Veitchii* should be grown transparently, not plastered against a wall. Any tall old tree would serve the purpose, an ancient pear or apple, or a poplar if you cannot command a silver birch; and I think the same advice would apply to many of the ornamental vines, such as *Vitis Coignettiae*, with its great shield-shaped leaves of pink and gold, or *Vitis purpurea*, whose name explains itself.[18]

While on the subject of snobbery, Farrer maintained that he had an almost snobbish passion for magnolias.

At least, is it not in the essence of snobbishness passionately to cultivate and ensure the acquaintance of gorgeous people who have no great desire for the compliment?[19]

Certainly there is no finer wall-plant, in the south of Britain at least, than *Magnolia grandiflora*, as Miss Sackville-West confirms.

The flowers of *Magnolia grandiflora* look like great white pigeons settling among dark leaves ... It is not always easy to know what to put against a new red-brick wall; ... the cool green of the magnolia's glossy leaves and the utter purity of its bloom make it a safe thing to put against any background, however trying. Besides, the flower in itself is of such splendid beauty. I have just been looking into the heart of one. The texture of the petals is of a dense cream; they should not be called white; they are ivory, if you can imagine ivory and cream stirred into a thick paste, with all the softness and smoothness of youthful human flesh; and the scent, reminiscent of lemon, was overpowering ...

Goliath is the best variety. Wires should be stretched along the wall on vine eyes for convenience of future tying ... [Otherwise] The time may come when you reach out of your bedroom window to pick a great ghostly flower in the summer moonlight, and then you will be sorry if you find it has broken away from the wall and is fluttering on a loose branch, a half-captive pigeon trying desperately to escape.[20]

The most popular shrub in gardens, by a very long way, is the rose. This popularity has been, for more than a hundred years, the spur to feverish efforts on the part of nurserymen to raise new varieties. Much of it was wasted labour, at least as far as Bowles was concerned, as, for him, 'the various species and their forms and hybrids are the real Roses ...' They appealed strongly to him because,

I do so enjoy the beauty of form in the flowers: the central mass or ring of stamens and the simple outlines of the five equal petals in their endless variations of relative positions are always worth drawing, and have an expression, a symmetry, that I can only compare with the charm of a beautiful and familiar face. Who wants to see the human object of their devotion improved by multiplicity of noses of varying sizes, the innermost being little more than slices of nose so as to pack into the centre? Then why should a Rose need doubling?[21]

There is no reason why it should, but there are plenty of very beautiful roses that are double, especially those which Miss Sackville-West called 'gipsy roses'. But before we get on to those, this is what she had to say about a lovely species, *Rosa moyesii*, which E.H. Wilson introduced from China in 1894 and which is one of the glories of Sissinghurst.

This is a Chinese rose, and looks it. If ever a plant reflected all that we had ever felt about the delicacy, lyricism, and design of a Chinese drawing, *Rosa Moyesii* is that plant. We might well expect to Meet her on a Chinese printed paper-lining to a tea-chest of the time of Charles II when wall-papers first came to England, with a green parrot out of all proportion, perching on her slender branches. There would be no need for the artist to stylise her, for Nature has already stylised her enough. Instead, we meet her more often springing out of our English lawns, or overhanging our English streams, yet *Rosa Moyesii* remains for ever China. With that strange adaptability of true genius she never looks out of place. She adapts herself as happily to cosy England as to the rocks and highlands of Asia.

'Go, lovely rose'. She goes indeed, and quickly. Three weeks at most sees her through her yearly explosion of beauty. But her beauty is such that she must be grown for the sake of those three weeks in June. During that time her branches will tumble with the large, single, rose-red flower of her being. It is of an indescribable colour. I hold a flower of it here in my hand now, and find myself defeated in description. It is like the colour I imagine Petra to be, if one caught it at just the right moment of sunset. It is like some colours in a rug from Isfahan. It is like the dyed leather sheath of an Arab knife—and this I do know for certain, for I am matching one against the other, the dagger-sheath against the flower. It is like all those dusky rose-red things which abide in the mind as a part of the world of escape and romance ...[22]

She had little time for the Hybrid Teas which she damned with extremely faint praise.

I am not here thinking of the Hybrid Teas, well-groomed, well-taught, compliant and as tidy as any lady of fashion. I can see their beauty and their usefulness, but it is the gipsy roses that take my heart. More primly, people now call them the shrub roses, which indeed is a right and proper name for a rose that is in fact a flowering shrub, but to me they are the gipsies of the rose-tribe. They resent restraint; they like to express themselves in all their vigour freely as the fancy takes them, free as the dog-rose in the hedgerows ...[23]

The gipsy roses, for her, were all those that came before the Hybrid Teas and the Floribundas—the Centifolias, the Albas, the Mosses, the Gallicas, the Musks, the Bourbons and the Damasks. She also loved the Hybrid Perpetuals, and a great many climbing roses. One of her most favourite climbers was a white rose raised in 1915 called 'Paul's Lemon Pillar'.

It should not be called white. A painter might see it as greenish, suffused with sulphur-yellow, and its great merit lies not only in the vigour of its growth and wealth of flowering, but also in the perfection of its form. The shapeliness of each bud has a sculptural quality which suggests curled shavings of marble, if one may imagine marble made of the softest ivory suede. The full-grown flower is scarcely less beautiful; and when the first explosion of bloom is over, a carpet of thick white petals covers the ground, so dense as to look as though it had been deliberately laid.[24]

There is a strain of roses not grown much these days, mainly because the roses are a little tender, of which Robinson was especially fond. These were the Tea roses, so called because of their scent; they are the ancestors of our modern bedding roses. Some are quite perpetual. He grew them in large numbers at Gravetye.

These roses of garden origin are the loveliest things raised or grown by man: sweet with all the delicate fragrance of the morning air on down or Surrey heath, having the colours of the cloud, and all that is loveliest in form of bud and bloom. But these precious roses are things of cultivation only. Without the good gardener's spade and knife they would soon become a tangle with less meaning and beauty than the Wild Brier.[25]

Among the best that he grew were 'Marie van Houtte' and 'Anna Olivier', both of which are still in cultivation today.

On the other hand, he did not at all care for standard roses, which were all the vogue then, and have lingered on in park and private garden alike.

A taking novelty at first, few things have had worse influence on gardening than the Standard rose in all forms. Grown throughout Europe and Britain by millions, it is seen usually in a wretched state, and yet there is something about it which prevents us seeing its bad effect in the garden, and its evil influence on the cultivation of the Rose, for we now and then see a fine and even a picturesque Standard, when the Rose suits the stock it is grafted on, and the soil suits each; but this does not happen often ...

While of the evil effect of the Standard Rose any one may judge in the suburbs of every town, its other defects are not so clear to all, such as the exposure high in the air to winter's cold of varieties more or less delicate. On the tops of their stick supports they perish by thousands even in nurseries in the south of England ... If these same varieties were on their own roots, even if the severest winter killed the shoots, the root would be quite safe, and the shoots come up again as fresh as ever; so that the frost would only prune our rose bushes instead of killing them and leaving us a few dead sticks from the Dog Rose.[26]

Miss Sackville-West was not enamoured of all roses, either.

In a gracious, small and ancient town near where I live, someone has had the imagination to plant a hedge of rambler roses. It occupies the whole of his road frontage, about one hundred and fifty yards I believe, and in the summer months people come from all over the county to see it. I must admit that it is an impressive sight; a blaze of colour; a long, angry, startling streak, as though somebody had taken a red pencil and had scrawled dense red bunches all over a thicket-fence of green. A splendid idea; very effective; but, oh, how crude! I blink on seeing it; and having blinked, I weep. It is not only the virulence of the colour that brings tears to my eyes, but the regret that so fine an idea should not have been more fastidiously carried out. [And what was the offender?]

The hedge is made of *American Pillar*, a rose which, together with *Dorothy Perkins*, should be forever abolished from our gardens.[27]

Not wishing to end this chapter on a sour note, however, here is some quaint wishful thinking on the morally uplifting virtues of roses from Miss Jekyll.

The back-door region and back-yard of many a small house may be a model of tidy dullness, or it may be a warning example of sordid neglect; but a cataract of Rose-bloom will in the one case give added happiness to the well-trained servants of the good housewife, and in the other may redeem the squalor by its gracious presence, and even by its clean, fresh beauty put better thoughts and desires into the minds of slatternly people.[28]

Notes

1. G. Jekyll, *A Gardener's Testament*, Francis Jekyll and G.C. Taylor (eds.) facsimile of 1937 edn (Antique Collectors' Club, 1982), pp. 65–6.

2. W. Robinson, *The English Flower Garden*, 6th edn (John Murray, 1898), p. 295.

3. Ibid., p. 295.

4. E.A. Bowles, *My Garden in Autumn and Winter*, 1st edn (T.C. and E.C. Jack, 1915), pp. 194–6.

5. G. Jekyll, *Wood and Garden*, facsimile of 1st edn (Antique Collectors' Club, 1981), pp. 50–1.

6. Robinson, *The English Flower Garden*, p. 328.

7. Jekyll, *Wood and Garden*, pp. 43–4.

8. G. Jekyll, *Colour Schemes for the Flower Garden*, facsimile of 1936 edition (Antique Collectors' Club, 1982), pp. 24–5.

9. V. Sackville-West, *In Your Garden Again*, 1st edn (Michael Joseph, 1953), pp. 149–51.

10. Bowles, *My Garden in Autumn and Winter*, p. 162.

11. Sackville-West, *In Your Garden Again*, pp. 136–8.

12. Bowles, *My Garden in Autumn and Winter*, p. 166.

13. Robinson, *The English Flower Garden*, p. 125.

14. E.A. Bowles, *My Garden in Spring*, 1st edn (T.C. and E.C. Jack, 1914), p. 178.

15. Ibid., pp. 179–80.

16. Jekyll, *A Gardener's Testament*, p. 64.

17. Robinson, *The English Flower Garden*, pp. 130–1.

18. V. Sackville-West, *In Your Garden*, 1st edn (Michael Joseph, 1951), pp. 69–70.

19. R.J. Farrer, *In a Yorkshire Garden*, 1st edn (Edward Arnold, 1909), p. 63.

20. Sackville-West, *In Your Garden*, pp. 93–4.

21. E.A. Bowles, *My Garden in Summer*, 1st edn (T.C. and E.C. Jack, 1914), p. 50.

22. Sackville-West, *In Your Garden (Some Flowers)*, pp. 191–3.

23. V. Sackville-West, *Even More for Your Garden*, 1st edn (Michael Joseph, 1958), p. 106.

24. Sackville-West, *In Your Garden Again*, pp. 91–2.

25. Robinson, *The Wild Garden*, 1st edn (John Murray, 1870), pp. 120–3.

26. Robinson, *The English Flower Garden*, pp. 186–7.

27. Sackville-West, *In Your Garden Again*, pp. 27–8.

28. G. Jekyll and E. Mawley, *Roses for English Gardens*, facsimile of first edn (Antique Collectors' Club, 1982), p. 210.

CHAPTER
ᕦ 12 ᕤ

Bulbs

To the botanist the word bulb means a swollen food-storing organ that is made up of fleshy, colourless leaves, like the tulip and the daffodil, whereas crocuses, which are swollen stems, are corms, and dahlias, which are swollen roots, are tubers. However, to the ordinary gardener, 'bulb' is a term used generally to mean any storage organ, and may even sometimes refer to a rhizome. In this chapter, the word bulb has a wide meaning for we are interested less in taxonomic classification than in ordinary garden cultivation.

Iris unguicularis is, in most gardens, the first one of the year to flower, and one peculiarly dear to our hearts because it means flowers to pick in the dead dark days of winter.

The Algerian iris [wrote Miss Sackville-West] is known to most of us as *Iris stylosa*. It should, in fact, be called *Iris unguicularis*, because this is the older botanical name for it, *unguiculus* meaning a small or narrow claw. Do we have to bother about that? Let us, rather, record that it is the native of stony ground in Algeria, Greece, Crete, Syria and Asia Minor, and that it accommodates itself very willingly to an island, flowering before Christmas sometimes, especially after a hot, dry summer, and continuing to flower in mild weather right into March. You should search your clumps of the grass-like leaves every day

for possible buds, and pull the promising bud while it still looks like a tiny, tightly-rolled umbrella, and then bring it indoors and watch it open under a lamp. If you have patience to watch for long enough, you will see this miracle happen.[1]

Admiration for this iris, of which he had several forms all flowering at slightly different times, led Bowles into extravagance:

Suppose [he supposed] a wicked uncle who wished to check your gardening zeal left you pots of money on condition you grew only one species of plants: what would you choose? I should settle on *Iris unguicularis* as in summer one could get whiffs of other folks' roses and lilies and all the dull season enjoy the flowers of this beautiful Iris. It was some twenty-four years ago I first saw it in the gardens at La Mortola. Sir Thomas Hanbury parted its forelock of long leaves and displayed a mass of lilac blossoms, and then and there I vowed I must find further suitable sites for them.

... Patience seems to be the only manure these Irises need, poor soil inducing flowering instead of production of leaf, and the older a clump grows the better it flowers, so long as it does not raise itself too much out of the ground to be able to get nourishment; but I have some old clumps that by pressing their rhizomes against the wall have climbed up it some six or seven inches; these aspiring individuals flower well and I respect their ambitious habit so long as the leaves look strong and vigorous and I receive my rent in flowers.

Last winter we picked about fifty buds a week from the time the frosts had killed off the Asters and outdoor Chrysanthemums until March brought us sufficient Daffodils to keep the dinner table supplied. As a producer of *ver perpetuum* during the dullest months of the year I feel sure no outdoor plant can beat *Iris unguicularis*.[2]

Sir Thomas Hanbury, by the way, is famous for buying the Wisley estate in 1903, after the death of the garden's creator, G.F. Wilson (a friend of Miss Jekyll's), and giving it to the Royal Horticultural Society at a moment when their Chiswick garden had become too small and unsatisfactory. We owe him a great deal. His garden, La Mortola, near Ventimiglia on the Italian riviera was the repository for many exotic and unusual plants. It is still in existence.

Iris reticulata, in its many forms, usually appears not long after *Iris unguicularis*; it will, with a little grit added to the soil, blossom and flourish for many years. It was certainly the only bulbous iris with which Farrer had any luck.

My conditions, in which Primulas and Gentians rejoice, is slow death to the bulbous Irids; they barely endure the long, soaking dreariness of autumn, the wet, open mildness of winter, and then, with early spring, they send up, perhaps, one hesitating, frail, flower. A slug takes it as a *hors d'oeuvre*, a mouse for dessert; what is left—a flapping torn relic—is washed threadbare with spring rains, and splashed with mud until its original design and colour can only be guessed. Next season, of course, the wretched bulb prefers death to another such unprofitable effort. One, only, has to be excepted from this dreary list. *Iris reticulata* approves of me, and occasionally, for some mysterious reason, prospers most unreasonably ... throughout the garden, I am liable to outbreaks of unsuspected *Iris reticulata* every season. Perhaps of all the bulbous species, too, *reticulata* is the loveliest, with its trim rush-like leaves and its three pronged flowers of intense violet, eyed with orange and scented with the fierce deliciousness of the violet whose colour it imitates.[3]

At the same time as these irises are flowering, the aconites begin to appear, to hearten the gardener when the winter seems never-ending.

The common one, *Eranthis hiemalis*, like *Chionodoxa*, is one of the test plants of the established maturity of gardens; your parvenu, architect-planned, and colour-schemed affairs can seldom include such a fine drift of its cheery yellow faces in their green Toby frills as one may see in the garden of many a parsonage or quiet old grange. It is difficult to establish a new colony of it unless one can rob an old one, for it is one of those plants which suffer terribly from being kept out of the ground any length of time, and here I find the best time to transplant it is during its period of flowering. Roots bought in winter are generally sick unto death.[4]

It is fascinating to observe what a difference personality makes to attitude. That was Bowles, and this is Farrer on the same subject:

... the winter Aconite is indeed the promise of things to come. My joy, though, in seeing him is rather for what he represents than for what he is. For I think his colour is almost dreadful, an acrid malevolent yellow verging towards green and duly expressive of the plant's poisonous properties.[5]

He held the view that, when there was so little to see in the garden, that which there was should be of a very high standard. This seems perverse, but then Farrer did occasionally fall into the way of wilful perversity for the sake of originality.

... if one is only to have one or two flowers, one desires those one or two to reach an almost impossible standard of perfection, and is doubly acute to notice any blemish they may have of shape or colour.[6]

He could not love the snowdrop either, calling the ordinary one a 'chaste cold virgin'. Miss Sackville-West liked it, but admired more the unusual sorts not commonly seen in gardens.

For instance, there is the finer rarity called *Galanthus nivalis viridi-apice*, or green tipped; and of course there is the double snowdrop, but I hope nobody would wish to grow that, for surely the whole beauty lies in the perfec-

19. The South Cottage Garden – Sissinghurst (see Ch. 5)

20. *Cardiocrinum giganteum* (see Chs. 8 and 12)

tion of line of the single bell. Then there is the tall, large-flowered *Galanthus Elwesii*, from the hills behind Smyrna, often seen in old cottage gardens but not so often planted by the modern gardener, a most graceful dangling thing, flowering rather later than the little *Galanthus nivalis*, the 'milk-flower of the snow'. For people who want something really unusual ... there is *Galanthus Ikariae* which has the romantic peculiarity of growing in a wild state in only one place in the world: the small island of Ikaria or Nikaria in the Aegean sea, where Hercules buried the ill-fated Icarus. It flowers in March, and much resembles the common snow-drop, except that the flower is a little larger and the leaves curl over backwards.[7]

Of that harbinger of the Spring, the crocus, there is much to say. Bowles, nick-named 'the Crocus King' by Farrer, was in his time the great authority on the genus, and his botanical and horticultural monograph, *A Handbook of Crocus and Colchicum*, is still referred to by bulb enthusiasts today. He had the rare gift of being able to bridge the gulf between the arcane milieu of the herbarium and the more workaday world of the garden. When addressing the subject in *My Garden in Spring*, he confessed;

> For me ... there are great searchings of heart, compared with which those of the division of Reuben were as nothing ... for me, the very inmost cockle of whose heart glows more for a crocus than for the most expensive Orchid, every cockle in me ... is full of searchings and divisions now to do justice to my first garden love and avoid wearying and driving away readers to whom my raptures may appear the vapourings of a love-sick monomaniac.
>
> We treat crocuses *au grand sérieux* in this garden, giving over two double-light frames to their service in the very sunniest part of the kitchen garden ...[8]

His friends apparently accused him of giving them 'Crocus fever'.

> ... but I assure you I do not. I give them Crocuses and I leave the fever to develop. It is not a dangerous disease, although if you get it badly it lasts throughout the year. It is not a germ I can carry about to infect you with; it is

simply the charm of the Crocus itself. So be warned, and if you do not want to have Crocus fever, do not look at Crocuses ...[9]

That charm for him lay chiefly in their flowering in the dullest months of the year, and also in the fact that it was possible to have crocuses flowering for seven months of the year outside. Crocuses in this context are, of course, the delicate fragile-looking, infinitely charming species crocuses or the hybrids between two species. We are not here thinking of the large Dutch crocuses, developed over a long period, with flowers as fat and yellow and somehow utilitarian as electric lightbulbs, which called forth this unbridled outburst from Farrer.

> ... anger clots the ink of my typewriter when I think of the contrast between these [*Crocus vernus*] and the fatties that we complacently cultivate in our gardens; only to be disdainfully pulled to pieces, it is true, by sparrows of an acuter artistic sense than our own, who cannot put up with those plump pantomime 'principal' boys who pretend to represent the real fairies of the snow. Ah, for what price has *Crocus vernus* sold its birthright, and from the frail and delicate grace of its fluted fine chalices, developed into bumpers like the coarsest claret glasses of a public house. Not that, in any circumstances, any crocus could achieve actual ugliness; the innate good breeding of the race is too strong. But the pure line of the wild species stands far beyond any comparison with the pampered obesity that flops about in gardens.[10]

Passionate as Bowles' interest in crocuses was, his love was not blind.

> One little yellow Crocus has an obnoxious trait in its character and is a little stinking beast, as Dr. Johnson defined the stoat. It is well named *graveolens*, and its heavy scent is generally the first intimation I get of its having opened its flowers. Sometimes I get a whiff of it even before I reach the Crocus frame— an abominable mixture of the odour of black-beetles and imitation sable or skunk, or one of those awful furs with which people in the next pew or in front of you at a matinée poison you. A dried specimen of this Crocus retains its scent for years, and so does the blotting paper it has been pressed in. I think it emanates

from the pollen grains, and I suppose it must be of some use to it in its native country—perhaps attractive to some insect of perverted olfactory tastes.[11]

He loved *Narcissus* too, both the little species and the garden varieties of daffodil, although he did draw the line at the larger cultivars, raised then, as now, with such enthusiasm by breeders. He had a favourite bicoloured daffodil, called 'Weardale Perfection', which he said was quite large enough for him. For:

I do not want to sit under a trumpet during a shower. Beyond a certain point, size nearly always means coarseness, and I greatly dislike the huge race of trumpet Daffodils, so much to the fore in some Dutch gardens. A small man might almost feel nervous of looking down some of their trumpets, for fear of falling in and getting drowned in the honey, and a life belt or two should be hung among the beds. As we have not yet come to viewing our gardens from aeroplanes, we can do without

Figure 12.1 A Drawing done by Bowles of Narcissus bulbocodium citrinus *for* A Handbook of Narcissus

Rafflesia Arnoldii [the largest flower known] in the rock garden and the Waterbutt Trumpet Daffodils for mixed borders. Even the loveliest of fair damsels, magnified to the size of two and a half elephants, would be an appalling object to the stock-sized suitor, and until I have to take to much stronger spectacles, Weardale is large enough for me.[12]

Bowles pretended not to be a great expert on daffodils, but he did write an excellent monograph, *A Handbook of Narcissus*, so we must assume that he knew very well what he was talking about. He hybridised them, as he did crocuses, but he claimed to find it a disappointing business.

After ten years of hope and mild admiration for a long bed of home-raised seedlings, we have decided to offer them for sale at a penny each for mother-bulbs and two a penny for rounds, [flowering bulbs, round in shape, and without any offsets] on the flower stall of the Parish Fête, hoping to be easily rid of them, and to benefit the Parish Fund simultaneously. Therefore, may I remind you of Mr. Punch's advice to those about to marry? It was 'Don't'.[13]

Bowles was fond of picking a curious little iris to put in vases amongst his daffodils.

Here and there among the broad-leaved flag Irises appears the long narrow leaves of the Little Widow, La Vedorina of Italian gardens, no longer allowed to be an Iris, and obliged even to change her sex and reappear as *Hermodactylus tuberosus* ... I love this weird little flower, made up of the best imitation I have ever seen in vegetable tissues of dull green silk and black velvet—in fact it looks as if it had been plucked from the bonnet of some elderly lady of quiet tastes in headgear.[14]

Miss Sackville-West liked to call it *Iris tuberosa*, although she did acknowledge its new name,

which being interpreted, means Finger of Hermes (Mercury), and *tuberosus* of course, refers to the tuberous root-stock which does indeed bear some resemblance to the fingers of the human hand. Having got thus far, I began to reflect on its familiar sobriquet, the

Snakeshead, and to wonder whether the current explanation was correct in attributing the name to a fanciful likeness to the head of a snake. Perhaps, I thought, there may be a double meaning, for although the sombre sinister colouring and spiteful shape do suggest the spitting head of a reptile, it is also true that Mercury's winged wand, the caduceus, that swift and elegant symbol of the most roguish of all the minor gods, was twirled round by two interlaced serpents. Would it be possible and even probable, I wondered, that the name might have a classical origin we never suspected? I like to think so. I like to think that the messenger of the gods, Hermes in Greece, Mercury in Rome, gave his symbol as the name to one of our messengers of spring.[15]

Yes, she would like to think so, for she had a firm attachment to romantic associations.

The Hermodactylus may be only an Iris-relative, as the botanists say, but there is a race of real rhizomatous irises, that test the mettle of the most skilful cultivator; they are the Oncocyclus irises from mountainous regions in Asia Minor and Iran. These strange and gloomily beautiful irises require a long period of rest in dry soil, and only a very short wet season, conditions which are not easy to reproduce in Britain. Whether they are worth the anxiety and trouble, the reader may like to decide from the following;

A high, proud race are the Oncocyclus Irises—a doomed, tragic line, in crapes and blacks and purples, sweeping by on their road to the grave. They belong to a bygone day, and none can marvel at their sombre glories without feeling that they are mourners at their own funeral—a sad, lonely group, royal to the last, but swiftly, sternly passing away from the world. And so (for my garden is a marriage-bed, not a burial-ground, if I can help it) I will have none of the Oncocylus Irises; let others tend these agonising princesses, and enjoy what brief triumphs they can (a triumph that, of course, is longer and brighter where sun is hot and winters dry, than here where the sun at the best is only warm and the winters damp as Niobe); while, for my part, not liking sick-beds, I stand against spoiling my garden by glass frames and fir-boughs and all the elaborate medicaments that must be ready for the need of the Oncocyclus.[16]

For those whose courage fails them at the thought of the 'Oncos', there is a strain of crosses between them and the more amenable Regelia irises which was raised in Holland by the same firm, van Tubergen, that named a Crocus seedling after Bowles; these have proved less fugitive in cultivation. Farrer, paradoxically, was rather dismissive.

The less impossible *Regelio-Cyclus* group, have somehow sold the honour of those silken sad uncertain queens, their mothers, for a mess of comfort in the garden. One is glad they are such comparatively willing captives, yet even their purchased affability one regrets as a betrayal. Nor is it, even in itself, so much to boast of; let them be in deep beds of cow-manure with a foot of hot sand on top; so they will thrive and bloom, but will not for long continue, unless glass and bells be put over them in winter, a set of precautions that turn the garden from a paradise into a kindergarten or reformatory; and are permissible when employed to help, as with the rare Gentians, but not as the only hopes of prolonging an artificial existence, as with the more fractious Irids of the East.[17]

If those fractious Irids need some care, so too does the spectacular Giant Lily, *Cardiocrinum giganteum*, or *Lilium giganteum* as both Miss Sackville-West and Miss Jekyll (see Chapter 8) called it.

Too splendid to be called vulgar, she is still very decidedly over life-size. Unconsciously, one sets oneself some kind of limit as to what size a flower ought to be and here is one which exceeds them all. It looks almost as though she had adapted herself to the proportions of her tremendous home. For I suppose that there is no scenery in the world so appallingly majestic as that of the great mountains of Central Asia. Reginald Farrer found her in Tibet, [though he was by no means the first to collect it] and any reader of his books will have formed some distant idea of that remote and lovely region scarcely travelled and practically unmapped, where men are few, but flowers are many, a ravishing population put there as it were to compensate for the rudeness of life, the violence of the climate and the desolation of the ranges.

So the Giant Lily, not to be outdone, has

matched her stature against the great fissures and precipices of nameless peaks. In an English garden she looks startling indeed, but out there a peculiar fitness must attend her, making of her the worthy and proportionate ornament, sculptural as she is with her long quiet trumpets and dark, quiet leaves. I do not know to what height she will grow in her native home, but in England she will reach twelve feet without much trouble, and I have heard it said that in Scotland she will reach eighteen.

A group of these lilies, seen by twilight or moonlight gleaming under the shadow of a thin wood, is a truly imposing sight. The scent is overpowering and seems to be the only expression of life vouchsafed by these sentinels which have so strange a quality of stillness. I should like to see them growing among silver birches, whose pale trunks would accord with the curious greenish-white trumpets of the flower spike.[18]

I wonder of how many plants Farrer wrote the following.

... in all the garden there are no plants that more completely take my heart.

On this occasion he was referring to the hardy cyclamen, which for me have great charm rather than conventional beauty. He continued:

They are so invariably, so indefatigably beautiful, their whole personality so winning and sweet. Exquisite they are when their pink blooms come fluttering up like little butterflies among the stones and herbage, but not a little less beautiful are they when only their leaves are above ground. Such wonderful leaves, too, rounded and violet-like in *europaeum*, ivy-shaped in *hederaefolium*; but always blotched and flaked with patterns of white upon their dark surface of grey-green, whose underside is of a deep red-purple like their stems. *Hederaefolium* has the bolder form, and the finer variation; but *europaeum* does not lag far behind. They both send up their butterflies in autumn, though *europaeum* is already doing so in July, and, perhaps does not continue so late as the other. I love them both with such a passion, that I am always myself discredit in other people's gardens, incurring unpopularity and scorn. For the

wealthy and learned convey me round among their rarities, and are filled with indignation when I break away from my dutiful raptures over some ugly elm-like shrub, exceedingly new, which bears no beauty, but produces rubber, in order to throw myself on my knees before a clump of *Cyclamen hederaefolium* profusely blooming amid its leaves in coarse grass at the foot of a tree. 'Oh that', they say, in tones of scorn, 'that grows everywhere!'[19]

Dahlias certainly did not take Bowles' heart. It is not surprising. There is no element of subtlety, no hidden charm, no scent. This passage is a restorative for anyone who has moments of self-doubt when he feels it is an unreasoning prejudice to take against them.

I should like to be strong-minded enough to dislike Dahlias and to shut the garden gate on one and all of them as a punishment to them and the raisers who have produced some of the horrors of modern garden nightmares. But as it would not make much stir in the world of Dahlias however tightly I barred it, and as I have a great affection for single Dahlias and all the true species I have been able to get, the family is still admitted. I cannot believe I shall ever be converted to a taste for Collarette Dahlias. The crumpled little pieces of flower that form the frill cause an itching in my fingers to pick them all out to see what the flower would look like without them; and latterly they have taken to themselves such appallingly virulent eye-jarring combinations of colour that I long to burn them, root and all. A screeching magenta Dahlia with a collarette of lemon yellow, or a mixture of cerise and yellow, I think only fit to be grown in the garden of an asylum for the blind. Even the name annoys me; it suggests a sham affair, a dickey or some lace abomination, a middle-class invention to transform useful work-a-day clothes into a semblance of those of afternoon leisure.

Then we have a new race of Paeony-flowered Dahlias that get larger and more violently glaring each season, and their poor stalks seem more and more unable to hold up the huge targets that grow out of them. They must be matchless for saving labour in decorating for Harvest Thanksgivings, one pumpkin with two Paeony Dahlias and one bud would be enough for the pulpit, and an extra large one would be all-sufficient for the font. I saw some magnificently grown last season, but so huge that I could not resist asking, in as innocent a tone as I could man-age, whether they fried or steamed them, and if the latter, were they best with a white sauce or brown gravy.[20]

Notes

1. V. Sackville-West, *In Your Garden*, 1st edn (Michael Joseph, 1951), p. 34.

2. E.A. Bowles, *My Garden in Spring*, 1st edn (T.C. and E.C. Jack, 1914), pp. 21, 30.

3. R.J. Farrer, *Alpines and Bog Plants*, 1st edn (Edward Arnold, 1908), p. 199.

4. Bowles, *My Garden in Spring*, p. 115.

5. R.J. Farrer, *In a Yorkshire Garden*, 1st edn (Edward Arnold, 1909), p. 3.

6. Ibid., p. 4.

7. V. Sackville-West, *In Your Garden Again,* 1st edn (Michael Joseph, 1953), pp. 35–6.

8. Bowles, *My Garden in Spring*, p. 262.

9. E.A. Bowles, 'Crocuses', *Journal of the Royal Horticultural Society*, vol. 61, part 6 (1936), p. 237.

10. R.J. Farrer, *Among the Hills*, 1st edn (Headley Brothers, 1911), p. 35.

11. Bowles, *My Garden in Spring*, p. 79.

12. Ibid., p. 123.

13. E.A. Bowles, *A Handbook of Narcissus*, 1st edn (Martin Hopkinson, 1934), p. 232.

14. Bowles, *My Garden in Spring*, p. 231.

15. Sackville-West, *In Your Garden*, pp. 47–8.

16. R.J. Farrer, *My Rock Garden*, facsimile of the fourth impression (Theophrastus, 1971), p. 280.

17. R.J. Farrer, *The English Rock Garden*, fourth impression (2 vols., T.C. and E.C. Jack, 1928), vol. 1, p. 439.

18. Sackville-West, *In Your Garden (Some Flowers)*, pp. 205–6.

19. Farrer, *Among the Hills*, pp. 289–90.

20. E.A. Bowles, *My Garden in Autumn and Winter*, 1st edn (T.C. and E.C. Jack, 1915), pp. 88–9.

CHAPTER
❧ 13 ❧

The Protected Garden

-*Greenhouses & Flower Arranging*

The impression one gathers from reading the writings of these five authors is that, if they were interested in indoor gardening, they certainly did not do much of it. Robinson, we know, was trained in greenhouse culture, because of the famous incident at Ballykilcavan, but he was the only one. The reason for this must be that while labour was still cheap, and energy costs manageable, (i.e. up till the Second World War, and in the case of the rich till the early 1970s) greenhouse work was predominantly the preserve of the employed gardeners. This was also true of the arrangement of flowers in the house, towards which much of the work in glasshouses was directed, although it is apparent that both Miss Jekyll and Bowles took a personal interest in that. Farrer, no doubt giving way gracefully to his propensity for exaggeration, leaves the impression that the bosses were not always entirely welcome in the greenhouses and that, in order to indulge his passion for orchids, he had to defer to the gardeners. In *In a Yorkshire Garden* he adopted the conceit of pretending to conduct the reader around his garden, but:

It is not my business to convoy you round the houses. It is, of course, only of courtesy, really, that I myself am allowed in and about, and insinuate new beautiful things from time to time, without consulting the Powers that rule, who are not always strong in the matter

of name (though appreciators of good things) and so make no bones once some new star of the first horticultural magnitude comes sailing up over their firmament from peach-house or vinery, without any clear recollection on their part of having ordered it.[1]

When Robinson was writing about the culture of alpines, he complained of the current practice of growing them mostly in pots, which was why, he maintained, so few survived for a long time.

So long as the exaggerated ideas of the difficulties of growing alpine flowers were prevalent, it was the custom, even in good gardens, to grow most of these plants in pots in frames.

This he very much deprecated, believing that a well-prepared rock-garden was the best place for alpines, even the difficult ones. He did however grudgingly admit that:

Occasionally, too, we see them, as in the Alpine House at Kew, shown for their beauty in the Spring, in cool houses. Where there is the least difficulty as regards climate, such as the smoke of the town, having them slightly protected in pots will often gain a point or two, and in cold districts there is some reason why the early habit of flowering of so many beautiful kinds, should not be taken advantage of. [In this way, we can] enjoy their beauty and save them from the vicissitudes of our often wretched Springs.[2]

Certainly in those days, pot-culture was less successful because so little was known of suitable composts and growth media, feeding regimes and water requirements but, despite all that, Farrer believed that the culture of alpines in the Alpine House had many advantages, not least because the watering could be so strictly regulated especially in the winter, when these plants in their native habitats would have been snugly under a blanket of snow. These days, thanks in large part to the publicity afforded them and to Alpine Houses by Farrer and his disciples, pot-culture of alpines has reached a high point. The most casual and short-sighted visitor to the Spring Show at the Royal Horticultural Society's Halls in Vincent Square, Westminster cannot but be profoundly impressed. If he knows anything his admiration will deepen, because these pots often contain plants as difficult to cultivate successfully as anything known to the gardener, which will curl up and die on contact with an ordinary garden soil.

The advantages of the Alpine House are two-fold. First it protects these mountain dwellers from damp conditions in winter, but allows the freest ventilation and secondly, it facilitates the best display of these wonderful plants. Many alpines flower in the late winter, the time when outside their glory would be diminished by sleet and snow, slug and mould.

> No pleasure ... is greater than a clean little house, airy and sweet, filled with clean, undamaged potfuls of Saxifrage, Iris, Adonis, and so forth, all shining in untarnished radiance, and developing under protection of the glass such unsuspected charms as the delicate fragrance exhaled, under these undisturbed conditions, by *Saxifraga Burseriana*.[3]

There is no doubt that the thoughtful methods of growing alpines advocated by Farrer and based on the knowledge which he gleaned from studying them in the wild, turned the culture of rock plants in this country from a specialist pursuit, where pain was all too often mixed with pleasure, into one that was universally capable of being enjoyed.

By the time Miss Sackville-West was writing in the 1950s enthusiasts had the culture of alpines under glass very much under their control. The next extract was written for the very general public, that is, the readers of a national Sunday newspaper. The Alpine House that she mentioned at Kew fortunately still stands, but has been supplemented by a large pyramidal structure of metal and glass, which, marvellous as it is for the rearing of inconspicuous cushion-plants from beyond the Arctic Circle, is nevertheless lacking a little in the charm of the earlier, wooden construction.

> At this time of year [mid April] ... a few pans of small, brightly coloured flowers give vast pleasure. If you want to see what I mean done on the grand scale, go to the Alpine House at Kew. No need to be so ambitious, for even half a dozen pans on the staging of a small greenhouse produce an effect of clean brilliance, which I suppose is enhanced by the light coming on all sides, and overhead, through glass; and also because each bloom is unsmirched by rain or soil-splash, unnibbled by slugs, and unpecked by birds. Furthermore, the greyness of the stone chippings with which you will, I hope, have sprinkled your pans, throws up the colours into strong relief. Ideally, the pans should be whitewashed, for no one can pretend that the red of a flowerpot is pleasing, or of an agreeable texture. [I am someone who can pretend quite easily. I like the red of a flowerpot, if, as I suppose, she meant the brick red of a clay pot. I find it not only pleasing but of an agreeable, gritty texture, that shines very little in sunlight, but absorbs the light. Whitewashing cannot be a good idea because the paint would glare in the sun, and very likely clog the pores in the pot and prevent the free movement of air; just what you would not wish to happen. But she continues with a rather attractive idea.]
>
> Some of the little primulas lend themselves very happily to this treatment [i.e. being grown in the Alpine House] *P. marginata*, for instance, or the lovely pale lavender *Linda Pope*; or even a clump of the ordinary blue primrose which suffers so from the mischief of birds when growing out of doors in the garden. I would like also to see a pan of larger size, interplanted with some of the choicer varieties of common bulbs, coming up be-

tween the primulas: the intensely blue hanging bells of *Scilla Spring Beauty* or the strange greenish-turquoise of the grape hyacinth called *Tubergeniana* or the pale blue of *Chionodoxa gigantea* which in spite of its adjectival name resembles a tiny lily. Endless variations could be played on different colourschemes; you could have a cool pan of yellow primroses interplanted with the white grape-hyacinth and the white chionodoxa; or, for something looking rich and ecclesiastical, a pan of that very ordinary magenta *Primula Wanda* with the inky blue *Muscari latifolium* amongst it.[4]

Far more common than the Alpine House, then as now, was the cool, that is frost-free, greenhouse or conservatory. It had grown as an idea, out of the Orangery; a place where tender plants could be grown successfully, with some accent on display and as an amenity for the owner and his visitors. It was somewhere to go to wander about and admire the vegetation, perhaps during an interminable 'Friday to Monday'. It always seems to me that the reason for the popularity of the night-flowering cactus, *Cereus*, is that it was something to take the guests to see when conversation flagged during a sticky dinner-party. Miss Jekyll rather frowned upon the showing off that often resulted from the possession of these houses, both by the owners and by those who worked in them. She particularly deprecated the excessive size of calceolarias, cinerarias and begonias displayed in conservatories and drawing-rooms. As usual her concern was with tasteful design.

How seldom does one see a conservatory arranged with good taste. The usual thing is a crowded mass of incongruous flowering plants; just anything that happens to be in bloom in the plant-houses; and they are arranged so as to bring the bloom all to one even surface, sloping up from front to back. It looks as if the largest amount of material was used in order to produce the least effect, for the quantity of ill-assorted flowers brought together without design is sure to prevent the full enjoyment of the beauty of any.[5]

Elsewhere she maintained that it was a rare thing to see a conservatory well arranged.

. . . it is easy to do it if one or two simple rules

are kept in mind. The most important thing is to have an abundance of good greenery. Here is the place for the Palms and for anything of the Orange, Lemon and Citron kind, and for Myrtles and Camellias with what serves as undergrowth represented by Aspidistra, Funkia [*Hosta*] and Ferns. With the green thing well disposed, a much smaller number of flowering plants will be required, perhaps not more than one-fifth of the number usually seen and yet the whole effect will be very much better.[6]

She had a clear mental impression of what she would like to see.

I take pleasure in picturing to myself various forms of pleasant winter gardens; of places where there shall be no discordant note of obtrusive staging or gaudy tile or bluewhite paint, or any ostentatious or unseemly elaboration; but where beautiful flowers and foliage should hold their own in undisputed possession. What groupings I would have of tropical Ferns and Orchids, overshadowed by great groups of Bananas, and how much better to give the needed shade by means of Bananas or tall Tree Ferns than by an artificial shading only. The artificial shading may be wanted as well, but the living leafage is more positively satisfactory as a means of representing the subdued light of a tropical forest.[7]

She must have known and approved of the Palm House at Kew, built in 1848 and true to that ideal. I feel sure she would also have approved of the modern practice, in public collections of plants at least, of 'landscaping' the interiors of glasshouses, where once stood serried ranks of pots full of thirsty, root-girdling sub-tropical vegetation. Large blocks of sandstone half hidden by expanses of crumbly soil now replace the former staging and, though this 'landscape' is not much more realistic as a habitat for foliage begonias or African violets, it is a great deal more congenial for their growth.

In the warmer houses, and perhaps in a lesser degree in the temperate region, the wall would in places be the background of an arrangement of rockwork for the better planting of Ferns, and temporary placing of Orchids and other plants on rocky shelves and niches hidden by the growing greenery.[8]

Miss Jekyll said of the Orangery, at a time (1900) when most were still used for their original purpose and not, as now, almost exclusively as teashops and gift stalls:

There is another class of structure, such as the large Orangeries attached to old houses, of the palatial class, that would demand more formal treatment, because the buildings themselves have a distinct architectural value that should be not only recognised but intentionally emphasised. These are nearly all on the same general plan, with one blank wall at the back [which tender climbers can colonise] and one main face pierced with large lights often with arched heads, and between them important pilasters that carry the cornice. And often this face was designed in relation to the adjoining parterre for its original purpose was that it should be a place for storing the large boxes or tubs of tender trees, such as Oranges or Oleanders, that would stand out on the terraces in summer.[9]

Handsome and aesthetically satisfying they are, but as structures for growing plants well they suffered from two major defects; the ratio of glass to brick, or stonework, was too low which meant less than sufficient light in winter and they were difficult to shade successfully in summer. As the formal garden declined in popularity, so too did the Orangery, with which it was inevitably associated.

It is liberating to find Miss Jekyll admitting openly that she disliked the Anthurium, the ugliest flower I know, with its red, shiny, plastic-looking spathe and most unappealing curved spadix. When discussing how she would design a range of greenhouses if she could 'have her head', she wrote:

In my tropical houses ... the aim would be to have the most beautiful plants beautifully arranged. Nothing would be admitted merely because it was curious or rare or costly. There should be no unbeautiful audacities like *Anthurium* [her proper way of saying that it looks phallic] no evil little curiosities such as *Stapelia*, [the Carrion Flower] no insignificant plants of unworthy price, such as people crowd to look at at shows because they are valued at a hundred guineas; none of the usual commonplace unworthinesses, as of houses full of the coarse nettle-like Coleus, most of

them of shocking colour; of hundreds of pots of Calceolaria and Cineraria; no stove half full of uninteresting *Achimenes*, a family of plants I confess to disliking; without grace or beauty of form, in colour either washy or distinctly displeasing, and needing to be tied up to an infinity of small sticks ...

But I would have ropes and swags of the scarlet Passion-flower (*P*[*assiflora*] *racemosa*), and plenty of that goodly white-flowered company, *Stephanotis* and *Gardenia* and *Eucharis* and *Pancratium*, and the glowing *Hibiscus rosa-sinensis*, and the great yellow *Allamanda*. And with them the large flowered Oriental Jasmines, and quantities of fresh-coloured tender foliage of the beautiful Ferns of the tropics.[10]

In the same passage she mentioned which of the many orchids she would like to have but, though enthusiastic, she was comparatively restrained. Farrer was not:

It is too hot to go into the Orchid House. And, probably, as you are most of you out-of-door gardeners, I imagine, you spit at the very name of an Orchid. I wish that I had always been able to be so stern. It is very difficult to be stern, when you are catholic in your love for all things that are beautiful, and not at all useful. I had a drunken-bout of Orchids once; now that I am sober again, I have a headache and sickness. I have no wish ever to see an Orchid flower—until I do. And then, well, I get drunk again upon the gorgeous weird beauty of it. But I think by now I am immune against frenzies of new intoxication. I think I can rest content with sips from my cellar.[11]

Greenhouses, whose purpose was to provide tender vegetation for the display houses, far outnumbered the display houses themselves. This was because all pots had to be removed when out of flower, and also because many were needed to decorate the family house itself.

In 1883, Robinson urged people to consider cutting hardy garden flowers for the house, instead of just those grown in the glasshouses. A reserve garden, in the kitchen-garden, for example, was capable, he said, of producing flowers for as long a period as eight months of the year.

The enemy in the way hitherto against plenty of cut flowers has, it must be confessed, been the gardener. But the poor fellow was confined in his cutting operations to a greenhouse or conservatory, which he naturally wished to have gay, and cutting flowers has been the bone of contention in many a place ... A supply equal to that of twenty plant houses can be got from an open square in the kitchen garden or any other piece of good ground. We noticed a vigorous bed of Carnations last year flowering for nearly three months, while baskets of flowers were taken from it every week. For eight months of the year there is a continual progress of open-air flowers, which can be grown easily in sufficient quantity to allow of plenty being cut for every want ... From this [the reserve garden] and the general open garden collections—the woods, hedgerows and copses—every charm of flower life might be culled in abundance, from one end of the year to the other, for the embellishment of our tables.[12]

This seems self evident but was by no means the case in 1883 when that extract was published. Bowles was enormously keen on flower arrangements in the house, and yet,

I believe there is a wider evil lurking in the apparently harmless practice of growing flowers chiefly for cutting. I mean that it tends towards regarding flowers merely as decorations, and plants are chosen because they will produce so many masses of colour of some particular shade, much as one would buy silks by the yard, and it seems to me a waste of energy, pelf, and intellectual powers to grow plants merely to fill a dozen large bowls with soft mauve or pale pink to place in the drawing-room because they go well with the curtains or wall-paper. The faculty for appreciating the habit and individuality of a plant is destroyed as one learns only to care for its decapitated heads in baskets, as some ancient tyrant might gloat over those of his enemies.[13]

Most people can quieten their conscience on this point, or may not even see the relevance of it. It was Bowles' Christian sensibilities which prompted him to write that. It shows him to have been a man of nice judgement and unyielding moral standards.

Having said that, Bowles rivalled even Miss Jekyll in his commitment to the task of cutting flowers properly. This is what he had to say on preserving cut Shirley poppies, which are notorious for dropping their petals at the first glimpse of a flower-vase.

It took me a long while to learn how to cut them for the house so that they would not flag and faint within an hour. They never flag now when cut, nor do they fail to last in full beauty for three days if I carry a jug of *hot* water (hot, not tepid) down to their bed in the evening after dinner for preference, and cut the buds that have straightened up their necks ready to open on the morrow or perhaps the day after, and any flowers that have just split the calyx lobes and are showing their colour. I put each one into my jug so that it is almost up to its neck in hot water as soon as I have cut it, and I put jug and all in the bathroom for the night, because I love to see them half open, bursting off the sepals, or even in freshly-escaped glory full of crinkles and folds, the first thing in the morning. Opened thus and transferred to other vases, they will generally last for three days ... and, moreover, will increase in beauty, for they grow in size daily, until the anthers and petals all descend with a rush and make what the housemaids declare to be a horrid mess, but is often a wonderful display of blended shades dusted over with golden pollen almost as good to look at as the young flowers themselves.[14]

One wonders how he kept the water *hot*, not tepid, in the garden while he cut the flowers.

Miss Jekyll when talking about poppies, amongst other difficult flowers, remarked:

These flowers ... have a fast-flowing milky juice that dries quickly and hardens over the cut as if it had been purposely sealed with a waterproof coating of india-rubber. Therefore, when I bunch up Oriental Poppies, the moment before the bunch is put into its deep pail, the ends are cut afresh, and the stalks are also slit up two or three inches, and as the juice flows out they are plunged into the water, which washes it away.[15]

Finding that the range of commercially available vases suitable for cut flowers was very limited, which was not surprising as the occupation was fairly new, Miss Jekyll designed a group of receptacles which fitted her requirements exactly.

Formerly, it was difficult to get useful glasses for holding cut flowers. They were nearly always of a trumpet shape, widest at the lip and tapering down to a point just where it is most desirable to have a large quantity of water ... It was so evident that flower glasses of useful shapes and good capacity were wanted that I drew some shapes and had them made in a non-expensive quality of glass ... They are known as Munstead flower-glasses, they are cheap and strong, they hold plenty of water, and are in a number of useful sizes.[16] [Would that they were still made.]

As for the treatment of the flowers once the vases were found, according to Robinson,

arrangement ... is not nearly so difficult if we seek unity, harmony, and simplicity of effect, rather than the complexities which we have all seen at flower shows and in 'table decorations', many of them involving much weari-

some labour, while a shoot of a wild rose growing out of a hedge or a wreath of honeysuckle would put the whole thing to shame from the point of view of beauty ... generally it is best to show one flower at a time, especially if a noble one like the Carnation, which varies finely in colour.[17]

Miss Jekyll found, too, that:

mixed arrangements are by no means the easiest to make. Of late years [this was published in 1907] there has been a wholesome avoidance of the older practice of putting together a number of different kinds of flowers without much thought about their relative form or colour. Then we went to the other extreme, and held that arrangements of one kind of flower at a time was best, or of two kinds at most. This is quite right and safe for those who have not had their eyes trained so as to know all the resources and possibilities of good colour harmonies, [that was a snub, presumably unintentional, for Robinson] but it is not enough for the garden artist who will be able to put together a wider range of colour

Figure 13.1 Christmas Roses in a Munstead Vase. (From First Edition of Flower Decoration in the House, *by Gertrude Jekyll)*

material, and yet keep within safe limits.

As an example, let there be taken white Snapdragons, pink China Roses, the tall *Ageratum mexicanum*, some pale lilac Pansies (their leaves must not show), some pure white Pansies, foliage of *Cineraria maritima*, a few sprays of Gypsophila and of one of the small hybrid Clematises of pale lilac colouring. Let these be put together, not tightly, but with a certain ease and freedom of outline; the white Snapdragons standing well above the rest; and it will be seen that there are no less than six different kinds of flowers agreeing together, and none too many.[18]

A useful example for those of us who do not claim to be garden artists.

Miss Jekyll described a sensation that many people must feel, especially if they have lived in the same house for a long time.

Anyone who is accustomed to arrange flowers in certain rooms year after year must have observed how, after a time, the room 'finds itself'. How, first of all, there are certain places where flowers always look well, so that one always puts a vase of flowers there; and how one gets into the way of putting other vases into other special places. Some day one thinks, perhaps, the putting of the same glass or bowl in the same place is only a habit or a piece of mental indolence. The thing is taken away—put somewhere else. It does not do so well in the new place and the old place calls out for it. It looks empty—unfurnished. One moves about the room, studying it from every point. Yes, it must go back to the old place. Then conscience is at rest. The thing has 'found itself'.[19]

She also believed that:

it should be borne in mind in the use of flowers indoors that one of the first and wholesome laws is that of restraint and moderation. So great is the love of flowers nowadays, and so mischievous is the teaching of that hackneyed saying which holds that 'you cannot have too much of a good thing', that people often fall into the error of having much too much of flowers and foliage in their rooms. There

comes a point where the room becomes overloaded with flowers and greenery. During the last few years I have seen many a drawing-room where it appeared to be less of a room than a thicket. Where a good mass of greenery is wanted in a house, it is best kept in the hall or some place near the entrance, and even in quite a large room, one very large arrangement of foliage and flower will probably be enough, though of pot-plants in suitable receptacles and if smaller things of carefully arranged and dispersed cut flowers, it may take a large number.[20]

She could not resist the occasional gentle dig at current trends, for elsewhere she wrote of the fashion for bulrushes in tall vases, and went on to say:

It was followed by the reign of the Pampas Grass. Now plumes of Pampas Grass, picked and prepared at the right moment and beautifully feathered are undoubtedly handsome things and are capable of being used in clean country places with great effect. But some years ago fashion decreed that they must be in every London drawing-room. The revolution was a long time coming, but it came at last, and then it was realised that after a winter in a London room the poor plumes had first lost their freshness of ivory-white and had then become loaded with that well-known, evil-smelling greasy grime that their form and texture seemed specially adapted for collecting and retaining . . .

Following close upon the Pampas Grass as a fashion came the Palm in a pot; it pervaded nearly every sitting-room and remains to this day . . .

. . . the poor Palm. How one pities those that are hacked about all through the London season; that pass their nights in crowded, overheated, unventilated rooms and their days in travelling from one town mansion to another on the tail-board of the decorator's van. Still more do I pity, and think grievously misplaced, the unhappy little Palms that grace the long saloon tables of passenger steamers, and that drag out their wretched lives in a perpetual state of quivering unrest from the vibration of the machinery.[21]

Notes

1. R. J. Farrer, *In a Yorkshire Garden*, 1st edn (Edward Arnold, 1909), p. 181.

2. W. Robinson, *Alpine Flowers for Gardens*, 4th edn (John Murray, 1910), pp. 79–80.

3. R. J. Farrer, *The English Rock Garden*, fourth impression (2 vols., T.C. and E.C. Jack, 1928), vol. 1, p. lxii.

4. V. Sackville-West, *In Your Garden Again*, 1st edn (Michael Joseph, 1953), pp. 63–4.

5. G. Jekyll, *Home and Garden*, facsimile of 1st edition (Antique Collectors' Club, 1982), pp. 205–6.

6. G. Jekyll, *Flower Decoration in the House*, 1st edn (Country Life, 1907), p. 52.

7. Jekyll, *Home and Garden*, p. 208.

8. Ibid., p. 211.

9. Ibid., p. 209.

10. Ibid., p. 212.

11. Farrer, *In a Yorkshire Garden*, pp. 182–3.

12. W. Robinson, *The English Flower Garden*, 1st edn (John Murray, 1883), p. lxxi.

13. E.A. Bowles, *My Garden in Summer*, 1st edn (T.C. and E.C. Jack, 1914), pp. 264–5.

14. Ibid., p. 128.

15. Jekyll, *Home and Garden*, p. 182.

16. Jekyll, *Flower Decoration*, p. 59.

17. W. Robinson, *The English Flower Garden*, 6th edn (John Murray, 1898), pp. 358–9.

18. Jekyll, *Flower Decoration*, p. 37.

19. Ibid., p. 47.

20. Jekyll, *Home and Garden*, p. 191.

21. Jekyll, *Flower Decoration*, p. 48.

CHAPTER ❧ 14 ❧

Water Gardens: Scent: the Seasons

Water Gardens

It is perhaps unfair to begin this chapter on water and bog gardens with some advice of a rather negative sort from Farrer, but anyone who has embarked on a grandiose scheme to create a stretch of cool shimmering water, pockmarked by feeding carp and surrounded by swaying flags and bulrushes, will know that of all branches of gardening this is the hardest work to achieve and, after that, to maintain.

> Advice to those about to build a Water-garden—DON'T. Not that the Water-garden is not a joy and a glory; but that it is cruelly hard to keep in order and control unless you are master of millions and of broad ample acres of pool and pond. Water, like fire, is a good servant, perhaps, but is painfully liable to develop into a master ... How many little ponds are unguardedly built, only to become mere basins of slime and duckweed? How many larger pools are made, only to fill with *Chara*, *Potamogeton*, and the other noxious growths that make its depths a clogged, waving forest of dull brown verdure? The fact is a pool, not an easy thing to build and set going—is of all things in the garden the hardest of all to keep in decent order. Some of its choice inmates devour and despoil the smaller ones; water weeds increase and multiply at a prodigious rate; dead leaves drift thick upon it

in autumn, slime and green horrors make a film across it in summer.[1]

Be that as it may, most gardeners feel tempted at one time or another to try. The knowledge that failure may well result rarely stops anyone in the first flush of horticultural enthusiasm. Farrer certainly resisted manfully everything but temptation.

> The Water-Garden is an invaluable adjunct to the rock-garden, if the outlines of the pool can be so schemed as to make it look harmonious and inevitable there. The cultivation of the inmates is of the simplest; they either will not thrive at all, or else, in ninety-nine cases out of a hundred, thrive you out of house and home. First of all, the lines of the pool and stream should be mapped out; they must be neither straight nor gratuitously wobbly, but as far as the eye and taste of the designer can achieve, should represent the real thrust and flux of naturally flowing water into bay and inlet. A nurseryman's usual idea of a pond is a thing shaped like a kidney-bean, or a figure of eight. But cape should answer to bay, not to brother cape, and bay must answer headland. At the same time the strictest economy should be observed in such flourishes, lest the outline of the pool become artificially undulating and

diverse, like the soul of man. One good point should be made, and emphasised once for all, in a headland with a beautiful outstanding boulder; but good points never bear repetition, and the finer the dominant feature, the quieter should be the lines of the rest.[2]

Miss Jekyll rather favoured the stream, which she harnessed to her scheme in several gardens that she designed. She understood perfectly well the attraction for the observer that running water has over still.

> Not only is it pleasant to see the clear pebbly bottom, but it makes more movement of water, and the movement brings forth that sweet babbling, the language of the water, telling of its happy life and activity ...
>
> Sometimes the only stream one has to deal with is running water in the bottom of a straight, deep, narrow ditch, with nearly vertical sides. Nothing can be less inspiring to the planter than such a ditch; yet on the other hand, nothing is more stimulating to his power of invention, and determination to convert unsightliness into beauty. The ditch, as it exists, is useless except as a drain, but there is the precious running water—the one thing most wanted. In such a case it is often advisable to make an entirely new channel, excavating a good width so as to gain plenty of space down at the water's edge, and to give the stream some other form than a straight one. A natural stream is seldom straight, and though in gardening in general straight lines have great value, yet there are often reasons for departing from them, especially in groundwork of the wilder sort.[3]

Bowles had more than a stream flowing through his garden, he had a river, although, from the point of view of growing aquatics, it did him very little good.

> So many people say, 'What splendid opportunities you must have for Water Lilies and aquatic plants with the New River running through the garden,'—so many, in fact, that some day I shall push one of them into it instead of explaining that, if I did plant a Water Lily in the River, the Water Board's officials would soon rake it out again, and, even if they did not, it would catch its death of cold ... The New River water comes chiefly

from chalk wells of great depth, and therefore is hard enough to look blue, and cold enough in summer to make you look blue if you were in it for long. Besides, its banks are made of clay, pounded and puddled and slapped and banged with wooden slappers to a degree of watertightness, solidity, and neat level appearance that admits of nothing but turf margins. So the River is banned, taboo, *verboden* for planting, but above all, unsuitable. The pond is almost as bad. It too owes its watertightness to puddled clay, and most of its water to the same sources as the River. So it is the more easily grown aquatics that do best in and around it.[4]

There is no more beautiful waterplant than the water lily, and it was fortuitous that at the time when these authors were gardening there was a considerable leap forward in the raising of hardy water lilies. The man responsible for so much of the experimental breeding was a French nurseryman from Temple-sur-Lot, called Joseph Bory Latour-Marliac. Before his pioneering work, there were few really hardy water lilies, and those that there were had small flowers. In 1879, he crossed two North American water lilies, *Nymphaea odorata* and *N. tuberosa* with the Swedish red *N. alba rubra*. The result was a strain of hardy pink lilies. These he hybridised with the tender, yellow *N. mexicana*, to achieve a group of vigorous and large-flowered hybrids, that had colours ranging from white and pink and red to yellow, orange and coppery-red. These *marliacea* hybrids rapidly became popular, on both sides of the Channel, and Robinson was responsible for much of the work of disseminating the good news. As a matter of interest Marliac named a hybrid of his raising *Nymphaea robinsonii*, which the eponymous gardener grew at Gravetye. In the fourth edition of *Alpine Flowers* of 1910, he wrote about Marliac's lilies:

> Of late years a precious aid has come to us in the shape of many beautiful uncommon things for the water-garden, and above all, the hardy water-lilies raised by M. Latour-Marliac, which give us in a cold country such beauty as at one time was thought to be only possible in sub-tropical countries. We now have water-lilies so bright in colour, as hardy as a Dock, and it is impossible to resist such beauties, especially when we may grow them in a small pool ... if such we desire.[5]

Farrer said of Water lilies:

Of the Water-lilies there are legion, species and hybrids all of gloriousness untellable, and ever-increasing from year to year, as more and more colossal pink and crimson beauties appear at more and more colossal prices ... the rock garden [however] has no business with them, but to look serenely down on a pond bedecked like the dream of some Indian princess of long ago, and see its own reflection there broken by great blossoms floating on the water, in rose and crimson and pink and pearl and copper and sulphur and saffron and snow, looking incredibly tropical to be, as they are, as hardy and even more vigorous than the poor little common white Water-lily that now seems so very remote and obscure a cousin of such regal gorgeousnesses. The obscurity of these, indeed, lies only in the causes that provoke their unfolding. Full sun is the usual notion of the key that unlocks them; and certainly so it often is; yet no less often have I gone by in the twilight of a sad grey day, or on a tranquil dull evening after rain, and found all the huge blossoms agape and glowing, with the rain still standing in globular diamonds over the marbled and mottled darkness of their leathern leaves.[6]

Water lilies are only the most spectacular of true aquatic plants. I have mentioned the arrowheads (*Sagittaria*) which turned Bowles' skin purple. Most of his waterplants were collected in the wild, a practice which is now thoroughly frowned upon. His best story concerns the collection of a plant which is now protected by law.

My Water Soldier, *Stratiotes aloides*, dates from a very pleasant cruise in a wherry from Lowestoft to Norwich, with occasional landings to hunt Natterjack Toads at Reedham, Lepidoptera in a fen near Brundell and plants from a Broad in the same neighbourhood. When we landed at Norwich it looked as though it were going to be difficult to carry the large, wet, pineapple-leaved Water Soldiers any further until my kind host offered his bath towel, the largest ever seen, for the purpose. With its four corners knotted together, it made a glorious receptacle for the muddy collection of plants, but I expect I looked a somewhat strange figure carrying it on my back, with black mud oozing out of its

lower parts, and with a breeding-cage full of toads under my arm; of course we met all our smartest acquaintances at every turn of the road and every station we had to change at. I don't care, and here are my Water Soldiers as lively as ever. They remain at the bottom of the pond eleven months of the year in a most peaceable manner, but during August they float up to the surface and protrude their swords and bayonets and warlike armour, and then their fleeting white flowers appear to be fertilised, and when this is accomplished the plant sinks down again.[7]

Water in a garden is a distinct asset, which Lutyens and Miss Jekyll exploited to the full in, for example, the formal garden at Hestercombe, near Taunton. Here water ran in the shallow channels called 'rills' between the lawns, descended into the semi-circular tanks between the terraces; its passage culminating in the small square tanks on the bottom terrace. This downward movement of water was echoed by the 'flowing' of plants grown in each terrace wall. In the tanks and channels were water lilies and in the channels *Mimulus*, irises, water plantain, arum lilies and forget-me-nots. I feel sure she was thinking, at least half-consciously, of Hestercombe when she wrote in the context of a discussion on bog-gardening,

though one may grow Water Lilies and some other beautiful aquatic and paludinous plants in tanks and channels that are severely architectural, yet it is impossible to think of a formal parterre of bog plants.

For her:

The thought of such plants carries the mind away to stretches of heathy waste and wild places far away from houses and cultivation; therefore the bog garden, if some of its natural expression is to be retained, should be in a place apart from any horticulture of the tamer kind. It is best of all when it can be in some good stretch of rough, wet peatland, cut off from all gardening where the design is of rectangular form, although planting of a sympathetic character may well approach it.[8]

That is the bog garden on its own, but of course in many places where there is a lake or pond, the area of ground surrounding the water

Figure 14.1 Water-Garden with Paved 'Rills', Hestercombe, Somerset. (From Fifth Edition of Wall and Water Gardens, *by Gertrude Jekyll)*

may be boggy, and will need planting. In this context Miss Sackville-West wrote:

> For the marshy swamp I would suggest a drift of the moisture-loving primulas; *Sikkimensis, Florindae, Japonica, Chionantha, Bulleyana, Helodoxa*, known as the Glory of the Marsh ... The tall clematis-like Japanese irises, *I. Kaempferi*, look most beautiful growing amongst them, but I always think their requirements are a little awkward to manage—wet in summer, dry in winter. Nature's water supply usually works the other way round. The blue *Iris laevigata*, on the other hand, does not mind boggy conditions all the year through. *Iris Sibirica*, less large and handsome than the Japanese, is exceedingly graceful and pretty, and most accommodating, though it does not like being too deeply drowned. *Iris Delavayi* resembles it, and is useful because it flowers later, when *Sibirica* is over ...
>
> These are all tall-growing, but if you can spare a special corner marking it off with a ring of rough stones, do try the little almost-black gold-veined *I. chrysographes*, a real gem; and *I. fulva*, a coppery-red.[9]

Bowles was very fond of Asiatic primulas,

too, especially the forms of *Primula japonica*.

Their idea of luxury is mud, and it suits their requirements as well as those of a cockle-gatherer. The margin of a pond and the bottom of a not too wet ditch provide a happy home for them, and failing these the richer and moister soil you can give them, the better will be the result. There are some good colour forms of *japonica*, a so-called salmon, which is much more like anchovy sauce if one must give it a fishy name, a pure white with large orange eye, one of the loveliest of Primroses, and a very deep coppery red one, so there is no need to tolerate the old magenta forms and still less the speckled and ring-straked abominations that a bad white strain produces so freely among its seedlings. Even *P. pulverulenta* is crude and twangy beside the best deep *japonica*. I planted some seedlings along the pond edge and grouped *pulverulenta* with the deep red and white *japonicas*, and directly I had done so was sorry, believing the Chinese *pulverulenta* would kill the colour of the Japanese. When they flowered it was the Chinese that were defeated, and had to be removed to a separate cantonment for sake of peace to the eye. By itself the Chinese, mealy-stemmed fellow is not bad, and among wildish grass on the edge of a small pool at the bottom of the rock garden I thought its crimson tiers quite lovely enough to leave them to seed if they will, as their own mother did higher up, by the trickle that overflows from one little pool and fills another. From there, poor lady, she was ejected as she was so cabbage-like in profusion of foliage and so smothering to choicer neighbours, white Calthas and *Cyananthus lobatus*, and this last, like the Princes in the Tower, died this very stuffy death before I noticed what was going on.[10]

Farrer made the point of how a friend in the bog garden can turn fiend, when it thrives inordinately. In the following extract he described a British native, *Cirsium heterophyllum*. He had had a form of it which he liked with leaves 'gashed and slashed' like those of Acanthus, and so:

Actuated then, by admiration and old love, I introduced the Melancholy Thistle from the woods above the Lake to the bog in the Old Garden. Immediately, however, the drooping creature cheered up in the most dreadful and depressing way. It grew and it grew and it grew, it spread and it spread and it spread; ever since I have been waging vain war with the invader, spudding it up today in one place only to find it burgeoning anew from another to-morrow. My combat is with a Lermean Hydra; the plant runs underground, and makes two shoots, it seems to me, for each one that I cut off. But still I love the Melancholy Thistle, wicked, fascinating creature, which is not content with the iniquity of ramping insatiably underground, and must needs also fill the air all summer through, with flying silver clouds of seed.[11]

Scent

E.A. Bowles was acknowledged in his day as having a more than usually acute and accurate sense of smell, quite out of the ordinary way; he had developed it by playing guessing games as a child. Late on in his life he recalled Henry Elwes (the celebrated plant-hunter and entomologist, who with Augustine Henry published *The Trees of Great Britain and Ireland* in seven volumes, and who gave his name to *Galanthus elwesii*),

causing quite a sensation at a show here [i.e. at the RHS in Westminster] many years ago when he shouted out 'Where's Bowles? He's the only man with a nose!' People expected to see someone with a nose like that of Cyrano de Bergerac and may have been disappointed.[12]

His olfactory refinement was all the more surprising and impressive, since he was subject to yearly bouts of hay-fever.

I generally arrange to be absent from my garden in mid and late June, for I am one of those badly finished off persons whose mucous membrane never got the last coat of paint, or the right tempering and hardening, or whatever was needful to enable it to resist the irritation of grass pollen that is called Hay-fever. I believe I have tried every remedy that has been put on the market, and though some alleviated my particular forms of sneezing and

eye-swellings, none made me feel well enough to be happy. I objected all along to have my nose cauterised, believing it dulls one's power of scent, which means so much to me that I would far rather snuffle and sneeze for one month and be able to smell clearly and keenly the other eleven than be robbed of any olfactory powers; and before the days of antitoxins and injections I discovered so pleasant a cure that Hay-fever has become quite a valuable asset in my scheme, for I must, 'absoballylutely must,' as Grossmith used to say, carry my poor nose away from the flowering grass meadows to Alpine heights where a breeze blows off the snow. Once I reach an altitude of 3000 feet I am cured and the sight of *Poa alpina* in its viviparous state by the side of a road assures me it is safe to draw in the breeze with expanded nostrils.[13]

At the same lecture he discussed the smell of the curry plant, *Helichrysum angustifolium*.

It gives out a most extraordinary smell like curry, and not only curry but a very good curry too with mango chutney in it. During the Kaiser's war [the First World War] I thought it might be useful to chop it up and put it into ordinary minced beef to turn it into a curry, but the flavour does not compare with the scent, and is unpleasantly bitter. This strong scent, however, especially as I pass by on a hot day, still makes me feel hungry.[14]

His powers of discernment were so highly developed that he could remark about the Moroccan Broom, *Cytisus battandieri*, that it

is a remarkable plant as the nature of its fragrance changes every few minutes. Sometimes it reminds me of strawberries, and at others of grapefruit and lemons, or of a fruit salad with a dash of maraschino or kirsch. You can get all these scents from the same bunch of blooms at different times of the day.[15]

He had strong dislikes. He considered the worst of all to be *Cotoneaster multiflora*, which smelled, in his opinion, like a fried fish shop, and one that used bad oil. As for *Allium siculum*, he likened it to a gas-leak or a new mackintosh.

It is no coincidence that Bowles' poor eyesight had a direct bearing on his acute sense of smell; it is well known that the atrophy of one sense very often leads to the development of another. This was also the case with Miss Jekyll whose sense of smell and hearing were excellent. One of her favourite scents was the wood violet because she considered it was never overdone.

It seems to me to be quite the best of all the violet-scents, just because of its temperate quality. It gives exactly enough, and never that perhaps-just-a-trifle-too-much that may often be noticed about a bunch of frame-Violets, and that also in the south is intensified to a degree that is distinctly undesirable. For just as colour may be strengthened to a painful glare, and sound may be magnified to a torture, so even a sweet scent may pass its appointed bounds and become an overpoweringly evil smell. Even in England several of the Lilies, whose smell is delicious in open air wafts, cannot be borne in a room. In the south of Europe a tuberose [*Polianthes tuberosus*, which Shelley thought the sweetest flower for scent] cannot be brought indoors, and even at home I remember one warm wet August how a plant of Balm of Gilead [*Cedronella triphylla*] had its always powerful but usually agreeably-aromatic smell so much exaggerated that it smelt exactly like coal-gas! ...

While on this less pleasant part of the subject, I cannot help thinking of the horrible smell of the Dragon Arum; and yet how

fitting an accompaniment it is to the plant, for if ever there was a plant that looked wicked and repellant, it is this; and yet, like Medusa, it has its own kind of fearful beauty.[16]

The reason is that the Dragon Arum, *Dracunculus vulgaris*, is pollinated by flies and hence smells of rotting meat. This was a fact which Miss Jekyll obviously hesitated to mention, not because of her own sensibilities, for she was extremely robust, but to spare the finer feelings of her readers. Bowles had no such compunction; he referred to a close relation of the Dragon Arum, *Helicodiceros crinitus*, as

the most fiendish plant I know of, the sort of thing Beelzebub might pluck to make a bouquet for his mother-in-law ... [it] looks as if it had been made out of a sow's ear for spathe, and the tail of a rat that died of Elephantiasis for the spadix. The whole thing is a mingling of unwholesome greens, livid purples, and pallid pinks, the livery of putrescence in fact, and it possesses an odour to match the colouring. I once entrapped the vicar of a poor parish into smelling it, and when he had recovered his breath he said it reminded him of a pauper funeral. It only exhales this stench for a few hours after opening, and during that time it is better to stand afar off and look at it through a telescope.[17]

Farrer would have disagreed with Miss Jekyll about the fact that scents could be excessive. As far as he was concerned it was not possible.

... I must own that I would do almost anything, and grow almost anything, for the sake of a fragrance. What use, what *raison d'être* has any flower without a scent ... People may swoon all round me from Jasmine or Gardenia: at each whiff I grow stronger, and my thoughts clearer, and my hopes higher, and my whole being strung to keener and keener intensities of effort and aspiration. What folly it is to ignore the curative, the stimulant powers of scent! I defy any one to remain mumpish, groovy or fanatical in a room full of Primroses; I defy the most pernicious anaemia to resist the odour of *Narcissus Tazetta*; I defy all vapours, low spirits, glooms, Lassitude and Languor (horrid hags!) not to pick up their skirts and scuttle from the room when a bowl of roses or Lilies-of-the-Valley comes in.[18]

Being so conscious of smells, pleasant or otherwise, could cause difficulties for Bowles.

The scent of fresh flowers in rooms is one of the joys of life if sufficiently understood and controlled. I have been poisoned olfactorily, which means headache and a fearful longing for a whiff of the clean outdoor smell of greenery, by rooms with too many *Lilium auratum* or *Azalea mollis* in them; and I do not think I could be polite and good-tempered for long in a room with many bunches of Phloxes in it. A dinner-table decorated heavily with Sweet Peas spoils my dinner, as I taste Sweet Peas with every course, and they are horrible as a sauce for fish, whilst they ruin the bouquet of good wine. I once cut a quantity of Almond blossom for a centre-piece, and six smaller vases for the dinner-table, and quite smothered out the charms of a good dinner with its aroma. Violets, Mignonette, Wallflower, Roses, Hyacinths, Stocks, and many other flowers lose their sweet scent after about twenty-four hours in a room, and need carefully testing day by day as well for freshness of odour as for colour effect, and yet, again, some flowers are never agreeable to my fussy old nose. Phloxes smell to me like a combination of pepper and pig-stye, most Brooms of dirty, soapy, bath sponge, Hawthorn of fish-shop, and Meadow Sweet of curry powder, so I much dislike being shut up in a house with them; while *Philadelphus coronarius*, Elder, and *Spiraea Aruncus* simply drive me out, for they generally produce a violent attack of hay fever.[19]

To dwell on those undesirable or unpleasant smells, however, would be an injustice to all the many that give pleasure.

Perhaps the most delightful of all flower scents [wrote Miss Jekyll] are those whose tender and delicate quality makes one wish for just a little more. Such a scent is that of Apple-blossom, and of some small Pansies, and of the wild Rose and the Honeysuckle. Among Roses alone the variety and degree of sweet scent seems almost infinite. To me the sweetest of all is the Provence, the old Cabbage Rose of our gardens. When something approaching this appears, as it frequently does, among the hybrid perpetuals, I always greet it as the real sweet Rose smell ...

But of all the sweet scents of bush or flower, the ones that give me the greatest pleasure are those of the aromatic class, where they seem to have a wholesome resinous or balsamic base, with a delicate perfume added. When I pick and crush in my hand a twig of Bay, or brush against a bush of Rosemary, or tread upon a tuft of Thyme, or pass through incense-laden brakes of Cistus, I feel that here is all that is best and purest and most refined, and nearest to poetry, in the range of faculty of the sense of smell.[20]

The Seasons

It is partly intimations of mortality, partly an appreciation of beauty and partly a sense of the certainty of seasons and their passage that turn reasonable men into gardeners. Gardening promises an understanding of the annual patterns of change, of birth and of decay, that sheds a chink of light on the mystery of being human. The realisation that all will continue, however short our own existences may be, is deeply satisfying to our agitated spirits. That is why description of the seasons is common to all these authors, except for Robinson, too intent on his polemical purpose perhaps, to set down his feelings very much.

Capturing a moment as evanescent as a blown bubble is possible but remarkably difficult. Gardeners have an equation: plants flowering, plus weather, equals season. We shall begin here with Spring, as all gardeners do in their calculation, although readers should by now be aware that Winter is not a dead season. Bowles, who had given a seasonal title to his trilogy, obviously had to explain himself at the beginning of each volume.

If a census of opinion were to be taken as to when Spring commenced, he began,

The majority of people would most likely declare that the 21st March was the first day of Spring, though there still exists a sentimental preference for the 14th of February, the feast of St. Valentine, while a large number of people over a certain age would insist that Spring no longer exists, and would probably endeavour to prove this assertion by lengthy reminiscences of halcyon days of yore, which provided early opportunities for picnics and thin raiment.

Who has not heard their great-aunt Georgina hold forth on the Indian muslins that in bygone Mays were all-sufficient for her comfort?[21]

Argument with such is useless, and it is much better to pile fresh logs on the fire and shut the windows to preserve her tweed-clad frame from a chill.[21]

In the end Bowles would only commit himself as far as proclaiming *Iris unguicularis* as the first flower of Spring; in some years this begins to appear in Autumn! He refused to be pinned down to a date, and how could he be? We all can recognise the first day of spring, when the air has a faint smell of soil warmed by the sun. However, Spring came in a different way to Farrer in the North of England. Then, in

cyclones of snow and ice, begins the spring. And such a spring. No wonder that Our Lady Persephone does not gladly nor promptly come up again into so ungenial a world as this of ours. The earth is in agony for her; great rents open and gape in all directions. The garden is a waste of dark crumbling clods, and the plants everywhere look inconceivably dead and hopeless and beyond thought of resurrection. Only the Tulips and Daffodils already poke up green noses of vitality; the Hellebores send up their pale ghosts of blossom—to be immediately spattered out of shape and colour by a storm, or else devoured piecemeal by a slug. Everything else is in the last and lowest hour of death, shrunk to its smallest proportions, with the vital principle lurking far down underground and out of harm's way. And on the dead rose bushes hang a thousand buds, like withered moths, dark amid the whirling snow-flakes.[22]

It is a matter of perception but that appears to me to be a good description of late winter.

Spring is an uncertain time, it must be conceded, and very treacherous for the gardener who is often tempted to put out tender plants too early. It is traditionally the time of greatest growth and tremendous optimism. Promissory notes are out from the Bank of Hope, but, as Miss Jekyll described, the weather can undermine confidence and even threaten foreclosure.

In the end of March, or at any time during the month when the wind is in the east or north-east, all increase and development of vegetation appears to cease. As things are, so they remain. Plants that are in flower retain their bloom, but as it were, under protest. A kind of sullen dullness pervades all plant life. Sweet-scented shrubs do not give off their fragrance; even the woodland moss and earth and dead leaves withhold their sweet, nutty scent. The surface of the earth has an arid, infertile look; a slight haze of an ugly grey takes the colour out of objects in middle distance, and seems to rob the flowers of theirs, or to put them out of harmony with all things around. But a day comes, or perhaps, a warmer night, when the wind, now breathing gently from the south-west, puts new life into all growing things. A marvellous change is wrought in a few hours. A little warm rain has fallen and plants, invisible before, and doubtless still underground, spring into glad life.[23]

Miss Sackville-West described a spring afternoon in her part of the world.

I had had occasion to drive across ten miles of Kent, through the orchard country. The apple blossom was not yet fully out; and it was still in that fugitive precious stage of being more of a promise than a fulfilment. Apple-blossom too quickly becomes overblown, whereas its true character is to be as lightly youthful as an eighteen-year-old poet. There they were, the closed buds just flushing pink, making a faintly roseate haze over the old trees grey with age; closed buds of youth graciously blushing as youth must blush in the presence of age, knowing very well that within a few months they themselves would turn into the apples of autumnal fruit.

But if the apple-blossom was no more than a pink veil thrown over the orchards, the cherry was at its most magnificent. Never had it looked more lavish than this year [1948] nor so white, so candidly white. This heavy whiteness of the cherry, always enhanced by the contrasting blackness of the branches, was on this particular afternoon deepened—if white may be said to deepen—by a pewter-grey sky of storm as a backcloth; and I thought, not for the first time, how perfectly married were these two effects of April: the dazzling blossom and the peculiarly lurid heaven which is only half a menace. Only half, for however wrathful it may pretend to be overhead, there are gleams of light round the edges, with lances of sun striking a church tower somewhere in the landscape. It is not a true threat; it is a temporary threat, put on for its theatrical effect—Nature's original of that most strange and beautiful of man's new inventions, flood-lighting.[24]

Bowles' favourite moment in the whole year came right at the end of the spring season, when it fades almost imperceptibly into summer. It was the time of his birthday and the Tulip Tea.

If a fairy godmother or a talking fish offered me three wishes I think one would be to have the clock stopped for six months on a fine morning towards the end of May. Then, perhaps, I might have time to enjoy the supreme moment of the garden. And I am not at all sure the second wish would not be used to extend the period. It must be after those plaguey Ice Saints have finished playing the fool with the weather, and when there comes a spell that is neither too hot nor too cold, but just the climate one would expect to meet with in Heaven, and in England sometimes comes to us in late May and September. The tall Tulips would be at their best, *Iris florentina* and its early companions in full glory. Lilacs and Apple-blossom, Hawthorn and Laburnum, all masses of flower. Trees full of tender green, yet not too densely clad to prevent our seeing the architecture of the boughs. The Mulberry would be in leaf and showing that frosts have ceased, for it is the wisest of all trees, and always waits till it is quite safe before it opens its buds.[25]

He confessed that he liked to have visitors to see his garden then before his plants began to burn up in his thirsty soil. Miss Jekyll, on the other hand, preferred June.

What is one to say about June—the time of perfect young summer, the fulfilment of the promise of the earlier months, and with as yet no sign to remind one that its fresh young beauty will ever fade? For my own part I wander up into the wood and say, 'June is here—June is here; thank God for lovely June!' The soft cooing of the wood-dove, the glad song of many birds, the flitting of butterflies, the hum of all the little winged people among the branches, the sweet earth-scents—all seem

to say the same, with an endless reiteration, never wearying because so gladsome. It is the offering of the Hymn of Praise! The lizards run in and out of the heathy tufts in the hot sunshine, and as the long day darkens the night-jar trolls out his strange song, so welcome because it is the prelude to the perfect summer night; here and there a glow-worm shows its little lamp.[26]

Farrer would have been proud of her for that passage.

Summer's lease, unfortunately, soon runs out and before gardeners can feel much irritation with droughty borders and yellowing lawns, autumn creeps in with chilly air and first heavy early morning dews.

In the garden Summer melts into Autumn [wrote Bowles] as gradually as the fading from one to another of the dissolving views that delighted the children and enlivened parish entertainments some half-century ago. A touch of gold or crimson on the heavy dark green foliage of late Summer, gives promise of the new picture that will grow clearer as the old one fades ...

Seed time and harvest is perhaps the best definition of the third season of the year; but for the good gardener it only expresses one side of its character. The cooling rains of Autumn produce a similar result to that wrought by the warming sunlight of Spring, and awaken so many bulbous plants to their annual round of growth, flowering, and seeding, that in gardens where good collections of them are grown a second Spring seems to fill the beds.[27]

The good gardener, in this context, is the one who has the sense to plant all the autumn crocuses and colchicums that Bowles so admired. He went on, optimistic in tone as always,

Some people prefer to read a sad note in Autumn and to dwell on the fading and passing of Summer's joys, and as it takes all sorts to make a world, and there must ever be those who *enjoy* bad health, who would miss their death's head as much as their salt-cellar on their dinner tables, we must allow them their minor harmonies and depressing remarks about departing swallows. But the good gardener should have no time to look back on departing joys; he should be all alive to take advantage of the yet warm soil, that, combined with a cool and moist atmosphere makes the days of September and early October the most propitious of all the year for planting out recently collected alpines ...[28]

Miss Sackville-West suggested that it was only as a portent that we deplored autumn, and that seems right.

> The autumn garden ... has its beauty; especially, perhaps, a garden with an old orchard attached to it. When I was very small, about four years old, I suppose, a line of poetry entered into my consciousness, never to leave it again.
>
> Rye pappels drop about my head.
>
> I had no idea what rye pappels might be, but they held a magic, an enchantment for me, and when in later life I identified them as the ripe apples of Andrew Marvell's poem they had lost nothing of their enchantment in the process of growing up.
>
> Coming home from abroad, after an interval when the season had time to change from late summer into autumn, it struck me how *pink* and green the autumn garden was. Not bronze and blue, the colours we associate with the turning woods and the hazy distance and the blue smoke of bonfires along the

hedgerows. The woods had not turned yet but in the orchard the apples were rosy and in the garden the leaves of the peonies were pink, and so were the leaves of *Parrotia persica* and the leaves of that other little tree with the lovely name *Liquidambar* and the leaves of *Prunus Sargentii*, so soon to drop, alas, from the row in which I had planted them along the top of a rosy-red brick retaining wall.[29]

It often seems that just as the autumn colour is at its best a series of sharp frosts puts paid to the display and heralds the start of winter. It would be tempting to end with a piece on the storms and ravages of winter which can dash the gardener's hopes, but it is more agreeable to finish with a cosy, comfortable view from Bowles.

> There is a wonderful beauty in the old stems, the kecksies, [hollow plant stems] of many plants in a soft winter evening's glow. A ruddy light on brown Grasses or Eryngium stems, or against bare Lime twigs, is a source of great pleasure when it is just too dark to see to weed or dig among the small plants ... Then again on a frosty morning, every stem, weed, blade of grass or cobweb has its edging of pearls or diamond dust, and I am always glad if I have not yet tidied away the dead stems that look so lovely in their coats of hoar-frost.[30]

Notes

1. R. J. Farrer, *Alpines and Bog Plants*, 1st edn (Edward Arnold, 1908), p. 259.

2. R. J. Farrer, *The English Rock Garden*, 4th impression (2 vols., T.C. and E.C. Jack, 1928), vol. 2, pp. xxxviii–xi.

3. G. Jekyll, *A Gardener's Testament*, Francis Jekyll and G.C. Taylor (eds.), facsimile of 1937 edn (Antique Collectors' Club, 1982), pp. 99–100.

4. E.A. Bowles, *My Garden in Summer*, 1st edn (T.C. and E.C. Jack, 1914), p. 157.

5. W. Robinson, *Alpine Flowers for Gardens*, 4th edn (John Murray, 1910), pp. 61–2.

6. Farrer, *The English Rock Garden*, vol. 2, p. 4.

7. E.A. Bowles, *My Garden in Summer*, 1st edn (T.C. and E.C. Jack, 1914), pp. 161–2.

8. Jekyll, *A Gardener's Testament*, pp. 102–3.

9. V. Sackville-West, *In Your Garden Again*, 1st edn (Michael Joseph, 1953), pp. 48–9.

10. Bowles, *My Garden in Spring*, pp. 146–7.

11. Farrer, *Alpines and Bog Plants*, p. 184.

12. E.A. Bowles, 'Fragrance in the Garden', *Journal of the Royal Horticultural Society*, vol. 78, part 3 (1953), p. 90.

13. Bowles, *My Garden in Summer*, pp. 202–3.

14. Bowles, 'Fragrance in the Garden', p. 88.

15. Ibid., p. 93.

16. G. Jekyll, *Wood and Garden*, facsimile of 1st edn (Antique Collectors' Club, 1981), pp. 316–18.

17. Bowles, *My Garden in Spring*, p. 280.

18. R. J. Farrer, *In a Yorkshire Garden*, 1st edn (Edward Arnold, 1909), p. 64.

19. Bowles, *My Garden in Summer*, p. 264.

20. Jekyll, *Wood and Garden*, pp. 316–8.

21. Bowles, *My Garden in Spring*, p. 1.

22. Farrer, *Yorkshire Garden*, p. 2.

23. Jekyll, *Wood and Garden*, p. 68.

24. V. Sackville-West, *In Your Garden*, 1st edn (Michael Joseph, 1951), pp. 62–3.

25. Bowles, *My Garden in Spring*, pp. 279–81.

26. Jekyll, *Wood and Garden*, pp. 115–6.

27. E.A. Bowles, *My Garden in Autumn and Winter*, 1st edn (T.C. and E.C. Jack, 1915), p. 1.

28. Ibid., p. 1.

29. Sackville-West, *In Your Garden*, pp. 131–2.

30. Bowles, *My Garden in Autumn and Winter*, pp. 256–7.

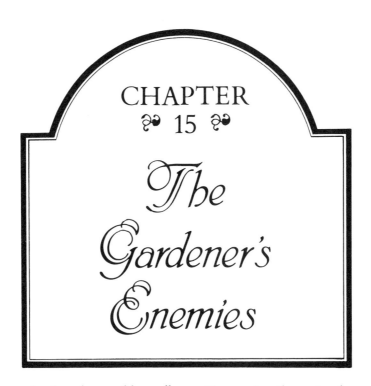

CHAPTER
❧ 15 ❧

The Gardener's Enemies

It is remarkable to what lengths sensible, well-balanced people will go in their efforts to create a garden, considering that, wherever they are, the odds against success are stacked so alarmingly against them. I find this no less remarkable for being true of myself as well, and therefore something to which I should by now have become accustomed. The untold millions of flying insects, the deadly pathogens ever present in the soil waiting for suitable hosts, the searing winds in winter, the no less debilitating droughts in summer, and worst of all, ineradicable as sin, the weeds. The pleasure of it all lies in triumph over adversity, but in most battles the victory is decidedly Pyrrhic. Success is compromised by misfortune, ignorance and error. We may never know what caused Miss Sackville-West's viburnums to cease flowering, nor that the reason our precious bulbs will not flower is that we have planted them upside down.

For some, it is true, the interest and stimulus of gardening stems not from overcoming difficulties, but from wallowing in them. Just as the enjoyment of ill health is a hobby for the hypochondriac, who takes pleasure in collecting medicines, so some gardeners derive great satisfaction from surrounding themselves with shelves full of chemicals, with which to attack every pest from cherry slugworm to Solomon's Seal sawfly. Fortunately for them, the garden will never be cured.

Slugs and snails must rank as some of the most destructive real enemies in the garden, and ones for which most gardeners have a convulsive and primitive distaste, which can lead them into ways of cruelty which they would thoroughly disapprove of in others. The damage done by these creatures seems particularly savage and indiscriminate in the rock-garden, because their unassuageable appetite for fresh shoots in the spring will more often send a tiny alpine to join its fathers, than the more robust delphinium or hosta. Farrer loathed them and had no qualms about using his precious tie-pin in the war against them. He had, as well, another remedy, although I myself doubt its efficacy.

The only enemy before whom C[ampanula] raineri goes down is the slug, against which the only sure remedy is nothing more or less than an orange—which, if cut across and eaten out with a spoon, then leaves you the squeezed drained halves to put about in the rock garden, where they will at once attract every slug for miles around, which can thus be captured by the hundred each morning and consigned to their just doom. [He does not elaborate.] It is true that this may make your garden look a little as if a beanfeast had there lately raged; however, even this is better than rings of zinc or bran, and incomparably better than finding your C. raineri in the morning a bare ruined choir where late the sweet birds sang—to say nothing of the economical fact that you have already had the felicity of eating your orange.[1]

Bowles favoured the hat-pin, going out after dinner armed with that and an acetylene lamp to spear them as they fed on his colchicums. Miss Jekyll was a great deal more fortunate, for

> we have one grand consolation in having no slugs, at least hardly any that are truly indigenous; they do not like our dry, sandy heaths. Friends are very generous in sending them with plants, so that we have a moderate number that hang about frames and pot plants, though nothing much to boast of; but they never trouble seedlings in the open ground, and for this I can never be too thankful.[2]

Bowles, as an enthusiastic entomologist, could be expected to take a great deal of interest in the pests that harried his plants. It was especially important in those days, before the invention of systemic insecticides, to have a good idea of the habits, proclivities and life-cycle of insect enemies. What is interesting is that gardeners seemed to cope as well with their pests, or at least keep them to manageable proportions, as they do today, with all the armoury of chemicals now at their disposal. This is only a strong impression but, either they had a higher tolerance for leaf and flower damage, or the natural balance maintained with the mammal and bird population served to keep the harm to reasonable proportions.

> I wish the Cabbage Moth (*Mamestra brassicae*) could be induced to realise that death and disaster will pursue its brood of caterpillars when asylumed on Romeyas, [beautiful white poppies with yellow centres from California] and therefore Cabbages are safer orphanages for motherless larvae. No one grumbles at a few holes in the outer leaves of Cabbages, and even if these little green pests would eat them up entirely it would save gardeners and cooks from cutting them off; but surely it is bad policy to bore into the white heart, for though it may be fat living it must often end in disaster under wrathful gardeners' feet or in boiling and posthumous execration by the would-be consumer of unadulterated Cabbage. Still

more rash is it to invade the Romeya of a keen gardener, to fret and filigree its leaves at first when small, and then to bore into fat buds so that they can only open as mere rags, like the tattered old flags preserved in cathedrals. If the keen gardener is enough of an entomologist to recognise his enemy's style of work, he will sally forth after dark with an acetylene bicycle lamp, and catch Master Cabbage Moth ... Caterpillars that are hidden in the ground or under leaves by day lie out at full length after a meal on the upper surfaces of leaves, feeling there is nothing to fear; or may be seen chewing away at the edge of leaf and bud, and are easily detected, as their colony is shown up by acetylene light in a wonderful way that renders them conspicuous in spite of the patterns that are useful for hiding them in daylight.[3]

Miss Sackville-West became so desperate about the damage caused by birds that she appealed to her newspaper readers for help.

> How does one protect the choicer sorts of primroses from the attack of sparrows? Has any reader of these articles a sovereign remedy against this naughty, wanton, wild destruction? Short of putting automatic cartridges amongst my primroses, I have done everything I can think of. I have made a sort of cat's cradle of strong black thread, pegged down in the hope that the birds would catch their nasty little claws in it as they alighted and thus be frightened and discouraged. It doesn't work. The sparrows don't seem to mind. I can suppose only that they crawl underneath the threads and nip the flowers off, scattering the buds and the heads all over the ground at dawn before I have got up in the morning.
>
> This is a real S.O.S. I have quite a collection of uncommon primroses, Jack-in-the-Green, Madame Pompadour, Cloth-of-Gold, and so on, but what is the good of that if the sparrows take them all? I would try not to grudge them their fun if it was of any benefit to them, but it isn't. They are mischievous hooligans who destroy for the sake of destruction.[4]

The answers she received ranged from pepper, powdered napthalene, saffron, quassia and soft soap to old nursery fireguards, confetti and gramophone records, splintered; she was even enjoined to try Christian Science. There is a point, however, when the remedy becomes less desirable than the *status quo*. Bowles also favoured quassia and soft soap, for sparrows were a great nuisance at Myddelton.

I have been unable to discover what are the enemies of such flowers [early crocuses] in their own homes, but judging from the evil habits of that vulgar little pest the sparrow, one is inclined to fancy they may be birds of sorts. But for the sake of those to whose charitable sentimentality all members of the avian fauna are the 'dear little birds', repaying winter doles of crumbs with spring carols, I will offer a scapegoat in the form of some beetle of the family of Cantharidae such as our British Oil Beetle, *Meloe Proscarabaeus*, to which a fresh young flower is a toothsome breakfast, for I notice that those who can overlook anything in a bird—'a dear little bird', of course, ostriches and eagles being outside their spheres of experience—are ever ready to denounce or bring about the destruction of 'nasty creeping things'. For myself, I am too light a sleeper to appreciate the cheeping of newly-awakened sparrows in the Wistaria round my window, and too fond of its flowers to forgive their chewing the swelling bloom-buds.[5]

Knowing, however, that he was powerless, more-or-less, against the ravages of birds, he rationalised his impotence in this way.

As one cannot preach honesty to the birds, nor would wish to banish their songs and cheerful presence from the garden, it is best to philosophise mildly, and reconcile oneself to the loss of gaily coloured fruits by reflecting that as an actual fact we owe the beauty of colouring of bright berries as much to the birds themselves as to the plants that bear them. The very *raison d'être* of attractive colouring in a berry is to advertise it as a desirable meal for a bird, in order that, in one way or another, the seeds in the fleshy pulp may be carried into suitable places for their germination.[6]

The saving grace of pests, such as it is, lies in their visibility to the gardener if he is observant. Soil-borne pathogens, on the other hand, defeat the most assiduous care and attention.

This last season brought some mysterious influence to bear on several of my vines. I had been inclined to complain of many of them because their leaves remained green until sharp frosts cut them, and they fell, a dingy, dishonoured mass of tarnished reputations, the colour of an over boiled Brussels-sprout. Last Autumn an old *Vitis coignetiae* that had never before got beyond the golden bronze of a new penny, astonished me by turning a rich purple in early September, and then proceeded to produce semi-transparent patches of the rich crimson I associate with carbuncles among gems and currant jelly among jams, wherever the sunshine fell on an exposed portion of leaf. For several weeks I made an afternoon pilgrimage daily to this pillar of fire, to stand with it between me and the westering sun, to catch the full glow of its tones of reds, growing more and more scarlet every day, and reminding me of Burne-Jones' wonderful window in Birmingham Cathedral ... But in the light of later events I can only account for their unwonted roseate hues by believing that some horrible fungus was at work among their roots. For when Spring came and it was time for their new leaves, these three Vines were found to be as dead as Rameses and as dry as his mummy.[7]

This mystery was never satisfactorily resolved, and nor was the case of the non-flowering viburnums.

... recently [August 1954] they seem to have developed a disheartening form of delinquency. A bad idea has seized them. They just don't flower.

I began to notice this failure in my own garden so long as four years ago and could not think what to attribute it to. It had nothing to do with the age of the plants ... [or] aspect ... [or] soil ... Yet in every case the flower-buds due for blooming the following spring started to form in summer, as they should, quite normally, and in every case they blackened, shrivelled, and finally came to naught. They turned into something like tiny black crabs with hooked claws, or like the corms of some anemones, instead of the handsome pink-and-white flower-head I had anticipated. Baffled, I blamed myself: what had I done wrong by them? Then, losing my temper, I blamed them: ungrateful things, why should they suddenly go back on me like this? Yet I worried, because one has a responsibility towards one's plants as towards one's children or one's animals.

I now discover that my experience is becoming widespread, and that inquiries are pouring into the R.H.S. office at Wisley ... It appears that the authorities ... have no explanation. Laboratory examination has given no result. No grub, bug, mite, thrip, fly or other noxious organism has revealed itself under the microscope. No spore, fungus, canker or other murrain. Nor can the trouble be attributed to the weather, say to an early autumn frost, since last autumn we enjoyed temperatures which sent the mercury too high to please the fore-sighted gardener. The mystery of the viburnums may sound like the title of a Sherlock Holmes story, but remains unsolved. And most provoking.[8]

Some gardeners ignore the difficulties posed by pests and diseases, and set their faces resolutely against any remedies mechanical or chemical to deal with them, settling down, more or less contentedly, with a garden of tattered and mildewed plants and an unpolluted atmosphere. Weeds, on the other hand, cannot be disregarded, because they can thwart by their excessive seeding and colonising, all attempts at beautiful effect. No one who calls himself a cultivator of gardens can ignore them.

Weeding is a delightful occupation, [Miss Jekyll began, controversially, although, in order not to lose her readers' sympathy, she did qualify that with] especially after summer rain, when the roots come up clear and clean. One gets to know how many and various are the ways of weeds—as many almost as the moods of human creatures. How easy and pleasant to pull up are the soft annuals like Chickweed and Groundsel, and how one looks with respect at deep-rooted things like Docks, that make one go and fetch a spade. Comfrey is another thing with a terrible root, and every bit must be got out, as it will grow again from the smallest scrap. And hard to get up are the two Bryonies, the green and the black, with such deep-reaching roots, that, if not weeded up within their first year will have to be seriously dug out later. The white Convolvulus, one of the loveliest of native plants, has a most persistently running root, of which

every joint will quickly form a new plant. Some of the worst weeds to get out are Goutweed and Coltsfoot. Though I live on a light soil, comparatively easy to clean, I have done some gardening in clay, and well know what a despairing job it is to get the bits of either of these roots out of the stiff clods ...

Goutweed [ground elder, *Aegopodium podograria*] is a pest in nearly all gardens and very difficult to get out. When it runs into the root or some patch of hardy plant, if the plant can be spared, I find it best to send it at once to the burn-heap; or if it is too precious, there is nothing for it but to cut it all up and wash it out, to be sure that not the smallest particle of the enemy remains. Some weeds are deceiving—Sow-thistle for instance, which has the look of promising firm hand-hold and easy extraction, but has a disappointing way of almost always breaking short off at the collar. But of all the garden weeds that are native plants I know none so persistent or so insiduous as the Rampion Bell-flower [*Campanula rapunculoides*]; it grows from the smallest thread of root, and it is almost impossible to see every little bit; for though the main roots are thick, and white, and fleshy, the fine side roots that run far abroad are very small, and of a reddish colour, and easily hidden in the brown earth.[9]

This plant received the rough edge of Farrer's pen. He called it

the most insatiable and irrepressible of beautiful weeds. If once its tall and arching spires of violet bells prevail on you to admit it to your garden, neither you nor its choice inmates will ever know peace again.[10]

Weeds fit into two categories; those plants that are part of the native flora, never allowed in and to be ruthlessly extirpated when they do find a way, and those cultivated plants, deliberately introduced but which prove difficult and obstreperous guests, the vegetable equivalents of H.M. Bateman's rotter who, when invited to make himself at home, did so. Those men, like Bowles, who were for ever experimenting with new untried plants, often recently introduced from overseas with glowing testimonials, but not yet awarded a badge for good and considerate behaviour, were in difficulties.

Some of the new Chinese Brambles have yellow fruits, but too small to be very attractive, and the wicked wandering ways of the coarse plants that bear them appear so aggressive that it seems best to march them off to the bonfire heap, before they fill the garden and push up through the floors and scratch one's legs under the dinner table. We have quite enough rough bramble stems in our own woods to trip us up and scratch us when taking short cuts, without wanting any more varieties, even though they come from China.[11]

and

If ever you want to provide an unending struggle for a brother gardener, and perhaps make a lifelong enemy of him, give him a morsel of the Blue Sowthistle, *Lactuca alpina.* It is so beautiful, and seems to grow so pleasantly for its first two seasons, making a compact carpet of handsome leaves and giving tall stems of lovely blue flowers, that anyone who knows not its wicked ways is sure to let it make itself at home—then he must spend the rest of his life striving to keep the trespasser from running over his whole garden.[12]

The other great immutable, against the baleful effects of which the gardener must exercise all his ingenuity and capacity for fortitude, is the weather. We have seen how it affects plant-hunters but, here at home too, it bulks large in the consideration of gardeners. Years of effort and care can be undermined by a harsh and damaging winter, or even an untimely frost; much of the thinking, scheming, and practical work centres around the protection of tender plants outside, and great is the rejoicing, in which all neighbours are asked to join, when plants too shy to flower in cold conditions are coaxed into blossom by favourable weather.

Farrer complained long and hard about the difficulties of gardening on the edge of the Pennines. He felt somehow aggrieved and hard done by, but he could hardly blame the plants for giving up the unequal struggle. Because of the wet winters and the lack of daylight,

the woolly children of the highest alps make haste to depart to their long home, sodden and putrid little heaps of brown decay; the Primulas pull first one foot out of the ground and then another, as if they meant to trot away

up to the fells. But then, having achieved so much, their strength or their courage fails them, and they lie drunkenly about on the soaking earth, with their long, white tentacles waving in the air or trailing useless across the soil.[13]

Howling winds were a speciality of the district, or so you would think to read him.

… if they lull, it is delusively: Spring moves forward in a blessed interval of peace and warmth; like the young woman in the *Graphic* she takes off some of her wrappings and reveals herself. And then the winds pounce, and she catches a mortal chill as they roar and whistle round her anew, ravenously, shouting for joy in having played her such a trick. Disagreeable, disagreeable, disagreeable are the first four months of our northern year. And in so speaking, I think I even flatter them.[14]

Bowles, gardening on a light soil, had also reason to curse winds early in the season, but more because they dried the soil too much than anything else.

A peck of dust in March, we have all been taught, is worth a king's ransom. The farmer may find it so; he generally wants it dry when others would like it wet, and then grumbles because some crop has not grown. He is always waiting for dry weather to get on the land himself or to get something off it, so he may put that hateful peck of what the schoolboy defined as mud with the juice squeezed out, on his credit side, but I do not suppose I am alone among gardeners in feeling it is more likely to cost a king's ransom to renew the plants it kills. Those cold, drying March winds do so much terrible damage, or at least they put a finishing stroke to many a struggling invalid, shaken but not killed by the winter's frosts. If only they would tide over another week or two the warmer ground would help along the growth of their new roots, and enough sap would run up to equalise their loss by transpiration, but with imperfect roots and an east wind they shrivel up and give up the struggle in an hour or two. An aged Cistus bush will often be the first to show the bill is coming in; Bamboos, Miscanthus, and Choisya jot down fresh items and you are lucky if the young green shoots of

Crown Imperials, Eremuri and precious lilies are not included. It is an anxious and trying time, not only because it roughens one's own skin, making shaving a painful bore, and the corners of one's smile less expansive, but it is then one notes day by day some pet plant's failure to put in an appearance, or the flagging and browning of a cherished specimen.[15]

Weather we can do little about, except to mitigate its worst effects, but sometimes human agency intervenes to ruin our best plans. Farrer suffered from garden-boys who could not water properly, which is hardly surprising since watering is one of the most skilled operations in the garden, and one that should not have been left to an apprentice anyway; nor was he any more fortunate in one of his relations. After an *Abutilon vitifolium* had been cut hard back in his absence, he wrote,

> For certain Activities, [which is a strange word for them] being in need of exercise one day, and having an energy untempered by knowledge, mistook that unlucky shrub for a weed, and went for it with billhooks in my absence with so good a will that when I returned there was nothing except the most lamentable stump remaining ... And everyone of you good people pray put into your prayers a petition that you may have fortitude to bear with energetic relations who assist your labours, very kindly, in your absence, by cutting all your best shrubs into tight fat balls, regardless of whether the poor things blossom on the old wood or the new.[16]

Miss Jekyll's problem, or at least one she felt many gardeners had, was not inexperienced and over-zealous help, but the stubborn, know-all employee whose old ideas could not be shifted.

Now [1899] that the owners of good places are for the most part taking a newly awakened and newly educated pleasure in the better ways of gardening, a frequent source of difficulty arises from the ignorance and obstructiveness of gardeners ... The gardener may be an excellent man, perfectly understanding the ordinary routine of garden work; he may have been many years in his place; it is his settled home, and he is getting well on into middle life; but he has no understanding of the new order of things, and when the master,

perfectly understanding what he is about, desires that certain things shall be done, and wishes to enjoy the pleasure of directing the work himself, and seeing it grow under his hand, he resents it as an interference, and becomes obstructive, or does what is required in a spirit of such sullen acquiescence that it is equal to open opposition ... Various degrees of ignorance and narrow-mindedness must no doubt be expected among the class that produces private gardeners. Their general education is not very wide to begin with, and their training is usually in one groove, and the many who possess a full share of vanity get to think that, because they have exhausted the obvious sources of experience that have occurred within their reach, there is nothing more to learn, or to know, or to see, or to feel, or to enjoy. It is in this that the difficulty lies ...[17]

She moderated the severity of these remarks by admitting that there were gardeners, five of whom were personally known to her, who had risen above small-minded vanity and who were eager to learn and try out something new. She was also forced by honesty to admit:

> But then on the other hand, frequent causes of irritation arise between master and man from the master's ignorance and unreasonable demands. For much as the love of gardening has grown of late, there are many owners who have no knowledge of it whatever ...
> I have had ... [a] visitor ... who, contemplating some cherished garden picture, the consummation of some long-hoped-for wish, the crowning joy of years of labour, said 'Now look at that; it is just right, and yet it is quite simple—there is absolutely nothing in it; now why can't my man give me that?'[18]

This view has vanished as completely as the men of which she complained, though it lingers on in a diluted and slightly shame-faced form in some private gardens where hired help can still be afforded.

Inasmuch as the professional gardener still exists he is now as likely to be found pricking out seedlings in a nursery. Nurseries were, and are, the repositories of marvellous plants, although with the transformation of many into garden centres much of their charm has gone. I do not think that these five authors would have approved of the ordinary garden centre, with its small range of foolproof 'lines' and the accent very much on shifting a volume of plants as quickly as possible before they have the chance to die under the inept and careless supervision. None was a stranger, however, to the commercial motivations of nurseries, never better exemplified than in catalogue descriptions. Like estate agents' particulars these were, of course, invitations to buy, not sworn affidavits of fact, so fun was to be had at the expense of the nurseryman. There was however an underlying genuine irritation at misleading comments, for they all suffered from descriptions too flattering and alluring. Talking of fritillaries, *Fritillaria*, Farrer said that catalogues were a guide to the reader of what was available,

> ... so long as it is remembered that catalogues do not always emphasize the miffy temper of the prizes they proclaim; and that a nod ought to be as good as a wink to a blind gardener, accordingly, in the way of 'should have sand' or 'is best if planted early'. Not to mention—a fact which catalogues rarely do—that an enormous number of *Fritillarias* have more or less stinking bells of dingy chocolate and greenish tones, which often appear transfigured by the enthusiasm of those who desire to get rid of them, as 'rich purple' or 'amaranthine violet'.[19]

On the subject of China Asters, Miss Jekyll opined that for years she had been hindered from getting the colours she desired because of inaccurate descriptions in seed-lists:

> Finally I paid a visit to the trial-grounds of one of our premier seed-houses, and saw all the kinds and the colourings and made my own notes ... The customer, in order to get the desired flowers, has to *learn a code* ... Thus, if I want a Giant Comet of that beautiful pale silvery lavender, perhaps the loveliest colour of which a China Aster is capable, I have to ask for 'azure blue'. If I want a full lilac, I must order 'blue'; if a full purple, it is 'dark blue'. If I want a strong, rich violet-purple, I must beware of asking for purple, for I shall get a terrible magenta such as one year spoilt the whole colour scheme of my Aster garden. It is not as if the right colour-words were wanting, for the language is rich in them—violet, lavender, lilac, mauve, purple:

these, with slight additions, will serve to describe the whole of the colourings falsely called blue. The word blue should not be used at all in connection with these flowers. [And she ended in such a way as to brook no argument.] There are no blue China Asters.[20]

As colour was very important to Miss Jekyll so botanical correctness was the least that Bowles required. He expatiated on the problem that

> so often confronts the good gardener who wishes to be sure of the names of his plants. To him it seems quite a simple matter. He has two things so utterly distinct for garden purposes, that he can never himself be in doubt as to which is which, either when in flower or leaf. But he wishes to get more roots of the form that pleases him most, and, having ordered a hundred or two, finds he has landed himself with a fresh lot of the kind of which he already has too much. He may reason with himself and conclude that if he gets the plant he doesn't wish for, as *Bloomingthingia Thisherei*, doubtless he will get the one he does want, under one of the other names *B. totheronei* or *B. dontcherwishyermaygetitii* (true!). So he orders from the lists offering these attractive goods, and after another season he finds yet more large patches of his undesired old superfluity.[21]

Miss Sackville-West blamed herself for being taken in by nurserymen's descriptions.

> Catalogues arrive by every post, and are as bewildering in their diversity as in their monotony. What shall we order this autumn? Bulbs, shrubs, flowering trees, herbaceous plants, or what? How tempting the lists are! And how easy they make gardening sound! If you believed half they say you would look forward next year to a garden something between Kew and the tropical garden of some legendary millionaire in Guatemala. It is difficult to keep one's head. I always lose mine. Year after year I am decoyed into experiments which I know are almost certainly doomed to failure. I cannot resist. Experience tells me that I ought to resist, but, like the poor mutt who falls to the card-sharper in the train, I fall to every list offering plants I cannot afford to buy and could not cultivate successfully even if I could afford them.[22]

Notes

1. R. J. Farrer, *The English Rock Garden*, 4th impression (2 vols., T.C. and E.C. Jack, 1928), vol. 1, pp. 192–3.

2. G. Jekyll, *Wood and Garden*, facsimile of 1st edn (Antique Collectors' Club, 1981), p. 348.

3. E.A. Bowles, *My Garden in Summer*, 1st edn (T.C. and E.C. Jack, 1914), pp. 206–7.

4. V. Sackville-West, *In Your Garden*, 1st edn (Michael Joseph, 1951), pp. 52–3.

5. E.A. Bowles, *My Garden in Spring*, 1st edn (T.C. and E.C. Jack, 1914), pp. 24–5.

6. E.A. Bowles, *My Garden in Autumn and Winter*, 1st edn (T.C. and E.C. Jack, 1915), p. 234.

7. Ibid., p. 163.

8. V. Sackville-West, *More for Your Garden*, 1st edn (Michael Joseph, 1955), pp. 112–3.

9. Jekyll, *Wood and Garden*, pp. 342–4.

10. Farrer, *The English Rock Garden*, vol. 1, p. 193.

11. Bowles, *My Garden in Autumn and Winter*, pp. 242–3.

12. Bowles, *My Garden in Summer*, p. 289.

13. R. J. Farrer, *In a Yorkshire Garden*, 1st edn (Edward Arnold, 1909), p. 1.

14. Ibid., pp. 8–9.

15. Bowles, *My Garden in Spring*, pp. 149–50.

16. Farrer, *Yorkshire Garden*, p. 259.

17. Jekyll, *Wood and Garden*, pp. 360–2.

18. Ibid., pp. 366–8.

19. Farrer, *The English Rock Garden*, vol. 1, p. 356.

20. G. Jekyll, *Colour Schemes for the Flower Garden*, facsimile of 1936 edn (Antique Collectors' Club, 1982), pp. 174–6.

21. Bowles, *My Garden in Autumn and Winter*, p. 80.

22. Sackville-West, *In Your Garden*, pp. 118–9.

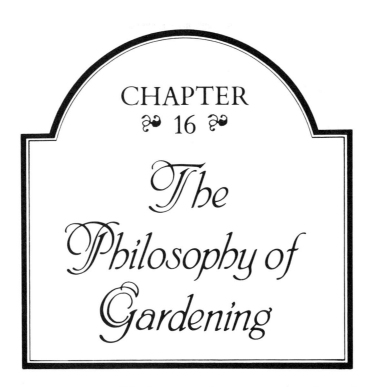

CHAPTER ❧ 16 ❧

The Philosophy of Gardening

In June 1918, Farrer wrote, apropos of the forms of the Harebell Poppy, *Meconopsis quintuplinervia* (see Chapter 6),

> if, amid the cataclysms of anguish that clamour round us everywhere nowadays, you declare that all this babble about beauty and flowers is a vain impertinence, then I must tell you that you err, and that your perspectives are false. Mortal dooms and dynasties are brief things, but beauty is indestructible and eternal, if its tabernacle be only in a petal that is shed to-morrow. Wars and agonies are shadows only cast across the path of man: each successive one seems the end of all things, but man perpetually emerges and goes forward, lured always and cheered and inspired by the immortal beauty–thought that finds form in all the hopes and enjoyments of his life. *Inter arma silent flores* is no truth; on the contrary, amid the crash of doom our sanity and survival more than ever depend on the strength with which we can listen to the still small voice that towers above the cannons, and cling to the little quiet things of life, the things that come and go yet are always there, the inextinguishable lamps of God amid the disaster that man has made of his life.

This is no idle fantasy: little happinesses may look little, and find no place in the plans of diplomats and prophets; but they outlast the worst catastrophes and survive the plans and the diplomats and the prophets and all. Dead bones in their grave lie Mary and Elizabeth, Queens, and dead dust of death is all they did; but the flowers they grew in their gardens still continue giving comfort and delight perpetually, down through the continuing generations, to whom the people of the past are mere phantasmal fictions in books, diaphanous, desiccated, as dried flowers themselves. All the wars of the world, all the Caesars, have not the staying power of a Lily in a cottage border: man creates the storms in his teacup, and dies of them, but there remains a something standing outside, a something impregnable, as far beyond reach of man's destructiveness as is man's own self. The immortality of marbles and of miseries is a vain, small thing compared to the immortality of a flower that blooms and is dead by dusk.[1]

Farrer felt, I am sure, that his mission in life was to impress on all receptive people the importance to our spiritual health of a love of beauty. Everything flows from that; not liking rarity for its sake alone, striving to cultivate plants as well as possible, searching always for the best and most felicitous effects with the plants available. Miss Jekyll agreed. At the beginning of *Wood and Garden*, her most influential work, which held, distilled, the essence of her garden philosophy, she said that she laid no claim to literary ability or botanical knowledge, or even knowing the best methods of cultivation, but that she felt that she had

> acquired certain instincts which ... are of the nature of useful knowledge ... [The lesson she had thoroughly learned] and wish to pass on to others, is to know the enduring happiness that the love of a garden gives. I rejoice when I see anyone, and especially children, inquiring about flowers, and making gardens of their own, and carefully working in them. For the love of gardening is a seed that once sown never dies, but always grows and grows to an enduring and ever-increasing source of happiness. [Her aim was gardening for beautiful effect.] A garden so treated gives the delightful feeling of repose, and refreshment, and purest enjoyment of beauty, that seems to my understanding to be the best fulfilment of its purpose; while to the diligent worker its happiness is like the offering of a constant hymn of praise. For I hold that the best purpose of a garden is to give delight and to give refreshment of mind, to soothe, to refine, and to lift up the heart in a spirit of praise and thankfulness. It is certain that those who practise gardening in the best ways find it to be so.[2]

For Robinson, the object of a garden was similar, that is to provide what he called 'high art', which he defined as 'power to see and give form to beautiful things'. To him, as for Miss Jekyll, close observation of Nature brought the best results. He inveighed against people who judged,

> pictures not by Nature, but by pictures, and therefore they miss her subtleties and delicate realities on which all true work depends.[3]

> The gardener should follow the true artist, however modestly, in his love for things as they are, in delight in natural form and beauty of flower and tree, if we are to be free from barren geometry, and if our gardens are ever to be pictures. The gardener has not the strenuous work of eye and hand that the artist has, but he has plenty of good work to do:—to choose from the thousand beautiful living things; to study their nature and adapt them to his soil and climate; to get the full expression

of their beauty; to grow and place them well and in right relation to other things, which is a life-study in itself, in view of the great number of the flowers and flowering trees of the world. And as the artist's work is to see and keep for us some of the beauty of landscape, tree or flower, so the gardener's should be to keep for us as far as may be, in the fulness of their natural beauty, the living things themselves. The artist gives us the fair image: the gardener is the trustee [this is an idea that has become increasingly prevalent in this century, but which must have been unusual in the 1890s] of a world of fair living things, to be kept with care and knowledge in necessary subordination to the conditions of his work.[4]

All this explains his abhorrence of 'decoration' and his desire to sweep away pattern-gardens.

> And as there is other and higher design than that of the decorator of flat surfaces with patterns, so there is an absolute and eternal difference between conventional form as he expresses it, and the true forms of cloud or hill, vale, stream, path, oak, palm and vine, reed and lily. And the first duty of all who care for the garden as a picture is to see these noble natural forms in every part of life and nature, and once they see them they will never mistake decorative patterns for art and beauty in a garden.[5]

For Bowles pictorial effect was important but not paramount. He was in what we would now call the plantsman's tradition.

> ... if only the owner of a garden will plant enough plants of the most different types and habits procurable, there ought to be never a day in which he cannot find some pleasure in maturing growth or decay, structure of bud, leaf, blossom, fruit or stem, no minute of the daylight hours of the working days in which there is no interesting and health-giving work to be done; and no bed of the garden that will not provide some offering for a friend, whether it be cut flowers, ripe seeds or divisions of roots. That is my idea of what a garden should provide for its owner and his friends, and my desire in writing these notes on my garden during the four seasons is that others besides myself, who like a plant for its associations and interest as well as for its own

individual beauty, may be encouraged to grow collections of plants that are often overlooked in the present-day desire for masses of colour. Of course I confess humbly that, owing to hindrances and limitations due to soil, climate, purse and space, the art of gardening for colour effect is too hard a one for me to attempt here. I do not wish to belittle the great successes others have achieved nor the pleasure I derive from seeing their beautiful gardens. I only wish to show how much pleasure I have derived from this by no means remarkable garden, and to encourage others somewhat similarly circumstanced to collect and grow plants of all kinds, to watch and note their peculiarities, mark their charms, and hand on the best of them to others who love a plant for its own sake.[6]

This is not a different viewpoint from Jekyll and Robinson and Sackville-West, merely a shift of emphasis, and one with which Farrer would have concurred. The latter did not, in any event, believe that all Nature was beautiful, and it followed that not all natural effects were exemplary either. Talking of the Order of Scrophularinae, he wrote,

Otherwise this Order leads worthily on to the dull desolation of *Labiatae*, though I know this is an unpopular view to take, and that nowadays it is good form to say that all plants are lovely, and that Nature can never be dull or plain. However, one must abide by one's own convictions, and I will honestly say that Nature not only can be both, but very frequently chooses to be so; so that real treasures are in an inconsiderable minority. As for the exalted truth that the emancipated mind can see beauties in Groundsel or Deadnettle, not for one moment will I deny it. But its prophets in popular literature seem too often to speak academically, as worshippers of the ideal, rather than as horticulturists with actual earthly, earthy gardens to cultivate ...[7]

When it came to expressing adequately his love of something beautiful, Farrer was in difficulties, or so he maintained.

For how many people, I wonder, feel with me, the difficulty of adequately appreciating? [He meant expressing that appreciation] I don't care what it is—whether it be flower of the field, or fluffy kitten, or human body. One stands in front, for instance, of a glory like the Siberian Columbine, and one thumps and throbs inside, and feels that there is something to be done in tribute, yet one cannot tell what. And so remains incomplete, frustrate, almost hurt with the impossibility of expression. One might perhaps say, 'How very pretty,' or words to that effect; or one might burst into tears as one certainly would have done if one had lived in the eighteenth century and cultivated sensibility.

But either course, after all, is wholly inadequate and silly. No, that is not enough. One wants and burns and pines to absorb the thing into oneself, crush it into one's own essence, make it everlastingly part of the everlasting flux of one's own personality. And yet all one can do is to look on at it in silence, and just stupidly in a sort of dazed anguish, contemplate that perfection from outside. And I wonder whether that inarticulate wait for incorporation of all beauty is what prayer really means; or, perhaps, they will tell me that any such passionate admiration is simply a development, however remote and obscure, of the sexual instinct, causing the delight of the eyes in every direction, to inspire one with the passion of personal possession. Well, I would rather have my cult for this Columbine than a passion *à la* Plato for a bashful young potato, or a not-too French French bean.[8] [There is a sweet irony in that passage, for Farrer of all people was capable of expressing his feeling for plants.]

All gardeners are faced sooner or later, and usually sooner, with the prospect of failure. It is the coming to terms with this which makes a man a true gardener. That and an unquenchable hope. Hope must triumph not only over experience but also over realisation. Farrer, when leading the reader around his garden, pointed to some big, old Tree-paeonies

just preparing to turn into a flaunt of gorgeousness. Probably now that I have said these words, this very night, there will come such a frost that it will destroy them all. At present, however, I may fairly enjoy the prospect of them; cruel fate may deprive us at will of our realisations; but not all the fates of the Pantheon, were they nine or ninety and nine, instead of three, could ever rob us of our hopes. And our hopes, when everything is said and done, are invariably more satisfactory and beautiful and precious than any amount of realisations. So that we have the best of the bargain, no matter how we may bewail ourselves in the anguish of disappointment. For, if your flowers *had* been allowed to bloom in glory, they would never and could never have managed to be as glorious as you saw them beforehand in imagination.[9]

Bowles, also, was prepared for failure but, in writing about his plants, he had a talisman. There is a warning here which we should all heed when success is so heady as to incline us to be boastful.

I rather pride myself on being free from superstitions about most things, and have even lectured at local debating societies on the inconsistency of superstitious fears with a Christian belief. But I believe most people, though able to make light of certain superstitions, and perhaps ready to walk under ladders, or dine comfortably though one of thirteen, cannot quite shake off some idea, probably an ingrained result of nursery teaching, that it is just as well to avoid giving and receiving scissors, or cutting one's nails on a Friday ... My greatest weakness of all, however, takes the form of an uncomfortable feeling, that the unseen powers lie in wait with trouble or failure for him who boasts of continued success ...

At no time am I more timid of these avenging fates than when openly rejoicing in some garden success, and more especially so in print. So often has dire calamity, sudden death, or uprooting by storm, followed the publication of a photograph and exultant note describing one of my best specimens, not only with Clematis, and Mezereon [*Daphne mezereum*] and such 'here to-day and gone to-morrow' subjects, but with many steady-going old plants, that I feel an uncanny dread creeping over me, that unless I touch wood in some way to disarm the overlooking witch and blind the Evil Eye, I had better not describe my successes. Now, as I do not wish for a blasted heath, or a landscape like that around the chemical works at Stratford, in place of my crowded old garden, and as I always use a stylograph pen made of vulca-

nite, and won't go back to a wooden pen-holder, my epistolary method of touching wood must consist of an assumed distrust in the future prosperity of my treasures, and so readers will please help me by understanding that the 'so fars' and 'apparently establisheds' I must sprinkle among my descriptions of flourishing colonies of healthy plants are amulets designed to protect my darlings from the maw of the mollusc and the blasting of the bacillus.[10]

What other qualities of the true gardener can we identify? Generosity, material and of spirit, is one. This is Farrer on the joy of giving, although it could have been any of the others.

... what pleasure is there greater than to go round one's garden on a sunny day with a fellow-enthusiast, and to sing that cheering Litany which runs, in strophe and anti-strophe, 'Oh, wouldn't you like a bit of this?'—'And I could send you a bulb of that'. Down delves the glad trowel into a clump, and it is halved—like mercy, blessing him that gives and him that takes ... There are few greater pleasures in life than giving pleasure with a plant; or getting pleasure again with a plant. And certainly there is none more bland and blameless.[11]

As essential as openhandedness is a proper humility:

... the true gardener is a lover of his flowers, not a critic of them. I think the true gardener is the reverent servant of Nature, not her truculent, wife-beating master. I think the true gardener, the older he grows, should more and more develop a humble, grateful and uncertain spirit, cocksure of nothing except the universality of beauty. It withers and affronts me to hear a gardener contemptuous of this little dear flower or that; to meet an arrogant and arid spirit stalking in its garden, with narrow specialist-talk of rarity, of rigid correspondence with man-made rule, and a cold sweeping of whole lovely classes and families into the outer darkness of his scorn.[12]

When I see this [wrote Miss Jekyll about a quantity of individual plants rather than a garden picture composed of a beautiful arrangement of those plants] in ordinary gardens, I try to put myself into the same mental attitude, and so far succeed, in that I can perceive that it represents one of the earlier stages in the love of a garden, and that one must not quarrel with it, because a garden is for its owner's pleasure, and whatever the degree or form of that pleasure, if only it be sincere, it is right and reasonable, and adds to human happiness in one of the purest and best of ways. And often I find I have to put upon myself this kind of drag, because when one has passed through the more elementary stages which deal with isolated details, and has come to a point when one feels some slight power of what perhaps may be called generalship; when the means and material that go to the making of a garden seem to be within one's grasp and awaiting one's command, then comes the danger of being inclined to lay down the law, and of advocating the ultimate effects that one feels oneself to be most desirable in an intolerant spirit of cock-sure pontification. So I try, when I am in a garden of the ordinary kind where the owner likes variety, to see it a little from the same point of view, and in the arboretum, where one of each of a hundred different kinds of Conifers stand in their fine young growth, to see and admire the individuals only, and to stifle my own longing to see a hundred of the sort at a time, and to keep down the shop-window feeling, and the idea of a worthless library made up of odd single volumes where there should be complete sets, and the comparison of an inconsequent jumble of words, with a clearly written sentence, and all such naughty similitudes, as come crowding through the brain of the garden-artist (if I may give myself a title so honourable), who desires not only to see the beautiful plants and trees, but to see them used in the best and largest and most worthy of ways.[13]

This passage suggests that she had not quite achieved that level of humility to which she aspired.

Bowles was a genuinely humble man, and a great giver too. His horticultural apprentice-ship, as it were, was served listening to men like Canon Ellacombe and Dr Lowe of Wimbledon, whose generosity in spreading around unusual treasures was legendary. Not that he would not have been a giver anyway, I feel sure, for such an outgoing Christian individual would be bound

to derive pleasure from seeing plants of his raising or finding, ornamenting the gardens of other keen gardeners. The only proviso was that gifts should be looked after well and diligently. Farrer felt that, too, about the plants he sold in his Craven Nursery.

> ... the one drawback of selling one's plants is not that it impairs one's happy unconscious-ness in talking about them, but that it lays such a load of responsibility upon one's conscience ... I can never see my officials despatching great hampers, without a wish to have references from their orderers ... to prove to me that they are indeed fit and know-ledgeable persons to be entrusted with the welfare of my precious little people.[14]

This obligation to do the best one could should extend to all forms of gardening.

> ... it is not enough to say in praise of a given method that it does not kill your plants ... The question is, Does your method make your plants the greatest possible degree of health and prosperity of which they are cap-able? It afflicts me to the heart, I declare when people rejoice and triumph over a wretched, ill-planted tuft, and congratulate themselves that it is 'doing', whereas it is merely surviv-ing, and very far from the health into which efficient culture would have brought it. 'Well, it is alive', they say. Ah, but it ought to be so very much more than that before you can call yourself a gardener, and your gardening a success. Many and many are the ways of ignorance, slackness and incompetence; it is quite likely that if their victim be naturally robust you will not kill it. But there is only one way of giving it a sound chance of show-ing you the best it can do. And that is to do the very best possible that you can do for it; with energy, thoroughness, and much painfully earned and diligently digested experience.[15]

As Miss Jekyll wrote, in the context of choos-ing the right internal fittings for her house but applicable generally.

> It takes more time, more trouble; it may even take a good deal of time and trouble, but then it is just right, and to see and know that it is right is a daily reward and a never-ending source of satisfaction.[16]

Doing the best that you can means very often paying close attention to soil and climate. There are gardeners, however, who have only to find themselves gardening on an alkaline soil for them ardently to wish to grow camellias, pieris and rhododendrons, and go to much time and effort with peat and iron chelates to achieve a few chlorotic and unhappy plants, having, so to speak, pitted themselves against the inexorable rigidity of natural law. The same people, put down on a heathy moor, will yearn to grow irises and pinks and roses well. It is personality and not circumstance that matters. For Robinson, who was no shirker provided he could see the point of it, it was wasted futile labour and his view has been echoed time and again by gardening writers since. For him,

> the best way in gardening is always to grow the flowers that thrive without great labour in the soil we have.[17]

> . . . a constant source of waste is the planting of things not really hardy in districts where they perish in hard winters, such as the Arbutus about London and in the midlands. And, even where things seem hardy, some of them, like Fuchsias, never give the charming effects we get from them in the west of Ireland, in Wales, and in warm coast gardens, whatever care we take. Such facts should not discourage because they only emphasise the lesson that the true way in a garden is for each to do what soil and climate allow of, and in that way we arrive at the most important artistic gain of all, i.e. that each garden has its own distinct charms.[18]

Robinson had difficulty overseeing his gardeners properly after his paralysing fall in 1910, and soon saw the need to employ a strong-minded head gardener. His choice was Ernest Markham; it was a decision he did not regret. He would have appreciated, therefore, what Miss Jekyll wrote on the subject of the employer keeping control of the garden. This is a salutary thought for those given to fits of blind nostalgia.

> I do not envy owners of very large gardens. The garden should fit its master or his tastes just as his clothes do; it should be neither too large nor too small, but just comfortable. If the garden is larger than he can individually garden and plan and look after, then he is no longer its master but its slave, just as surely as

the much-too-rich man is the slave and not the master of his superfluous wealth. And when I hear of the great place with a kitchen garden of twenty acres within the walls, my heart sinks as I think of the uncomfortable disproportion between the man and those immediately around him, and his vast output of edible vegetation, and I fall to wondering how much of it goes as it should go, or whether the greater part of it does not go dribbling away, leaking into unholy back-channels; and of how the looking after it must needs be sub-divided; and of how many side-interests are likely to steal up, and altogether how great a burden of anxiety or matter of temptation it must give rise to. A grand truth is in the old farmer's saying, 'The master's eye makes the pig fat'; but how can any one master's eye fat that vast pig of twenty acres, with all its minute and costly cultivation, its two or three crops a year off all ground given to soft vegetables, its stores, greenhouses, orchid and orchard houses, its vineries, pineries, figgeries, and all manner of glass structures?[19]

This same impulse, on a smaller scale, led her to stress the importance of observing closely, whether it be embroidery, painting or gardening. She emphasised it particularly in her book *Children and Gardens* for she obviously considered that no one was too young to learn this.

> Now if you will take any flower you please and look it carefully all over and turn it about, and smell it and feel it and try and find out all its little secrets; not of flowers only but of leaf, bud and stem as well, you will discover many wonderful things. This is how to make friends with plants, and very good friends you will find them to the end of your lives.[20]

Practising what she preached stood her in good stead for her eyesight was so bad that its natural focal length was only two inches.

She did have comforting words for anyone who may have become daunted by these counsels of perfection on his way to becoming a true gardener.

> Let no one be discouraged by the thought of how much there is to learn. Looking back upon nearly thirty years of gardening (the earlier part of it in groping ignorance with scant means of help), I can remember no part

of it that was not full of pleasure and encouragement. For the first steps are steps into a delightful unknown, the first successes are victories all the happier for being scarcely expected, and with the growing knowledge comes the widening outlook, and the comforting sense of an ever increasing gain of critical appreciation. Each new step becomes a little surer, and each new grasp a little firmer, till, little by little by little, comes the power of intelligent combination, the nearest thing we can know to the mighty force of creation.

And a garden is a grand teacher. It teaches patience and careful watchfulness; it teaches industry and thrift; above all it teaches entire trust. 'Paul planteth and Appolos watereth, but God giveth the increase.' The good gardener knows with absolute certainty that if he does his part, if he gives the labour, the love, and every aid that his knowledge of his craft, experience of the conditions of his place, and exercise of his personal wit can work together to suggest, that so surely will God give the increase. Then with the honestly-earned success comes the consciousness of encouragement to renewed effort, and, as it were, an echo of the gracious words, 'Well done, good and faithful servant.'[21]

Notes

1. R. J. Farrer, *The Rainbow Bridge*, 3rd impression (Edward Arnold, 1926), pp. 225–6.

2. G. Jekyll, *Wood and Garden*, facsimile of 1st edn (Antique Collectors' Club, 1981), pp. 15–16.

3. W. Robinson, *The English Flower Garden*, 6th edn (John Murray, 1898), pp. 3–4.

4. Ibid., p. 8.

5. Ibid., p. 8.

6. E.A. Bowles, *My Garden in Autumn and Winter*, 1st edn (T.C. and E.C. Jack, 1915), pp. 262–3.

7. R. J. Farrer, *Alpines and Bog Plants*, 1st edn (Edward Arnold, 1908), pp. 145–6.

8. R. J. Farrer, *In a Yorkshire Garden*, 1st edn (Edward Arnold, 1909), pp. 131–2.

9. Ibid., p. 129.

10. E.A. Bowles, *My Garden in Spring*, 1st edn (T.C. and E.C. Jack, 1914), pp. 35–6.

11. Farrer, *Yorkshire Garden*, p. 18.

12. Ibid., p. 11.

13. G. Jekyll, *Home and Garden*, facsimile of 1st edn (Antique Collectors' Club, 1982), pp. 346–8.

14. Farrer, *Yorkshire Garden*, p. 46.

15. Ibid., p. 302.

16. Jekyll, *Home and Garden*, p. 15.

17. Robinson, *The English Flower Garden*, p. 105.

18. Ibid., pp. 121–2.

19. Jekyll, *Wood and Garden*, pp. 242–3.

20. G. Jekyll, *Children and Gardens*, facsimile of 1st edn (Antique Collectors' Club, 1982), p. 80.

21. Jekyll, *Wood and Garden*, pp. 20–1.

❧ *Bibliography* ❧

Allan, M. *E.A. Bowles and his Garden at Myddelton House [1865–1954]* (Faber and Faber, 1973)

—— *Plants that Changed Our Gardens* (David and Charles, 1974)

—— *William Robinson 1838–1935 Father of the English Flower Garden* (Faber and Faber, 1982)

Berrall, J.S. *A History of Flower Arrangement* (Thames & Hudson, 1968)

Bowles, E.A. *My Garden in Spring* (T.C. and E.C. Jack, 1914)

—— *My Garden in Summer* (T.C. and E.C. Jack, 1914)

—— *My Garden in Autumn and Winter* (T.C. and E.C. Jack, 1915)

—— 'Autumn Crocuses', *Journal of the Royal Horticultural Society*, vol. 48, parts 2 and 3 (1923), pp. 161–7

—— *A Handbook of Crocus and Colchicum for Gardeners* (Martin Hopkinson, 1924)

—— *A Handbook of Narcissus* (Martin Hopkinson, 1934)

—— 'Crocuses', *Journal of the Royal Horticultural Society*, vol. 61, part 6 (1936), pp. 237–45

—— 'Books for a Gardener's Library', *Journal of the Royal Horticultural Society*, vol. 63, part 2 (1938), pp. 68–74

—— 'Features of My Garden—VI. Reminiscences of Myddelton House, Enfield', *Journal of the Royal Horticultural Society*, vol. 66, part 7 (1941), pp. 225–9.

—— 'Fragrance in the Garden', *Journal of the Royal Horticultural Society*, vol. 78, part 3 (1953), pp. 87–95

Brown, J. *Gardens of a Golden Afternoon—The Story of a Partnership, Edwin Lutyens and Gertrude Jekyll* (Allen Lane, 1982)

—— *Vita's Other World* (Viking, 1985)

Coats, A. *The Quest for Plants* (Studio Vista, 1969)

Cox, E.H.M. *Farrer's Last Journey. Upper Burma, 1919–20* (Dulau and Co., 1926)

—— 'Reginald Farrer's Garden', *Country Life*, 13 August 1927

—— 'Reginald Farrer, 1880–1920', *Journal of the Royal Horticultural Society*, vol. 67, part 9 (1942), pp. 287–90

—— (ed.) *The Plant Introductions of Reginald Farrer* (Bibliography by W.T. Stearn) (New Flora and Silva, 1930)

—— *Plant-hunting in China* (Collins, 1945)

Denham, H. 'Footnote to Farrer', *Journal of the Royal Horticultural Society*, vol. 67, part 9 (1942), pp. 290–3

Elliott, Dr B. 'Some Sceptical Thoughts about William Robinson', *Journal of the Royal Horticultural Society*, vol. 110, part 5 (1985), pp. 214–17

Farrer, R. J. *Alpines and Bog Plants* (Edward Arnold, 1908)

—— *In a Yorkshire Garden* (Edward Arnold, 1909)

—— *Among the Hills* (Headley Brothers, 1911)

—— *On the Eaves of the World* (2 vols., Edward Arnold, 1917)

—— *The Void of War: Letters from Three Fronts* (Constable and Co, 1918)

—— *The Rainbow Bridge*, 3rd impression (Edward Arnold, 1926)

—— *The English Rock Garden*, 4th impression (2 vols., T.C. and E.C. Jack, 1928)

—— *My Rock Garden* (Theophrastus, 1971)

—— *The Dolomites* (Cadogan, 1985)

Fisher, F.H. 'Reginald Farrer, author, traveller, botanist and flower-painter; with additional notes by E.H.M. Cox and W.E.T. Ingwersen', *Alpine Garden Society Bulletin*, vol. 1, no. 10 (1933), pp. 1–38

Fitzherbert, M. *The Man who was Greenmantle* (John Murray, 1983)

Glendinning, V. *Vita* (Weidenfeld and Nicolson, 1983)

Hadfield, M. *A History of British Gardening*, 3rd edn (John Murray, 1979)

—— *Pioneers in Gardening* (Routledge & Kegan Paul, 1955)

Hobhouse, P. *Gertrude Jekyll on Gardening* (The National Trust and Collins, 1983)

Jacob, Rev. J. 'Myddelton House: its Garden

and its Gardener', *The Garden*, vol. 53 (June 1909), p. 315

Jekyll, F. *Gertrude Jekyll, a Memoir* (Jonathan Cape, 1934)

Jekyll, G. *Flower Decoration in the House* (Country Life, 1907)

—— *Wall and Water Gardens*, 5th edn (Country Life, 1913)

—— *Annuals and Biennials* (Country Life, 1916)

—— *Wood and Garden* (Antique Collectors' Club, 1981)

—— *Children and Gardens* (Antique Collectors' Club, 1982)

—— *Colour Schemes for the Flower Garden* (Antique Collectors' Club, 1982)

—— *Garden Ornament* (Antique Collectors' Club, 1982)

—— *A Gardener's Testament*, Francis Jekyll and G.C. Taylor (eds.) (Antique Collectors' Club, 1982)

—— *Home and Garden* (Antique Collectors' Club, 1982)

—— and Mawley, E. *Roses for English Gardens* (Antique Collectors' Club, 1982)

—— and Weaver, L. *Gardens for Small Country Houses* (Antique Collectors' Club, 1981)

Jellicoe, G. 'Garden Design in England 1804–1954', *Journal of the Royal Horticultural Society*, vol. 79, part 10 (1954), pp. 488–95

Koppelkamm, S. *Glasshouses and Wintergardens of the Nineteenth Century*, trans. Kathrine Talbot (Granada, 1982)

Massingham, B. *Miss Jekyll, Portrait of a Great Gardener* (Country Life, 1966)

—— *A Century of Gardeners* (Faber and Faber, 1982)

Nicolson, N. *Portrait of a Marriage* (Weidenfeld and Nicolson, 1973)

Nicolson, P. *V. Sackville-West's Garden Book*, 4th impression (Michael Joseph, 1971)

Perry, F. 'E.A. Bowles and Myddelton House Garden', *Journal of the Royal Horticultural Society*, vol. 79, part 11 (1954), pp. 512–19

Robinson, W. *Gleanings from French Gardens*, 2nd edn (Frederick Warne, 1869)

—— *Alpine Flowers for English Gardens* (John Murray, 1870)

—— *The Wild Garden* (John Murray, 1870); 4th edn (John Murray, 1894); 5th edn (John Murray, 1903)

—— *Hardy Flowers* (Frederick Warne, 1871)

—— *The Subtropical Garden* (John Murray, 1871)

—— *The English Flower Garden* (John Murray, 1883); 3rd edn (John Murray, 1893); 6th edn (John Murray, 1898); 16th edn (Roy Hay ed.) (John Murray, 1956)

—— *Garden Design and Architects' Gardens* (John Murray, 1892)

—— *Alpine Flowers for Gardens*, 3rd edn (John Murray, 1903); 4th edn (John Murray, 1910)

—— *The Garden Beautiful, Home Woods and Home Landscape* (John Murray, 1906)

—— *Gravetye Manor: or, Twenty Years' Work round an Old Manor House* (John Murray, 1911)

—— *The Virgin's Bower: Clematis, Climbing Kinds and their Culture at Gravetye Manor* (John Murray, 1912)

—— *Home Landscapes* (John Murray, 1914)

Sackville-West, V. *The Land* (Heinemann, 1926)

—— *Sissinghurst* (Hogarth Press, 1931)

—— *The Garden* (Michael Joseph, 1946)

—— 'Hidcote Manor', *Journal of the Royal Horticultural Society*, vol. 74, part 11 (1949), pp. 476–81

—— *In Your Garden* (Michael Joseph, 1951)

—— 'Wild and Natural Gardening', *Journal of the Royal Horticultural Society*, vol. 76, part 6 (1951), pp. 182–8

—— *In Your Garden Again* (Michael Joseph, 1953)

—— 'The Garden at Sissinghurst Castle, Cranbrook, Kent', *Journal of the Royal Horticultural Society*, vol. 78, part 11 (1953), pp. 400–8

—— *More for Your Garden* (Michael Joseph, 1955)

—— *Even More for Your Garden* (Michael Joseph, 1958)

—— 'Roses in the Garden', *Journal of the Royal Horticultural Society*, vol. 86, part 10 (1961), pp. 426–33

Scott-James, A. *Sissinghurst, The Making of a Garden*, 6th impression (Michael Joseph, 1983)

Sitwell, O. *Noble Essences* (Macmillan, 1950)

Stearn, W.T. 'E.A. Bowles (1865–1954), The Man and his Garden. Part I and II', *Journal of the Royal Horticultural Society*, vol. 80, parts 7 and 8 (1955), pp. 317–26, 366–76

Stevens, M. *V. Sackville-West: A Critical Biography* (Michael Joseph, 1973)

Taylor, G. *Some Nineteenth Century Gardeners* (Skeffington, 1951)

—— *The Victorian Flower Garden* (Skeffington, 1952)

❧ Indices ❧

General Index

A Handbook of Crocus and Colchicum see E.A. Bowles

A Handbook of Narcissus see E.A. Bowles

Alpine Flowers for English Gardens see William Robinson

Alpine Flowers for Gardens see William Robinson

Alpine Garden Society, The 52

Alpine houses *see* greenhouses

Alpines 10, 90, 115–32 *passim*, 168
  Farrer's definition 127
  for a dry wall 124
  for a moraine 125
  grown in pots 151
  in Alpine House, Kew 152–3
  'natural' grouping 129
  on Farrer's Cliff 126

Alpines and Bog Plants see Reginald Farrer

Alps, Da-Tung 49, 71, 72

Alps, European 72, 76, 117, 131
  Mont Cenis 37, 73, 74

Among the Hills see Reginald Farrer

Annuals, hardy 107, 112
  half-hardy 111
  unsuitability for rock garden 127

Austen, Jane 50

Backhouse, James 115

Ballykilcavan 13, 151

Barry, Sir Charles 139

Beckford, William 115

Bedding-out 27, 79, 81, 82–3, 111–12, 117
  at Myddelton House 41
  example of modern bedding-out Plate 4

Biennials 107

Bitton, Gloucestershire 15, 36, 42, 112

Blomfield, Sir Reginald 16
  controversy with Robinson 86–7

Bog-gardens 159, 161–3 *passim*

Bowles, E.A. 9–11, 35–44, 50, 52, 69, 70, 140–9 *passim*, 162–8 *passim*, 170–4, 178–81, Plate 9, Figs. 3.1, 3.3
  becomes a gardener 36
  character assessment 38–9; in plantsman's tradition 178–9; proneness to hay-fever 163; sense of smell 163–5
  childhood 35; illness 35

dies 38

elected to Council of RHS 37

goes to Jesus College, Cambridge 36

interest in flower-arrangement 151, 155

on autumn colour 136

on bedding plants 82–3, 111

on cottage gardens 90

on crocuses 145–6

on raising crocus seedlings 102–3

parents 35

philanthropic work 36–7

plant-hunting trips 37; with Farrer 47, 74–5, 131

plants named after him 44

published works: *A Handbook of Crocus and Colchicum* 37, 145; *A Handbook of Narcissus* 37, 146; *My Garden in Autumn and Winter* 37, 44, 136; *My Garden in Spring* 37, 125, 145, Preface, 47, 50, 93, 117–19; *see also* Crispian Row; *My Garden in Summer* 37, 42

suffers family tragedy 36

trains for ordination 36

see also Crispian Row, Myddelton House

Bowles, Henry Carrington (father) 35, 39

Bowles, Henry Ferryman (brother) 36, 39

Brabazon, H.B. 24

Buchan, John 46, 49

Burma, Upper 49–50, 76

Carpet-bedding 80–2, 119

Chatsworth, Derbyshire *see* Sir Joseph Paxton

Chelsea Show 112, 119, 120

Children and Gardens see Gertrude Jekyll

Colour in the Flower Garden, see Gertrude Jekyll

Colour schemes 93–5

Colour Schemes for the Flower Garden see Gertrude Jekyll

Conservatories *see* greenhouses

Correvon, Professor Henri 51, 120

Cospoloi 58, 67
  see also Vita Sackville-West

Cottage garden, the 90–1, Plate 3

Cottage Gardening see William Robinson

Country Life 27

Cox, E.H.M. 49, 50, 52

Craven Nursery *see* Ingleborough House

Crisp, Sir Frank 37, 38, 119–20, Fig. 10.4

Crispian Row, the 47, 119–20, 121

Crystal Palace 79, 85

Douglas, David 133

Drayton, Middlesex *see* Mrs Lawrence

Edinburgh, Royal Botanic Gardens 71, 121

Ellacombe, Canon H.N. 14, 24, 112, 137, 181, Fig 3.2
  encourages the young Bowles 36
  see also Bitton, Gloucestershire

Even More for Your Garden see Vita Sackville-West

Farrer, Reginald J. 9–11, 36–9, 42, 45–54, 69–77, 92, 99–105 *passim*, 107, 115–32 *passim*, 139, 144–8 *passim*, 151–2, 159–63 *passim*, 164, 166, 169–75 *passim*, 177–81 *passim*, Plate 13, 14, Figs 4.1, 4.4
  achievements 51–2
  becomes Buddhist 46
  Burma expedition 49
  character assessment 50–1
  criticises Robinson's disciples 87–8
  dies 49
  expedition to China 47, 49
  goes up to Balliol College, Oxford 46
  makes first rock-garden 45
  on his Cliff 126–7
  on the moraine 124–5
  plant-hunting trips to European Alps 47
  Preface to *My Garden in Spring* 47, 117–19; *see also* E.A. Bowles, Crispian Row
  published works: *Alpines and Bog Plants* 46; *Among the Hills* 36, 47; *In a Yorkshire Garden* 37, 46, 52, 124, 151; *My Rock Garden* 42, 46, 52, 120; *On the Eaves of the World* 47; *The Dolomites* 37, 47; *The English Rock Garden* 49, 50, 52, 120, 129; *The Rainbow Bridge* 49, 50, 51; *The Rock Garden* 47; *The Void of War* 49
  publishes *My Rock Garden* 46; *The English Rock Garden* 49
  travels in Far East 46

works for Ministry of Information
49
see also E.H.M. Cox, Ingleborough
House, William Purdom
Flora and Sylva see William Robinson
Flower Decoration in the House see
Gertrude Jekyll
Fonthill *see* William Beckford
Forestry Commission, The 21, 136
Forrest, George 49, 69, 137
Friar Park, Henley 119, 120, 122

Garden-Craft, Old and New see John
Sedding
Garden Design and Architects' Gardens see
William Robinson
Garden Ornament see Gertrude Jekyll
Gardening Illustrated 15, 38, 47, 120
Gardens for Small Country Houses see
Gertrude Jekyll
Glasnevin (Irish National Botanic
Gardens) 13, 121, 134
Gleanings from French Gardens see
William Robinson
God's Acre Beautiful see William
Robinson
Gravetye Manor see William Robinson
Gravetye Manor 11, 15–17
garden 18–21, Plates 1, 2, Figs. 1.4,
1.6, 1.7 Alpine Meadow 19; East
Garden 21; Formal Garden (West
Garden) 19; Lakes 19; oval kitchen
garden 21; Playground 19
Great Dixter 29
Greenhouses 151–7 *passim*
Alpine house, the 151–2
Conservatory, the 153
Orangery, the 153, 154
Groundcover 101

Hanbury, Sir Thomas 144–5
Hardy Flowers see William Robinson
Herbaceous borders 88–9, 93–4, 102
see also Gertrude Jekyll, William
Robinson
Herbaceous plants 100, 107–10 *passim*
division 102
Herbert, Aubrey 46, 50
Herbert, Peter 18
Hestercombe *see* Gertrude Jekyll
Hidcote Manor 29, 63, 89
Hole, Reverend Samuel Reynolds 14,
24, Fig. 1.2
Home and Garden see Gertrude Jekyll
Home Landscapes see William Robinson
Hooker, Sir Joseph 16, 69
Hudson, Edward *see Country Life*
Hybridising plants 102–3

In a Gloucestershire Garden see Canon
Ellacombe
In a Yorkshire Garden see Reginald
Farrer
Ingleborough House 45, Fig. 4.2
garden 18, 50, 52–4, Figs. 4.5, 4.6,

10.6; Cliff 52, 54, 126; Craven
Nursery 51, 53, 181; Lake 52, 54,
126; Old and New Rock-Gardens
52–3
Ingleborough mountain 125, 128
In Your Garden see Vita Sackville-West
In Your Garden Again see Vita
Sackville-West

Jacob, Reverend Joseph 39, 44
see also E.A. Bowles, Myddelton
House
Jekyll, Gertrude 9–11, 14–18 *passim*,
23–34, 59, 61–3, 69, 79, 82–99
passim, 102–4 *passim*, 107–13
passim, 120, 123–4, 133–9 *passim*,
142, 151, 153–7 *passim*, 160, 161,
164–7 *passim*, 170, 172, 174–5,
177–83 *passim*, Figs. 2.1, 8.1
and Lawrence Weaver *Gardens for
Small Country Houses* 28, 30
born 23
building of Munstead Wood 24–5
character assessed 28–9
childhood 23
confined to Munstead 27
contributes to *The Garden* 24
describes her flower border 93–4
dies 28
edits *The Garden* 15
eyesight deteriorates 25
influence on Vita Sackville-West 62
gardens of Lutyens/Jekyll
partnership 25; Deanery Garden,
Sonning 24, 26; Folly Farm,
Sulhampstead 26; Hestercombe
25, 26, 161, Plates 7, 8, Figs. 2.3,
14.1; Lindisfarne 24; Millmead 26,
28
meets Edwin Lutyens 24; William
Robinson 14
on cottage gardens 90–1
on herbaceous borders 88–90
on making garden pictures 91
on relation of garden to house 86
on seasonal gardens 88
partnership with Lutyens 25
portrait painted by William
Nicholson 28
published works: *Children and
Gardens* 27, 182; *Colour in the
Flower Garden see next entry*; *Colour
Schemes for the Flower Garden* 27,
93; *Flower Decoration in the House*
27; *Garden Ornament* 28; *Home and
Garden* 27; *Lilies for English
Gardens* 27; *Old English Household
Life see next entry*; *Old West Surrey*
27, 62; *Roses for English Gardens* 27;
Some English Gardens 27; *Wall and
Water Gardens* 27; *Wood and Garden*
27, 28, 177
receives V.M.H. 27
studies art 24
work commissioned by Duke of
Westminster 24

see also Munstead Wood, William
Robinson
Johnson-Walsh, Reverend Sir Henry
Hunt 13
Johnston, Major Lawrence 63, 89

Kew, Royal Botanic Gardens 36, 47,
112
Alpine House 151, 152
Palm House 153
Rock-garden 115, 121
Kingdon-Ward, Frank 51, 69
Knole, Sevenoaks, Kent 57, 59

Lamport Hall, Northamptonshire 115
Lanchow, China 49, 50, 120
Lawrence, Mrs 115, 117
Lea Valley Regional Park Authority *see*
Myddleton House
Lilies for English Gardens see Gertrude
Jekyll
Long Barn 58, 59, 63, 105
see also Vita Sackville-West
Loudon, John 117
Lowe, Dr 112, 181
see also E.A. Bowles
Lutyens, Sir Edwin 23–8 *passim*, 30, 32,
58, 62, 86, 161
Lytton, Lady Emily *see* Sir Edwin
Lutyens

Markham, Ernest 16, 182
see also Gravetye Manor, William
Robinson
Marliac, Joseph Bory Latour- 19, 160
Marnock, Robert 14
Mont Cenis *see* Alps, European
Moon, H.G. 15, Fig. 1.7
Moore, David 13
see also Glasnevin
Moraine, the 51, 124–6
see also E.A. Bowles, Reginald
Farrer
More for Your Garden see Vita
Sackville-West
Mortola, La 143, 144
Mosaic-culture *see* carpet-bedding
Munstead flower vases 156, Fig. 13.1
Munstead Heath 15, 24
Munstead Wood 9, 17–18, 24–30
passim, 58
garden 30–4, 87, Figs. 2.2, 2.4, 2.5,
2.7, 2.8, 7.2; 'Cenotaph of
Sigismunda' 30; Grey garden 95;
Main Flower Border 30, *see also*
herbaceous borders; Michaelmas
Daisy Garden 30, 110; Nut Walk
30, 107; Spring Garden 30–2, 94;
Woodland Garden 32–4
house built 24
The Hut 30, 32
The Thunderhouse 32
see also Gertrude Jekyll
Myddelton House 35–8 *passim*, Fig. 3.4
garden 18, 35–44, 111, Figs. 3.5, 3.6,
3.7, 3.8, 3.9; Alpine Meadow

43–4; Crocus frames 36, 44; Iris
Beds 43; 'Lunatic Asylum' 41,
137; Market Cross 42, Fig. 3.7;
New River, The 35, 41, 42, 108,
160; Rock Garden 38, 39, 42, 92;
Rose Garden 42; Tulip Beds 41
see also E.A. Bowles
My Garden in Autumn and Winter see
E.A. Bowles
My Garden in Spring see E.A. Bowles
My Garden in Summer see E.A. Bowles
My Rock Garden see Reginald Farrer
My Wood Fires see William Robinson

National Trust, The 18, 61
Nesfield, W.A. 81
New River Company 35, 36
see also E.A. Bowles
Nicholson, Sir William 28, 104, Figs.
2.1, 8.1
see also Gertrude Jekyll
Nicolson, Ben *see* Vita Sackville-West
Nicolson, Harold Sir 58–64 *passim*,
Fig. 5.5
see also Vita Sackville-West
Nicolson, Nigel 18, 58, 61
see also Vita Sackville-West
Nymans 29

Observer, the 59, 101
see also Vita Sackville-West
Old English Household Life see Gertrude
Jekyll
One-colour gardens 95–6
On the Eaves of the World see Reginald
Farrer

Paxton, Sir Joseph 79
Pepita see Vita Sackville-West
Perry, Frances 37
Plant-groupings 96
of alpines 129
Portrait of a Marriage see Nigel Nicolson
Purdom, William 47, 50, 71, 72, 75–6,
Fig. 4.3

Regent's Park, The 14
Reserve garden, the 154–5
Robinson, William 9–11, 13–21 *passim*,
24, 37, 38, 47, 51, 69, 72, 76, 79–90
passim, 96–7, 99, 111, 115, 119–23,
129, 133–5 *passim*, 137–9, 141, 151,
154–5, 156, 160, 165, 174, 178,
179, 182, Figs. 1.1, 1.3
becomes journalist 14
birth 13
buys Gravetye Manor 15
character assessment 16–17
dies 16
dispute with Blomfield 86–7
elected Fellow of Linnaean Society
14
employment at The Regent's Park
14
first jobs 13
founds *The Garden* 14

his part in Crispian Row 120–1
influence on Vita Sackville-West 62
is paralysed 16
leaves abruptly for Dublin 13
meets Gertrude Jekyll 14
on bedding-out 79–83
on cottage gardens 90
on herbaceous borders 88–9
on Michaelmas daisies 110
on shrub borders 89, 101, 137
on the 'Wild Garden' 83–4
patron of artists 15
periodicals: *Cottage Gardening* 15;
Flora and Sylva 15; *The Garden* 14,
15, 17, 24, 39
published works: *Alpine Flowers for*
English Gardens 11, 80, 115, 117,
129; *Alpine Flowers for Gardens* 14,
120, 160; *Garden Design and*
Architects' Gardens 86; *Gleanings*
from French Gardens 14; *God's Acre*
Beautiful 15; *Gravetye Manor* 16,
18; *Hardy Flowers* 11, 14, 88; *Home*
Landscapes 16; *My Wood Fires* 15;
The English Flower Garden 11, 15,
16, 17, 83, 93; *The Garden Beautiful*
86; *The Subtropical Garden* 14,
79–80; *The Wild Garden* 14
publishes influential books 14
Rock-garden, the 104, 115–32 *passim*,
151, 159
Alpine lawns 127
dry walls 123
Rock-plants *see* alpines
Roses 42, 67, 140–2
Roses for English Gardens see Gertrude
Jekyll
Royal Horticultural Society 27, 36, 37,
39, 59, 144
gardens in South Kensington 81
Spring Show at Vincent Square 152
see also Wisley Gardens
Ruskin, John 14, 15, 24, 47

Sackville, Lady (Victoria) 57, 58, 61
Sackville, Lord 57
Sackville-West, The Hon. Vita 9–11,
16, 18, 27, 39, 57–67 *passim*, 69,
89, 99, 101, 105–6, 109, 133, 136,
139, 140, 143, 146–7, 147–8, 151,
152, 162, 166–75 *passim*, 179, Figs.
5.1, 5.2, 5.5
affair with Violet Keppel 58
born at Knole 57
buys Long Barn 58
buys Sissinghurst 59
character assessment 61–3
childhood 58
children born 58
engagement and marriage to Harold
Nicolson 58
influences on 62, 108
on colour-schemes 94–5
on cottage gardens 90–1
on her White Garden 95–6
plant preferences 63

published horticultural works: *Even*
More for Your Garden 59; *In Your*
Garden 59; *In Your Garden Again*
59; *More for Your Garden* 59; *The*
Garden 59, 62
receives V.M.M. 59
wins prizes for poetry 59
writes for *Observer* 59
writing style 59–60
writings 59
St John's College, Oxford 123
rock-garden 46
Sedding, John 16, 86
Shrub borders *see* William Robinson
Shrubland Park, Suffolk 15, 81, 139
Sissinghurst 59, Fig. 5.6
garden 10, 18, 29, 58, 61, 63–7
passim, 89, 101, 106, Plates 17, 18,
19, Figs. 5.3, 5.4, 5.7, 5.8; Cottage
Garden 63, 67; Nuttery 62, 67,
108; Rose Garden and Rondel 64;
Spring Garden (Lime Walk) 63,
64, 67; Thyme Lawn 61, 67; White
Garden 61, 64, 95
Sitwell, Osbert 46
Some English Gardens see Gertrude
Jekyll
Stearn, W.T. 37
Stern, Sir Frederick 37

Tate Gallery, the 28
The Formal Garden in England see Sir
Reginald Blomfield
The Garden (periodical) *see* William
Robinson
The Garden (poem) *see* Vita
Sackville-West
The Garden Beautiful see William
Robinson
The Gardener's Chronicle 14, 15, 37, 49
The Land see Vita Sackville-West
The Rainbow Bridge see Reginald Farrer
The Rock Garden see Reginald Farrer
The Void of War see Reginald Farrer
The Wild Garden see William Robinson
Tibet 72–5 *passim*, 147
Topiary 85–7
Trefusis, Violet *see* Violet Keppel
Turner, J.M.W. *see* Gertrude Jekyll

University of London, School of
Pharmacy *see* Myddelton House

van Tubergen 103, 147
Victoria Medal of Honour 27, 37

Wall and Water Gardens see Gertrude
Jekyll
Warley Place 9, 120, 121
Weaver, Lawrence *see* Gertrude Jekyll
Westminster, Duke of 24
Westonbirt Arboretum 136
Wild gardening 32, 83–4
Wildsmith, William 16
Willmott, Miss Ellen 9, 38, 120, 121,
Fig. 10.5

Wilson, E.H. 69, 137, 140
Wisley Gardens 144, Plate 16
  Bowles' Corner 104

rock-garden 115, 122, 123
  see also Royal Horticultural Society
Wolley-Dod, Reverend C. 24, 124, 125

Wolseley, Viscountess 16
Wood and Garden see Gertrude Jekyll
Woolf, Virginia 58

Short Index of Plant Names

Acanthus (various) 109–10
Acer griseum 136
Allium siculum 164
Alpines 90, 119, 122, 124, 125, 127, 152–3
  see also same entry, *General Index*
Ampelopsis veitchii 139
Anemone alpina 74
Anemone robinsoniana 128, Fig; 10.7
Arbutus menziesii 136
Aster frikartii 'Monch' 67
Asters *see* Michaelmas daisies
Asters, China 175

Balm of Gilead (*Cedronella triphylla*) 164
Bedding-plants (half-hardy annuals) 41, 82, 83, 89, 111
Betula albo-sinensis var. septentrionalis 136
Betula japonica 136
Birch, silver 135–6
Bog-plants 162–3
Buddleia alternifolia 47, 51
Buddleia farreri 47

Campanula raineri 169
Cardiocrinum giganteum see Lilium giganteum
Cheiranthus 'Bowle's Mauve' 44, 112
Chionodoxa gigantea 153
Cirsium heterophyllum 163
Cistuses 32
Clematises 139
Climbing plants 64, 139–40
Cob-nuts (*Corylus avellana*) 62
Colchicum 67, 167
Columbine, Siberian 179
Conifers 133–5
Corylus maxima 30
Cotoneaster multiflora 164
Crocus 44, 145
Crocus chrysanthus
  'Bullfinch' 103
  'Snowbunting' 44, 103
  'Yellowhammer' 44, 103
Crocus chrysanthus pallidus 'E.A. Bowles' 103, Plate 9
Crocus graveolens 145
  see also Spring bulbs
Crocus sieberi 'Hubert Edelsten' 44
Crocus tomasinianus var. pictus 44
Crocus vernus 145
Cyclamen europaeum 148
Cyclamen hederaefolium 148
Cytisus battandieri 164

Dahlias 67, 148–9
Daphne rupestris 74

Daphne tangutica 47
Dictamnus fraxinella 113
Dragon Arum (*Dracunculus vulgaris*) 164

Edelweiss (*Leontopodium alpinum*) 131–2
Eranthis hiemalis 144
Eritrichium nanum 37, 70, 74–5, 125, 130–1, Plate 14
Evil-smelling plants 164

Farreria pretiosa 51
Fritillaries 175
Fragrant plants 164–5

Galanthus (various) 144–5, Plate 12
  see also Spring bulbs
Gentiana farreri 49, 71, Plate 13
Gentiana verna 71, 129, Plate 5
Geranium farreri 49, 51
Greenhouse plants 152–4

Hazel, twisted 137
Helichrysum angustifolium 163
Helicodiceros crinitus 164
Helleborus niger 107
Helleborus orientalis 107–8, Plate 6
Herbaceous plants, hardy 64, 65, 67, 81, 82, 84, 89, 93, 94, 96, 102, Fig. 2.5
  see also same entry, *General Index*
Hermodactylus tuberosus (syn. *Iris tuberosa*) 146–7

Iris chrysographes 162
Iris delavayi 162
Iris foetidissima 109
Iris fulva 162
Iris kaempferi 52, 162
Iris laevigata 162
Iris pallida dalmatica 108–9
Iris reticulata 144
  var. 'Cantab' 44
Iris sibirica 162
Iris unguicularis 143–4, 166, Plate 10
Irises, bearded 42
Irises, Oncocyclus 147, Plate 15
Irises, Regelio-cyclus 147
Isopyrum farreri 51

Jasminum farreri 49
Juniperus communis 134–5
Juniperus coxii 49

Kalmia 30

Lactuca alpina (Blue Sowthistle) 173
Lilium farreri 54

Lilium giganteum (syn. *Cardiocrinum giganteum*) 85, 99, 147–8, Plate 20
Limes, pleached 64
Liquidambar 168
Lobelia 111

Magnolia grandiflora 140
Meconopsis quintuplinervia 54, 72
Michaelmas daisies 19, 30, 100–1, 110–11
Milium effusum 'Aureum' 44
Mimosa pudica 113
Mirabilis jalapa 113
Muscari latifolium 153
Myosotis rupicola 129

Narcissus see Spring bulbs
Narcissus bulbocodium citrinus 146, Fig. 12.1
Narcissus 'Weardale Perfection' 146, Plate 11
Nasturtiums 95
Nymphaea marliacea hybrids 19, 160
Nymphaea robinsonii 160

Orchids 15, 53, 153, 154

Paeonia suffruticosa 49
Palm, the 157
Pampas Grass 157
Pansies, Tufted 101
Parrotia persica 168
Penstemon 'Myddelton Gem' 41
Physostegia virginiana 113
Phyteuma comosum 74
Poppies, Oriental 155
Poppies, Shirley 155
Potentilla fruticosa 47
Primrose 'Miss Massey' 105
Primroses, Munstead bunch 30, 32, 62, 108, Fig. 2.6
Primula acaulis var. rubra 108
Primula bowlesii 37
Primula bulleyana 162
Primula chionantha 162
Primula × crucis
  'Blue Bowl' 131
  'Bowles' 37, 131
Primula farreriana 51
Primula florindae 162
Primula helodoxa 162
Primula japonica 162
Primula marginata 152
  'Linda Pope' 152
Primula pulverulenta 162
Primula reginella 51
Primula sikkimensis 162
Primula sonchifolia 49
Primula 'Wanda' 153

Prunus sargentii 168
Prunus serrula 136
Pyrethrum uliginosum 90–1
Pyrus salicifolia 'Pendula' 64

Rhododendron calostratum 49
Rhododendrons 135–6
Romneya 170
Rosa centifolia 63
Rosa farreri 47
Rosa filipes 'Kiftsgate' 67
Rosa gallica 'Rose des Maures' *see* Rose
  'Sissinghurst Castle'
Rosa moyesii 140
Rose 'American Pillar' 60, 142
Rose 'Dorothy Perkins' 142
Rose 'Madame Alfred Carriere' 67
Rose 'Paul's Lemon Pillar' 141
Rose 'Sissinghurst Castle' 67
Rose, the Austrian Copper 95

Rose 'The Garland' 32
Roses *see under same entry, General Index*

Sagittaria 38, 161
Sauromatum guttatum 113
Saxifraga aeizoon 70
  'Rex' 51, 129
Saxifraga bellardii 75
Saxifraga burseriana 152
Saxifraga florulenta 51, 74
Saxifrages 124, 125, 126–7, 129–30
Scilla 'Spring Beauty' 153
Scilla tubergeniana 153
Shrubs, evergreen 137
Spring bulbs 19, 36, 42–4, 64, 67
Spring flowers 30, 32, 85, 166–7
Stratiotes aloides 161

Taxodium distichum (Swamp Cypress)
  136

Thymus serpyllum 67
Tree-paeonies 32, 179
Tuberose (*Polianthes tuberosus*) 164
Tulips 41, 91
  see also Spring bulbs

Viburnum farreri (syn. *V. fragrans*) 49,
  51, 54
Viburnums 171–2
Viola 'Bowles's Black' 44, 112
Violet, Wood 164
Vitis coignetiae 139, 171
Vitis purpurea 139

Wallflowers 112–13
Water-lilies 161 *see also Nymphaea*
Water-plants 159–63
Weeds 172–3
Wisteria floribunda var. macrobotrys 41

Yew (*Taxus baccata*) 42, 134